Our Journey with Jesus

Discipleship according to Luke-Acts

by

Dennis M. Sweetland

A Michael Glazier Book
THE LITURGICAL PRESS
Collegeville, Minnesota

About the Author

Dennis M. Sweetland received his Ph.D. from the University of Notre Dame. He is a professor of theology at St. Anselm College, Manchester, N.H. He is the author of the companion volume *Our Journey with Jesus: Discipleship according to Mark,* and has had articles appear in *Biblica, Catechist, The Bible Today, Biblical Theology Bulletin,* and *Perspectives in Religious Studies.*

A Michael Glazier Book

published by

THE LITURGICAL PRESS

Typography by Brenda Belizzone

1	2	3	4	5	6	7	8	9

Library of Congress Cataloging-in-Publication Data

Sweetland, Dennis M.
    Our journey with Jesus : discipleship according to Luke-Acts / by Dennis M. Sweetland.
        p.   cm. — (Good news studies ; v. 23)
    "A Michael Glazier book."
    Includes bibliographical references and index.
    ISBN 0-8146-5688-9 (pbk.)
    1. Bible. N.T. Luke—Criticism, interpretation, etc. 2. Bible.
N.T. Acts—Criticism, interpretation, etc. 3. Christian life-
-Biblical teaching. I. Title. II. Series.
BS2589.S84   1990
226.4'06—dc20
                                         90-62035
                                            CIP

❧

In loving memory
of my father,
Raymond J. Sweetland (1920-1988)

❧

Table of Contents

Abbreviations

AB	The Anchor Bible
AnBib	Analecta Biblica
BAGD	W. Bauer, W. F. Arndt, F. W. Gingrich, and F. Danker, eds., *A Greek-English Lexicon of the New Testament and Other Early Christian Literature* (Chicago: University of Chicago, 1969)
BTB	*Biblical Theology Bulletin*
BZ	*Biblische Zeitschrift*
CBQ	*Catholic Biblical Quarterly*
ETL	*Ephemerides Theologicae Lovanienses*
EvT	*Evangelische Theologie*
HTR	*Harvard Theological Review*
ICC	International Critical Commentary
IDB	*Interpreter's Dictionary of the Bible* (Nashville: Abingdon, 1962)
JBL	*Journal of Biblical Literature*
JSNTS	Journal for the Study of the New Testament-Supplement Series
NovT	*Novum Testamentum*
NTS	*New Testament Studies*
PRS	*Perspectives In Religious Studies*
RB	*Revue Biblique*
RevRel	*Review for Religious*
RNT	Regensburger Neues Testament
SBLDS	Society of Biblical Literature Dissertation Series
SBLMS	Society of Biblical Literature Monograph Series
ScEccl	*Sciences Ecclésiastiques*
SJT	*Scottish Journal of Theology*
SNTSMS	Studiorum Novi Testamenti Societas, Monograph Series

TB	*Tyndale Bulletin*
TBT	*The Bible Today*
TDNT	G. Kittel and G. Friedrich, eds., *Theological Dictionary of the New Testament* (10 vols.; Grand Rapids: Eerdmans, 1964-1976)
THKNT	Theologisches Handkommentar zum Neuen Testament
TS	*Theological Studies*
TynNTC	Tyndale New Testament Commentary
TZ	*Theologische Zeitschrift*
ZNW	*Zeitschrift für die neutestamentliche Wissenschaft*

Preface

What does it mean to be a disciple of Jesus Christ? What does "following" Jesus entail in terms of one's daily life? This book looks at how the author of Luke's Gospel and the Acts of the Apostles answers these questions. As we examine Luke's two-volume work it will become clear that discipleship is one of his most important themes. Luke tells his readers what it means to "follow" Jesus not only in the call and commissioning stories, but throughout the Gospel and Acts. Because the person and activity of Jesus Christ are at the center of Lukan theology, one's understanding of discipleship and one's ability to follow as a disciple are directly dependent on one's understanding of Jesus. Thus we will be led to discuss Christology and its relationship to discipleship. Hearing the words of and about Jesus should lead an individual to repentance, belief, and baptism. This is in accordance with the plan of God, who has made salvation available to all. The recognition that there is a communal dimension to discipleship will lead us into a discussion of the structure of the Christian community in Luke-Acts. As we examine the community more closely we will see that celebration of the Eucharist and prayer are important elements of discipleship, that "following" Jesus has radical implications for one's attitude toward possessions, and that through his example Jesus calls upon his disciples to reject the use of violence as they set out to creatively transform the world. Jesus, the Servant of God who is also the Son of God, said to his disciples, "I am among you as one who serves." The Christian disciple, therefore, must adopt a lifestyle that follows Jesus' example of service to all.

This book is directed to the informed and educated general reader as well as to the college theology student. Although not primarily written for the specialized scholarly community, I believe that it also will be of use to this constituency.

Research for this volume was made possible by a Saint

Anselm College Summer Research Grant and a sabbatical leave. I would like to thank the members of the Grant Review Committee and the Governing Board of the College for their confidence and support. A debt of gratitude is also owed to Fr. Peter J. Guerin, O.S.B., Dean of the College, Dr. James McGhee, and my other colleagues in the Theology Department for their support and encouragement over the years. The members of the faculty and staff of Saint Anselm College as well as the students in my classes also deserve my thanks for their thought provoking questions which have assisted me in presenting my positions more carefully. Thanks are due, also, to the members of the Catholic Biblical Association's Luke-Acts Task Force who have helped me clarify my interpretation of Luke's theology.

Special thanks go to my good friend Dr. Patrick F. O'Connell of Villa Maria College for his valuable stylistic and exegetical suggestions. His assistance has resulted in numerous improvements; any remaining errors are my responsibility.

Finally, I would like to express my indebtedness to my wife, Jan, and my children, Susan and Karen. Without their support this book could not have been written.

1

Introduction

Before studying the nature of discipleship in Luke-Acts it is important to be aware of the relationship of Luke's writings to the gospel tradition. This knowledge will help us to determine the extent of Luke's activity in arranging and editing the traditional material he had at his disposal and in composing new material. It will also make it easier to identify the theological motifs at work in Luke-Acts and to understand Luke's unique theological point of view.

In the first verses of the Gospel, Luke admits that the story he is about to tell is not the first narrative ever written about the life of Jesus. The reader is told that many others have "undertaken to compile a narrative of the things which have been accomplished among us" (Lk. 1:1) and that these accounts "were delivered to us by those who from the beginning were eyewitnesses and ministers of the word" (1:2). In the prologue to the Gospel, therefore, Luke acknowledges his dependence on early Christian tradition.

The attempt to identify more precisely the sources behind Luke's version of the good news leads inevitably to what has come to be known as "The Synoptic Problem." Briefly stated, the problem is how to explain the mixture of similar and dissimilar material in the first three Gospels. Why do Matthew, Mark, and Luke have so much material in common? Why, if they narrate many of the same things, do they differ so much in content, order, and detail?

There have been various attempts to solve this problem

during the past century, but one solution in particular has gained widespread support among scholars.[1] It is generally accepted that Matthew and Luke had the Greek text of Mark available to them and used this earlier Gospel as one of their primary sources.[2] Scholars also postulate a Greek written source for more than 200 verses common to Matthew and Luke but not found in Mark. This source, which consists primarily of Jesus' sayings, is referred to as "Q," the first letter of the German word for "source" (quelle).

Scholars generally agree, therefore, that when Luke composed his Gospel, he had available to him at least a written copy of Mark's Gospel and a written (document) or oral (source) collection of material known as Q. Because the Two-Document Hypothesis or Two-Source Theory does not account for all the material in Luke's Gospel, it has been argued that this evangelist had a third source available to him. This material, unique to Luke, is referred to as "L" (that exclusive to Matthew is known as "M").[3] While many scholars are willing to speak about L and M, most are not convinced that these were written documents.

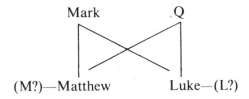

Luke is both faithful to the early Christian tradition which he had at his disposal and innovative. Much of the Jesus material handed on by the Christian community was known to Luke in the form and structure given to it by Mark. Nonetheless, Luke felt free to restructure the story by including material from Q and from his own special source. These additional stories and sayings are not included in a random fashion, but are used by Luke, who is both an editor and an author, to present to his readers a new perspective on Jesus.

The place and importance of Jesus in God's plan of salvation are presented in a story which for the most part follows the sequence found in Mark's Gospel. While Luke has added a

prologue and birth stories (Chapters 1-2) and included resurrection appearances in Jerusalem (Chapter 24), the most significant expansion he has made to the Markan narrative occurs
when he creates a companion volume to the story of Jesus.
The common authorship of the Gospel according to Luke and
the Acts of the Apostles is so widely admitted by modern
scholars that it will be taken for granted in this volume. In
Acts, Luke narrates the spread of Christianity from Jerusalem
to Judea, Samaria and "the end of the earth" (Acts 1:8), i.e.
Rome.

While the hypotheses of several decades ago concerning the
sources of Luke's Gospel continue to have substantial support,
those which sought to identify the sources of Acts do not
enjoy similar scholarly allegiance today. The advent of redaction and composition analysis has made it difficult to argue
convincingly for the existence of Jerusalemite and Antiochene
collections of traditions, or Hellenistic and Hebrew sources, or
accounts asssociated with individual Christian missionaries
(e.g., Peter, Paul, Philip).[4]

The traditional identification of a source behind the so-
called "we" sections in Acts has also been called into question.
Certain passages in the second part of Acts (16:10-17; 20:5-
21:18; 27:1-28:16) have been written in the first person plural
form. This seems to suggest that the material included in these
sections was composed by an eyewitness to the events and that
the author of Acts has not altered his source by reporting these
events in the third person.

Who, then, was this eyewitness? While it has been suggested
that the author of Acts employed as a source the diary of an
eyewitness distinct from himself,[5] the tradition has preferred to
identify the eyewitness as the writer of Acts himself. There is
little support today for the former theory, because there is no
perceptible difference in style between the "we" sections and
the rest of Acts. Does this mean that a diary kept by the writer
of Acts himself served as the source for the "we" sections?
Those who answer yes to this question, usually identify this
individual as Luke, the beloved physician (see Col. 4:14) and
companion of Paul (see Phm. 24; 2 Tim. 4:11).

It has been shown recently, however, that the first person
style of these "we" sections does not necessarily point to the

use of an eyewitness source. Sea-voyage narratives in Greek and Roman literature customarily include first person plural narration. It would be quite natural, therefore, for an author writing in the Hellenistic milieu near the end of first century A.D. to employ the first person plural style within the sea voyage genre.[6] It is likely, therefore, that these passages are neither an eyewitness account nor the diary of a companion of Paul.

Modern scholarship continues to question the traditional identification of the author of Luke-Acts with Luke the beloved physician and companion of Paul.[7] Because it makes little difference to the study of discipleship in Luke-Acts, we will continue to use the traditional name "Luke" to refer to the author of Luke-Acts while leaving open the question of the author's identification with Luke the companion of Paul.

While the vast majority of scholars admit that Luke made use of sources in composing Acts, there is little agreement on the identification or delineation of these sources. Dupont's conclusion summarizes the current situation well: "Despite the most careful and detailed research, it has not been possible to define any of the sources used by the author of Acts in a way which will meet with widespread agreement among the critics."[8]

It would be useful to know the sources Luke had at his disposal in composing Acts, but such information is not essential. What is important is to recognize the developmental character of Luke's two-volume work and to see Acts as a continuation of the Gospel. Because Acts is neither an afterthought nor merely another work by the same author, but an integral part of the author's original plan and purpose,[9] it is impossible to understand Luke's teaching on discipleship without taking Acts into account.

This study, therefore, assumes: (1) that one author is responsible for the Gospel according to Luke and the Acts of the Apostles, (2) that this author intended the Gospel and Acts to be read in sequence, (3) that the author drew on sources while composing Acts, but that these sources are not able to be defined, and (4) that Luke used as sources in the composition of the Gospel, the Greek version of Mark's Gospel, Q, and a variety of stories from his own unique source.

2

Call and Commissioning Stories: The Gospel

When one wants to discover what Christian discipleship entails, the logical way to start is by looking at the call and commissioning stories in the Gospels. It is there that Jesus explicitly calls individuals to follow him and they respond either positively or negatively. As we examine these stories we will discover that the disciples of Jesus are expected to continue his ministry of preaching and healing both within the early Christian community and outside of it, as a part of the missionary enterprise. While it is the earthly Jesus who issues the call to discipleship during his ministry, in the post-resurrection period the invitation to become a Christian comes from Jesus, the risen Lord, through his followers during their missionary travels. Because of this, our summary of the demands of discipleship contained in the Third Gospel's call and commissioning stories will necessarily be followed, in the next chapter, by an investigation of the "call stories" in Acts. In this way we will be able to determine if any changes were made in the requirements for discipleship by the post-Easter church.

The Call of the First Disciples (Lk. 5:1-11)

In Mark's Gospel, the call of the first disciples occurs as Jesus is passing along by the Sea of Galilee (Mk. 1:16-20).[1] The first words of Jesus, "The time is fulfilled, and the King-

dom of God is at hand; repent, and believe in the gospel"
(1:15), are followed almost immediately by his invitation to
Simon and Andrew, "Follow me and I will make you become
fishers of human beings" (1:17). After noting that these two
fishermen immediately left their nets and followed Jesus, Mark
informs the reader that the sons of Zebedee, James and John,
also followed Jesus immediately after he called them (1:18-20).
The call of the first disciples is not reported in the first
twenty verses of Luke's Gospel as it is in Mark's Gospel. Nor
does it immediately follow the first words of Jesus. Unlike
Mark, Luke begins his narrative with material related to the
infancy and early childhood of Jesus (Lk. 1-2).[2] And it is
during the episode about the twelve year-old Jesus in the
temple that Jesus speaks for the first time in Luke's Gospel
(2:49). Jesus also speaks several times during the temptation in
the wilderness (4:1-13), although no words of Jesus are re-
corded in the shorter Markan version of this episode (Mk.
1:12-13). When Luke continues his story by announcing that
Jesus returned to Galilee and began teaching in the synagogues
there (Lk. 4:14) he seems to be following his Markan outline
(cf. Mk. 1:14). What follows, however, are not the words of
Jesus in Mark 1:15 about the inbreaking of the Kingdom, but
a reading from the prophet Isaiah (Isa. 61:1-2; 58:6; Lk. 4:18-
19) which Jesus announces has been fulfilled that very day
(Lk. 4:21). After elaborating on his comment that "no prophet
is acceptable in his own country" (4:24), Jesus went down to
Capernaum where he taught with authority on the sabbath,
exorcised a possessed man in the synagogue, and healed
Simon's mother-in-law. Luke adds that although it was late in
the day Jesus continued his ministry of exorcising and healing
(4:31-41; cf. Mk. 1:21-34). The next day Jesus went to a lonely
place, but he was followed and hounded by the people who
wanted to keep him from leaving (Lk. 4:42; cf. Mk. 1:35-37).
Jesus then says to these people, "I must preach the good news
of the Kingdom of God to the other cities also; for I was sent
for this purpose" (Lk. 4:43; cf. Mk. 1:38). After informing his
readers that Jesus preached in the synagogues of Judea (Lk.
4:44), Luke then narrates the call of the first disciples.

5[1]While the people pressed upon him to hear the word of

God, he was standing by the lake of Gennesaret. ²And he saw two boats by the lake; but the fishermen had gone out of them and were washing their nets. ³Getting into one of the boats, which was Simon's, he asked him to put out a little from the land. And he sat down and taught the people from the boat. ⁴And when he had ceased speaking, he said to Simon, "Put out into the deep and let down your nets for a catch." ⁵And Simon answered, "Master, we toiled all night and took nothing! But at your word I will let down the nets." ⁶And when they had done this, they enclosed a great shoal of fish; and as their nets were breaking, ⁷they beckoned to their partners in the other boat to come and help them. And they came and filled both the boats, so that they began to sink. ⁸But when Simon Peter saw it, he fell down at Jesus' knees, saying, "Depart from me, for I am a sinful man, O Lord." ⁹For he was astonished, and all that were with him, at the catch of fish which they had taken; ¹⁰and so also were James and John, sons of Zebedee, who were partners with Simon. And Jesus said to Simon, "Do not be afraid; henceforth you will be catching human beings." ¹¹And when they had brought their boats to land they left everything and followed him.

According to Luke, Jesus does not call and commission his first disciples as he is passing along by the Sea of Galilee, but while in a boat on the Lake of Gennesaret (Lk. 5:1-11).³ In the Markan pericope (passage, story) there appears to be only a small group by the sea (Simon and Andrew, James and John, Zebedee and the hired servants), but Luke implies that a much larger group is present when he reports that "the people pressed upon" Jesus (5:1), that Jesus "taught the people from the boat" (5:3), and that "all" that were with Simon were astonished at the catch of fish (5:9). By transposing and editing his Markan source,⁴ Luke emphasizes several themes that he will develop throughout the Gospel and Acts.

(1) Individuals are presented as following Jesus only after they have heard his words and observed his powerful deeds. This is more plausible than the Markan account where the first disciples follow Jesus apparently without having previously seen him or heard him preach (Mk. 1:16-20). Luke

alters Mark's story about Jesus in the synagogue at Capernaum (Mk. 1:21-28; Lk. 4:31-37), which now precedes the call story, rather than following it as in Mark, by referring to the teaching of Jesus only at the outset of the pericope, in 4:32-34 (cf. Mk. 1:21-22, 27). By substituting "word" (λόγος) for "teaching" (διδαχή) in the crowd's response to the miracle (Lk. 4:36; cf. Mk. 1:27), Luke transforms the reaction of the crowd into a reaction to the miracle alone. In this way, Luke suggests that the authority (ἐξουσία) of Jesus is present in both his teaching and his miracles (Lk. 4:32, 36).[5] A balance is struck between proclamation and miracle-working, as Luke does not subordinate one activity to the other.

Both these elements are present in this call story as well. The importance of listening to Jesus will be discussed further below; it is enough to point out here that because the authority of Jesus' word has already been established (Lk. 4:32), Luke is able to present Simon as lowering his nets simply in response to Jesus' "word" (5:5).[6] In this pericope Luke also pictures Jesus as speaking "the word of God" (5:1) and notes that Jesus "taught the people from the boat" (5:3). After performing various exorcisms and healings in Capernaum (4:31-37), Jesus heals Simon's mother-in-law (4:38-39) *before* Simon, James, and John follow him (not after as in Mk. 1:21-34). Luke realizes that miracles are ambiguous (Lk. 11:14-19) and can be performed by non-Christians (Acts 8:9-11), but on many occasions in the Gospel[7] and Acts[8] he emphasizes that a miracle can be a catalyst for faith.[9] This appears to be what Luke intends the reader to understand when: (a) he places the healing of Simon's mother-in-law prior to the call of this well-known fisherman and (b) he records the miraculous catch of fish immediately prior to Peter's confession of faith and the following of the first disciples.

(2) Jesus associates with sinners and other outcasts. When Luke records Peter's comment, "Depart from me, for I am a sinful man, O Lord" (Lk. 5:8), he is pointing out Peter's sense of unworthiness and fear in the presence of the one who has worked such a tremendous miracle. While Jesus' words of comfort, "Do not be afraid" (5:10), may function as a declaration of forgiveness in the present context,[10] the more important fact is that Jesus calls a confessed sinner to follow him. Far

from being an impediment to discipleship, this recognition of sinfulness is a necessary prerequisite. Although Jesus' behavior would have shocked many first century Jews (cf. 5:30), Luke understands it to be a necessary part of the divine plan. The salvation of God is to be offered to all, especially sinners (cf. 5:32). Throughout the Gospel, Jesus associates with social outcasts and sinners, offering them forgiveness and reconciliation.

(3) The call to discipleship includes a missionary responsibility. By the end of this pericope it is clear that discipleship involves following Jesus on his way and that during the course of this following Jesus' disciples will save other human beings as they too become his disciples.[11] This missionary motif occurs explicitly later in the Gospel when Jesus, as the risen Lord, says to his disciples, "Repentance and forgiveness of sins should be preached in his name to all nations, beginning from Jerusalem. You are witnesses of these things" (Lk. 24:47-48). Jesus repeats this prophecy in Acts 1:8 when he says, "You shall receive power when the Holy Spirit has come upon you; and you shall be my witnesses in Jerusalem and in all Judea and Samaria and to the end of the earth." The fact that Jesus explicitly tells only Peter (cf. Lk. 6:14) that henceforth he "will be catching human beings" (5:10) points forward both to the leadership role Peter will play in the early church and to his future missionary activity.[12] One must not forget, however, that James and John also leave everything and follow Jesus. It is commonly accepted that Luke understands these words of Jesus about future missionary activity to be addressed to Peter's companions as well as to Peter himself.[13] The fact that Peter is unable to haul in his catch without the assistance of his companions (5:6-7) indicates that the symbolic referent has a community dimension right from the start.

Implicit in Jesus' words about the future missionary enterprise is the call to service, which will be stressed throughout the Gospel. Luke reports that at the Lord's Supper Jesus himself said, "I am among you as one who serves (διακονεῖν)" (Lk. 22:27), as he urges the leaders among his disciples to follow his own example and become servants (22:26). The missionary theme, Jesus as Servant, and the structure of the early Christian community according to Luke-Acts will be discussed further below.

(4) Christian discipleship can be described as "following" Jesus. Discipleship, according to Luke, characteristically takes the form of a journey.[14] The picture of Jesus as a purposeful traveler is seen most clearly in Luke's Travel Narrative (Lk. 9:51-19:44).[15] At the outset of this section, Luke informs the reader that Jesus has steadfastly set himself to go to Jerusalem, where his ascension will occur (9:51; cf. 9:31 and Acts 1:11). This is not the first time that Luke has drawn the reader's attention to the movement of Jesus, however. From the beginning of his ministry in Galilee Jesus is pictured as in the midst of one journey or another (Lk. 4:16, 31, 44; 5:12; 6:1, 12, 17; 7:1, 11; 8:1, 26, 40; 9:10, 28).[16] To be a disciple of Jesus one has to follow him along the way that he walks from Galilee to Jerusalem and ultimately to God.[17]

In his story of the call of the first disciples, Luke has not included Jesus' command "Follow me" (δεῦτε᾽ ὀπίσω), from his Markan source (Mk. 1:17). Commentators see this omission as insignificant, however, since Luke's remark that Simon and his companions left everything and followed (ἀκολουθεῖν) Jesus is its equivalent.[18] While ἀκολουθεῖν is only one of several words used by Luke to convey the idea of close personal attachment to the person of Jesus, it should be noted that Luke's first use of ἀκολουθεῖν occurs in this call story (Lk. 5:11). When Jesus says to individuals "Follow me" (5:27; 9:59; 18:22; cf. 9:23), he is inviting them to become intimately and personally attached to him as he journeys toward his goal.

Luke did not invent the journey motif; he found it in his Markan source and expanded upon it. Mark emphasizes that discipleship means leaving one's own way and following Jesus on his way. Discipleship, therefore, seems to be dynamic and not static, to involve mobility. This theme is present in the initial call stories (Mk. 1:16-20; 2:14f.) but it is more fully developed in the central section of Mark's Gospel (8:22-10:52).[19] Luke is following Mark's lead when he uses "to follow" (ἀκολουθεῖν) as a figurative expression for discipleship (Lk. 5:11; 9:49, 57, 61; 18:28). For Luke, as for Mark, this term involves not only physical accompaniment but intimate personal attachment.[20]

(5) The one who chooses to follow Jesus must adopt a radical stance toward possessions. When Luke tells the reader that Peter, James, and John "left everything" in order to follow Jesus (Lk. 5:11), he is intensifying the teaching about possessions that he found in his source. Instead of merely "leaving their nets" (Mk. 1:18), the disciples, according to Luke, "left everything." As we will see below, Luke stresses elsewhere in the Gospel (e.g. Lk. 5:28; 14:33; 18:22, 28; 21:3-4) and in Acts (e.g. Acts 2:45; 4:34; 5:1ff.) that the Christian disciple must adopt a radical stance toward possessions. The question we will have to address below is whether or not the total abandonment of one's possessions is a prerequisite for discipleship.

This first call/commissioning story thus provides the initial perspective on the key elements of discipleship according to Luke. Individuals are presented as "following" Jesus only after they have heard his words and observed his powerful deeds. This journey motif suggests that Christian discipleship is dynamic, not static. More than mere physical accompaniment is involved, however, as traveling "with" Jesus means intimate personal attachment to the person of Jesus. Recognition of one's own sinfulness does not preclude this personal attachment; such an awareness is not an impediment, but rather a prerequisite for discipleship. The one who joins Jesus on his journey also incurs a missionary responsibility, must adopt a radical stance toward possessions, and must be aware that there is a communal dimension to discipleship.

The Call of Levi (Lk. 5:27-32)

Shortly after learning about how Simon, James, and John left everything (family, jobs, possessions) to follow Jesus, the reader meets a tax collector named Levi who reacts similarly. The call of Levi (Lk. 5:27-32), obviously dependent on Mark 2:13-17, is preceded (as in Mk. 1:40-45; 2:1-12) by two pericopes in which the reader learns that Jesus, the authoritative miracle worker, restores social outcasts to community (Lk. 5:12-14) and forgives sinners (5:17-26).[21] The present story reinforces this understanding of Jesus and reminds the reader about the kind of individuals who followed Jesus as his disciples.

5²⁷After this he went out, and saw a tax collector, named Levi, sitting at the tax office; and he said to him, "Follow me." ²⁸And he left everything, and rose and followed him. ²⁹And Levi made him a great feast in his house; and there was a large company of tax collectors and others sitting at table with them. ³⁰And the Pharisees and their scribes murmured against his disciples, saying, "Why do you eat and drink with tax collectors and sinners?" ³¹And Jesus answered them, "Those who are well have no need of a physician, but those who are sick; ³²I have not come to call the righteous, but sinners to repentance."

Luke presents Jesus as welcoming sinners and, by having Jesus eat with them, may intend to imply symbolically that Jesus bestows forgiveness upon them.²² When he says "Follow me" (ἀκολούθει μοι), Jesus is inviting Levi to form a close personal relationship with him and to join him on his way (Lk. 5:27; cf. 9:23, 59; 18:22). In order to do this, Levi has to resign permanently from his position as a tax collector.²³ Luke stresses "his decisive break with his old life (aorist participle) followed by his continuing life of discipleship (imperfect indicative)."²⁴ The Lukan addition, that Levi "left everything" (5:28; cf. Mk. 2:14), makes this point and agrees with the response of the first disciples (Lk. 5:11). Discipleship for Levi means forsaking all in order to follow Jesus.

After he leaves his tax office, Levi invites many tax collectors and sinners to a great feast at his house (Lk. 5:29f.). There is no conflict between this and Luke's previous statement that Levi "left everything" in order to follow Jesus. The meal is meant to be a means of introducing Levi's business associates to Jesus, and "this motive is in no way inconsistent with his decision to give up his lucrative trade in order to become a disciple."²⁵ Some suggest that Levi, by inviting those who need the gospel to his house where the gospel is proclaimed (5:32), is being presented by Luke as engaged in the missionary activity of "catching human beings" (5:10).²⁶

Luke's inclusion of "left everything" (Lk. 5:28) is not the only significant change he makes in this pericope. Where Mark 2:16 says that the scribes said *to* Jesus' disciples, "Why does he eat with tax collectors and sinners?" in Luke the Pharisees and their scribes murmured *against* Jesus' disciples saying "Why do you eat and drink with tax collectors and sinners?" (Lk. 5:30). Here the complaint of eating with tax collectors and sinners is made to, and about, the disciples. By this alteration, Luke shows that the disciples are like their Master. Jesus comes to their defense, replying on their behalf, as he does later in Luke 6:2-3, where the Pharisees question his disciples, but it is Jesus who responds (a uniquely Lukan alteration). Luke's presentation of Jesus as one who is prepared to eat with sinners in order to bring them to repentance, foreshadows the situation in Acts where the early church associates with Gentiles who were believed to be unclean by orthodox Jews (Acts 10:1-11:18).[27]

The last significant addition to the Markan version of this story occurs when Luke tells his readers that Jesus has come to call sinners "to repentance" (εἰς μετάνοιαν LK. 5:32). By adding these words to his source, Luke has brought out an element that is integral to the teaching of Jesus. In a general sense, μετάνοια involves a radical conversion from all that is evil and a total commitment to God.[28] Luke understands this not as a once-for-all total change, but as a process to be worked out within the Christian community.[29] By his addition of μετάνοια, Luke appears to be bringing out what is latent in Mark and should not be seen as teaching that repentance is required before a person can associate either with Jesus or with the Christian community. Throughout the Gospel, Jesus is pictured as eating with sinners in order to lead them to repentance.[30]

Although there is no clear indication that Levi had heard or seen Jesus prior to receiving his invitation to "Follow me," the four other motifs singled out in the call of the first disciples are all present here. (2) Jesus' invitation to the tax collector Levi is reminiscent of his association with the confessed sinner Simon. Levi would have been considered a sinner by first century Jewish orthodoxy simply because of his occupation.[31] He is implicitly referred to as a sinner by Jesus when Jesus says, "I have not come to call the righteous, but sinners to repentance" (Lk. 5:32). Also supporting this is the fact that the following two pericopes focus on Jesus' defense of his disciples against charges that they are sinners, i.e. that they do not fast (5:33-39) and that they break the law (6:1-5). (3) The missionary dimension of discipleship, explicitly referred to as "catching human beings" in 5:10, is implicitly present when Levi invites tax collectors and sinners to attend his great feast at which Jesus preaches the good news. (4) Luke's comment that Levi "left everything" (5:28) as he responded (5) to Jesus' invitation, "Follow me" (5:27), parallels the concluding verse of the first call story, "they left everything and followed him" (5:11). Although Peter, James, John, and Levi apparently abandoned all their possessions in order to follow Jesus, this may not be required of every would-be disciple. These disciples voluntarily left all; they were not commanded by Jesus to leave all. Jesus tells the Pharisees and their scribes that he has come to call sinners to repentance (5:32); he makes no mention of any requirement that these repentant sinners totally abandon all their possessions.

The Choosing of the Twelve (Lk. 6:12-16)

Immediately after Jesus responds to the accusation that his disciples eat with the wrong kind of people (Lk. 5:30), he is confronted with a new charge. The questioners now suggest that the disciples of Jesus should spend more time fasting and praying, like the disciples of John and the disciples of the Pharisees, and less time eating and drinking (5:33; cf. Mk. 2:18). Luke continues to follow his source (Mk. 2:19-3:6; cf. Lk. 5:34-6:11) when he includes Jesus' response to these charges along with two controversy stories that deal with Jesus' attitude toward the observance of the sabbath. In the first sabbath story reported here (Lk. 6:1-5), Jesus defends the right of his hungry disciples to pluck and eat grain on the sabbath. In the second (6:6-11), he demonstrates that it is permissible to do good on the sabbath as he heals someone's withered hand. The Pharisees and the scribes who witnessed this healing "were filled with fury and discussed with one another what they might do to Jesus" (6:11). In the verses which immediately follow, Luke narrates the choosing of the Twelve.

6¹²In these days he went out into the hills to pray; and all night he continued in prayer to God. [13]And when it was day, he called his disciples, and chose from them twelve, whom he named apostles; [14]Simon, whom he named Peter, and Andrew his brother, and James and John, and Philip, and Bartholomew, [15]and Matthew, and Thomas, and James the son of Alphaeus, and Simon who was called the Zealot, [16]and Judas the son of James, and Judas Iscariot, who became a traitor.

The importance of this scene is indicated when Luke tells the reader that it was only after praying all night that Jesus "called his disciples, and chose from them twelve, whom he named apostles" (Lk. 6:13). Luke's stress on the choice of the Twelve and his specific reference to them as "apostles" indicate that this is an important stage for him in the development of the community of disciples. Those who will be witnesses to his resurrection and messengers of the gospel are the companions of Jesus early in his ministry (cf. Acts 1:2, 8, 26; 2:37, 42-43; 4:32-37; 6:2-6). While this pericope is dependent on Mark 3:13-19, there are some significant differences.[32]

(1) Luke has rewritten Mark's opening verse and introduced the motif of prayer. It is widely recognized that in the Gospel Luke portrays Jesus as one who prays. The choosing of the Twelve (Lk. 6:12), the confession of Peter (9:18), the transfiguration (9:28, 29), and the betrayal (22:39-46) are all preceded by a comment that Jesus was praying (cf. also 5:16; 11:1; 23:34,46). Luke also records that when Jesus "had been baptized and was praying, the heaven was opened, and the Holy Spirit descended upon him" (3:21-22; cf. 11:1-13). Jesus teaches his disciples a prayer (11:2-4) and urges them to pray always and not lose heart (11:5-8; 18:1-8; cf. 22:40). In Acts the early church is pictured as following Jesus' teaching and example concerning faithfulness in prayer (e.g. Acts 1:14, 24; 2:42, 46, 47; 4:24-31; 12:5, 12; 20:36; 21:5).[33] This has led many to conclude that Luke considers prayer to be among the more important elements of discipleship.[34]

(2) Luke distinguishes between a larger group of disciples and the Twelve, whom Jesus calls "apostles."[35] This explains the separate missions of the Twelve (Lk. 9:1-6) and of the Seventy (10:1ff.), and will be important for our discussion

concerning leadership in the Lukan community. The choice of the Twelve clearly refers to the twelve tribes of Israel and the eschatological hope of Israel for the complete restoration of the people of God in the last days (cf. Ezek. 37; 39:23-29; 40-48). Jesus' choice of the Twelve, therefore, is a symbolic prophetic action.[36] The Twelve point beyond themselves to what God is doing through Jesus, rebuilding his people Israel. The Twelve also function as witnesses who guarantee the authenticity of the church's message because they have been with Jesus from his baptism to his ascension (Acts 1:21-22).

(3) Luke has omitted both Mark's comment that the Twelve are called to "be with" Jesus and his reference to their assigned missionary tasks, "to preach and have authority to cast out demons" (Mk. 3:14-15). Although Luke omits reference to specific tasks (which he will include later in Jesus' missionary charge to the Twelve, Lk. 9:1-5) he retains a focus on mission through the use of the term "apostles" ($\dot{\alpha}$ $\pi\dot{o}\sigma\tau o\lambda o\iota$ = people sent out). Since "to be with him" *($\mu\epsilon\tau$' $\alpha\dot{v}\tau o\tilde{v}$ $\epsilon\dot{\iota}\mu\dot{\iota}$)* is a technical expression for discipleship in Luke's sources (cf. Mk. 3:14; 5:18; 14:67; Mt. 12:30) as well as in Luke-Acts (Lk. 8:38; 11:23; 22:56, 59; Acts 4:13),[37] it is seen by some as "inappropriate in conjunction with the election of the twelve apostles, who are *already* disciples. Furthermore *all* of the $\mu\alpha\theta\eta\tau\alpha\dot{\iota}$ (disciples) have been called 'to be with' Jesus, so that the phrase cannot designate a function reserved to the Twelve."[38] Because Luke later defines an "apostle" as a witness who guarantees the historical continuity and authenticity of Jesus' message (Acts 1:21-22), it is important that this group be established prior to the Sermon on the Plain (Lk. 6:20-49), one of the major speeches of Jesus in this Gospel. The witness role is not exclusive to the Twelve, however, as will be seen below.

Many of the themes we have previously identified as important are recalled in this pericope. (1) Simon, James, and John follow Jesus only after they have witnessed the miraculous catch of fish (Lk. 5:1-11; cf. 4:38-39). While it is not stated explicitly that the other members of the Twelve had heard or seen Jesus previously, it is clear that Luke intends the reader to understand that this is indeed the case. Luke informs the reader that after Jesus had taught and had exorcized an unclean demon in Capernaum reports of his authoritative words and deeds "went out into every place in the surrounding region"

(4:37). "Great multitudes gathered to hear and to be healed of their infirmities" (5:15; cf. 4:31ff.,40-42,44; 5:1ff.). Luke undoubtedly intends the reader to understand that the members of the Twelve were among these great multitudes who had heard and seen Jesus, or who had at least heard about him. Luke states explicitly that the Twelve are disciples (6:13), a group that had been with Jesus for some time and that had been verbally attacked by the Pharisees on at least two previous occasions (5:30ff.; 6:1-5). (2) The label "sinner," applied specifically to Simon (5:8), can be applied to Jesus' other disciples in general. This is suggested when Jesus announces that he has not come to call the righteous, "but sinners to repentance" (5:32). Presumably the future members of the Twelve, like Simon and Levi, were sinners who responded to Jesus' call. (3) The missionary dimension of discipleship is suggested by the name given to the Twelve, ἀπόστολοι, which means "people sent out." (4) Three of the Twelve (Peter, James, and John) have been "following" Jesus for some time (5:11). (5) While it is not explicitly stated that the Twelve must adopt a radical attitude toward possessions, the reader knows that three of their number (5:11), plus Levi (5:28), have already "left everything" to follow Jesus.

The Sending of the Twelve (Lk. 9:1-6)

In Mark's Gospel, the Mission of the Twelve (Mk. 6:7-13) is preceded by four miracles (4:35-5:43) and the story of the rejection of Jesus at Nazareth (6:1-6). The point of this arrangement seems to be that miracles do not necessarily lead to faith. Luke's use of this material directs the reader to a somewhat different conclusion. The account of the rejection of Jesus has been relocated by Luke and is found in the Nazareth story (Lk. 4:16-30), which occurs much earlier in the Gospel. The result is that the Sending of the Twelve (9:1-6) now follows immediately after Jesus performs these four miracles (8:22-56). The power *(δύναμις)* and authority *(ἐξουσία)* Jesus possesses (cf. 4:32,36; 5:17,24; 6:19; 8:46), and has used both to exorcise and to heal, are thus demonstrated prior to his giving power *(δύναμις)* and authority *(ἐξουσία)* to the Twelve (9:1).

9¹And he called the Twelve together and gave them power and authority over all demons and to cure diseases, ²and he sent them out to preach the Kingdom of God and to heal. ³And he said to them, "Take nothing for your journey, no staff, nor bag, nor bread, nor money; and do not have two tunics. ⁴And whatever house you enter, stay there, and from there depart. ⁵And wherever they do not receive you, when you leave that town shake off the dust from your feet as a testimony against them." ⁶And they departed and went through the villages, preaching the gospel and healing everywhere.

Deviating from his source (Mk. 6:7-13),[39] Luke informs the reader that Jesus sent out the Twelve specifically "to preach the Kingdom of God" (Lk. 9:2; cf. 9:6). This commission closely associates the Twelve with what Jesus has said is his main role: "I must preach the good news of the Kingdom of God to the other cities also; for I was sent for this purpose" (4:43). It foreshadows the well-known commission of the risen Lord, "that repentance and forgiveness of sins should be preached in his name to all nations, beginning from Jerusalem" (24:47).

Luke's unambiguous portrayal of Jesus and the Twelve as carrying out the same ministry is scarcely accidental. As the Twelve are given power and authority *before* being sent to preach and heal, so later, the risen Jesus will tell his disciples to wait until they "are clothed with power ($\delta\acute{u}\nu\alpha\mu\iota\varsigma$) from on high" (Lk. 24:49; Acts 1:8) before beginning their post-resurrection missionary task. The sending of the Twelve, therefore, also foreshadows the experience of the church in Acts.[40] Once the universal mission begins, it is the power of Jesus that enables these early Christian missionaries to be successful (e.g. Acts 3:12,16; 4:7-12) as they preach the Kingdom of God (Acts 8:12;19:8; 20:25; 28:23,31) and heal the sick (e.g., Acts 5:15; 19:12), just as he sent them out to do (Lk. 9:2,6).

Another significant difference between the Markan and Lukan accounts of the Sending of the Twelve concerns what these missionaries can take along on their journey. Mark, as narrator, reports that Jesus "charged them to take nothing for their journey except a staff ... but to wear sandals" (Mk.

6:8-9). Luke places more emphasis on the charge by trans-forming the narrative into direct discourse and having Jesus himself say, "Take nothing for your journey" (Lk. 9:3). Sandals are not worn (cf. 22:35) and Jesus specifically states that they are to take no staff (9:3). At the same time that they experience the power and authority given to them by Jesus, the Twelve also begin to experience the life of poverty, dependence upon God and rejection which was lived by Jesus and which will be their lot as missionaries.[41]

From the time that they were chosen, the Twelve have heard Jesus' authoritative words (e.g., Lk. 6:20-49) and wit-nessed his powerful miracles (e.g. 7:11-17). They appear to have left everything (cf. 8:1-3; 9:34) in order to follow Jesus, who continues to associate with outcasts and sinners (e.g. 7:36ff.).

An Invitation to Discipleship (Lk. 9:57-62)

The second pericope (cf. Lk. 5:27; 18:22) in which Jesus explicitly says to an individual "Follow me" ($\dot{\alpha}\kappa o\lambda o\acute{v}\theta\epsilon\iota$ $\mu o\iota$) occurs shortly after the Travel Narrative has begun and Jesus and his disciples have set off toward Jerusalem.

> 9[57]As they were going along the road, someone said to him, "I will follow you wherever you go." [58]And Jesus responded, "Foxes have holes, and birds of the air have nests; but the Son of Man has nowhere to lay his head." [59]To another he said, "Follow me." But that person said, "Lord, let me first go and bury my father." [60]But he responded, "Leave the dead to bury their own dead; but as for you, go and proclaim the Kingdom of God." [61]Another said, "I will follow you, Lord; but let me first say farewell to those at my home." [62]Jesus answered, "No one who puts a hand to the plow and looks back is fit for the Kingdom of God."

Luke's editorial activity in this passage, found only here and in Matthew 8:19-21, is significant. In the Matthean version of this story Jesus dialogues first with a scribe and then with one of his own disciples. Luke omits the reference to the scribe (Mt. 8:19) and the disciples (8:21) and includes a third dialogue (Lk. 9:61-62). The result is that in Luke's Gospel all these sayings of Jesus about the difficult demands of discipleship are addressed to would-be followers.

Several themes which have been pointed out before as important for Luke are also found in this pericope. The cost of discipleship, although not explicitly referred to as "leaving everything," is obvious in these verses. Equally clear is the fact that discipleship is expressed in terms of "following" Jesus. The first person mentioned in this pericope says to Jesus, "I will follow (ἀκολουθεῖν) you wherever you go" (Lk. 9:57). A second is invited by Jesus to "Follow me" *(ἀκολούθει μοι,* 9:59). And a third echoes the words of the first saying, "I will follow *(ἀκολουθεῖν)* you, Lord" (9:61).

In the first dialogue (Lk. 9:57-58) Jesus, who has recently been rejected by some Samaritan villagers (9:51-56), tells a would-be disciple that one of the consequences of following him wherever he goes is homelessness. In order to be a follower of Jesus one must be willing to forsake the security of a settled home life.

Luke has significantly altered the second dialogue by: (a) having Jesus take the initiative in summoning another individual to follow him (cf. Mt. 8:21-22) and (b) including Jesus' missionary charge to "go and proclaim the Kingdom of God" (Lk. 9:60; cf. 4:43; 8:1; 9:2). By means of these changes Luke has emphasized the motif of discipleship as "following," the missionary dimension of discipleship, and the relationship between the mission of Jesus and that of his disciples (cf. 4:43; 9:2).

By including the third dialogue Luke has further stressed the radical nature of Christian discipleship. Jesus told the second would-be follower that going and proclaiming the Kingdom of God takes precedence over one's obligation to bury the dead. In this third exchange the reader learns that the demands of discipleship preclude even taking the time to say goodbye to one's living relatives. It is widely recognized that Luke 9:61-62 alludes to 1 Kings 19:19ff. and that Luke is implicitly drawing attention to the fact that the demands of Jesus are more stringent than those of Elijah.

The dialogue between Jesus and these three individuals informs the reader that a would-be follower of Jesus must be willing to sacrifice security, forsake important religious obligations, and recognize that accompanying Jesus and assisting him in his missionary task take priority over certain responsibilities one has to one's family, both living and dead. The active nature of Christian discipleship is also suggested when Luke uses the image of the laborer (one who is plowing) who is not distracted from the work at hand to represent the faithful disciple.

The Mission of the Seventy (Lk. 10:1-20)

The mission of the Seventy follows immediately after the previous passage and elaborates on three of the themes found there—journey (Lk. 10:1), proclamation (10:9), and labor (10:2). Luke is the only Gospel writer to mention the mission of the Seventy, which is generally said to foreshadow the universal mission.[42] Most scholars agree that this pericope (10:1-20) is a Lukan construction, based on material from both Q (See Mt. 9:37-38; 10:7-16; 11:21-24; cf. 10:40) and Mark, and is patterned after the sending of the Twelve.[43]

> 10[1]After this the Lord appointed seventy others, and sent them on ahead of him, two by two, into every town and place where he himself was about to come. [2]And he said to them, "The harvest is plentiful, but the laborers are few; pray therefore the Lord of the harvest to send out laborers into his harvest. [3]Go your way; behold, I send you out as lambs in the midst of wolves. [4]Carry no purse, no bag, no sandals; and salute no one on the road. [5]Whatever house you enter, first say, 'Peace be to this house!' [6]And if a child of peace is there, your peace shall rest upon him/her; but if not, it shall return to you. [7]And remain in the same house, eating and drinking what they provide, for laborers deserve their wages; do not go from house to house. [8]Whenever you enter a town and they receive you, eat what is set before you; [9]heal the sick in it and say to them, 'The Kingdom of God has come near to you.' [10]But whenever you enter a

town and they do not receive you, go into its streets and say, [11]"Even the dust of your town that clings to our feet, we wipe off against you; nevertheless know this, that the Kingdom of God has come near.' [12]I tell you, it shall be more tolerable on that day for Sodom than for that town. [13]"Woe to you, Chorazin! woe to you, Bethsaida! for if the mighty works done in you had been done in Tyre and Sidon, they would have repented long ago, sitting in sackcloth and ashes. [14]But it shall be more tolerable in the judgement for Tyre and Sidon than for you. [15]And you, Capernaum, will you be exalted to heaven? You shall be brought down to Hades.

[16]The one who hears you hears me, and the one who rejects you rejects me, and whoever rejects me rejects the one who sent me. [17]The seventy returned with joy, saying, "Lord, even the demons are subject to us in your name!" [18]And he said to them, "I saw Satan fall like lightening from heaven. [19]Behold, I have given you authority to tread upon serpents and scorpions, and over all the power of the enemy; and nothing shall hurt you. [20]Nevertheless do not rejoice in this, that the spirits are subject to you; but rejoice that your names are written in heaven."

This passage foreshadows the Gentile mission in Acts 13-28 just as the movement of Jesus into Samaritan territory, reported a few verses earlier (Lk. 9:52-56), looks forward to the Christian mission into Samaria in Acts 8.[44] It is also widely acknowledged that Luke is directing much of this material specifically to the Christian community he is addressing. The teaching of the Christian community at the time of Luke, therefore, is seen as rooted in the teaching and command of Jesus himself. The instructions that Jesus gives the Seventy are seen as relevant to Christian missionaries in the last quarter of the first century.[45]

Several other things are important to note here:

(1) One of the most striking facts about this passage is that individuals other than the Twelve are involved in the missionary enterprise. In fact, the mission that symbolizes universality is not carried out by the Twelve. This foreshadows the situation in Acts when numerous members of the early

church, who are not members of the Twelve, will be actively involved in the universal mission. The reader of this pericope soon discovers that the Seventy (Lk. 10:3-4), like the Twelve (9:3), are to be totally dependent on God for their protection and sustenance. They are to set forth on their missionary journey without any equipment as a sign of their faith that God will supply what they need. The Christian missionary is also urged to accept the hospitality of one household and not beg from house to house (9:4; 10:5-7; cf. Acts 16:15). This is widely understood to mean that the disciples are entitled to their food and drink.

In their missionary travels these emissaries of Jesus should not be concerned about the Jewish food laws, since Jesus tells them to "eat what is set before you" (Lk. 10:8). Paul gives the Corinthians similar advice when he writes, "If one of the unbelievers invites you to dinner and you are disposed to go, eat whatever is set before you without raising any question" (1 Cor. 10:27). Such advice would be particularly appropriate for those Christians engaged in the mission to the Gentiles.

(2) These seventy missionaries, like the Twelve, are closely associated with the mission of Jesus. They use the authority *(ἐξουσία)* that Jesus gives them (Lk. 10:19; cf. 9:1) in order to exorcise (10:17) and heal (10:9), and, like Jesus and the Twelve, they preach the Kingdom of God (10:9,11). This motif is further emphasized when Jesus says, "The one who hears you hears me, and the one who rejects you rejects me, and whoever rejects me rejects the one who sent me" (10:16). Jesus' instruction to the Seventy, concerning what action to take if they are rejected during the missionary enterprise (10:11), should remind the reader of Jesus' similar instruction to the Twelve (9:5). The fact that the work of the Lord is so closely connected with the work of his disciples (cf. Acts 9:4) suggests that the teaching of Luke's community is rooted in the teaching of Jesus.

(3) The previously mentioned themes of hearing Jesus (Lk. 10:16; cf. 10:24), repentance (10:13), and prayer (10:2), are all referred to in these verses. As was stated earlier, in the discussion of the call of the first disciples, proclamation of the Kingdom takes place by both word and deed (10:9). The first disciples followed Jesus only after having heard his words and

observed his powerful deeds. Those who listen to the preaching of the Christian missionary are hearing Christ himself (10:16) as the missionary carries on the work of Jesus, who was sent to "preach the good news of the Kingdom of God" (4:43). Luke uses the verb "to hear" (ἀκούειν) in this verse (10:16) to mean more than mere passive listening. The ones who hear are expected to accept the message and incorporate these words into their lives (cf. 6:46-49).[46]

In the call of Levi (Lk. 5:27-32), discussed above, Jesus announces that he has come to call sinners to repentance. The Mission of the Seventy shows that repentance can be evoked by deeds as well as by words: "If the mighty works done in you had been done in Tyre and Sidon, they would have repented long ago" (10:13). This passage also looks forward to the risen Lord's command that "repentance and forgiveness of sins should be preached in his name to all nations" (24:47). In his second volume, Luke tells the reader that this is exactly what happens (Acts 2:38f.; 3:17-20; 5:31; 10:42f.; 13:38-41). Likewise, when Luke has Jesus urge his disciples to pray that God will provide sufficient numbers of laborers for the missionary enterprise (Lk. 10:2), he is foreshadowing the activity of the early church in Acts, specifically the missionary work of Paul and Barnabas (cf. Acts 13:1-3).

(4) These missionaries are told to employ a variation of an ancient Semitic greeting, "Peace be to you" (*shalom leka* in Judg. 6:23; cf. 19:20), when they visit each household. This is the same greeting that Jesus uses when he appears to his disciples after the resurrection (Lk. 24:36).[47] It is not an empty formality or a wish, but "a gift which is either received or rejected as such."[48] This gift, which remains with the recipient if that person is a child of peace, is associated with the coming of the salvation of God. It is an effect brought about by the Christ-event and refers to the salvation which is offered to those willing to receive it (2:14,29; cf. 19:42; Acts 10:36).[49]

(5) The Christian disciple should rejoice and be joyful (Lk. 10:17,20; cf. 10:21). The atmosphere of joy, wonder, praise, and blessing, that pervades the Infancy Narrative (e.g. 1:14, 28,46,58; 2:10) is found throughout the Gospel[50] and Acts,[51] and should characterize the disciple's attitude toward God's work in human history.[52] What the disciples are to be especially

joyful about, according to Luke 10:17-20, is not that they have power over the demons, but that their names are "written in heaven." This suggests that there is a certain complementarity between the outer-directed and inner-directed (others and self) aspect of being witnesses to and proclaimers of the Kingdom. The Seventy, like the Twelve sent out earlier by Jesus, work miracles, preach the word of God, and demand a decision from the members of their audience. Those who hear the authoritative words of these missionaries and/or witness their powerful deeds must either accept or reject them and their message of salvation. In this passage, however, the reader also learns that those who reject the missionary reject Jesus and that those who reject Jesus reject God.

The Rich Ruler (Lk. 18:18-30)

The last pericope in the Gospel in which Jesus explicitly calls an individual to follow him is the story of the Rich Ruler (18:18-30):[53]

> 18[18]And a ruler asked him, "Good Teacher, what shall I do to inherit eternal life?" [19]And Jesus said to him, "Why do you call me good? No one is good but God alone. [20]You know the commandments: 'Do not commit adultery, Do not kill, Do not steal, Do not bear false witness, Honor your father and mother.'" [21]And he said, "All these I have observed from my youth." [22]And when Jesus heard it, he said to him, "One thing you still lack. Sell all that you have and distribute to the poor, and you will have treasure in heaven; and come, follow me." [23]But when he heard this he became sad, for he was very rich. [24]Jesus looking at him said, "How hard it is for those who have riches to enter the Kingdom of God! [25]For it is easier for a camel to go through the eye of a needle than for a rich person to enter the Kingdom of God." [26]Those who heard it said, "Then who can be saved?" [27]But he said, "What is impossible with human beings is possible with God." [28]And Peter said, "Lo, we have left our homes and followed you." [29]And he said to them, "Truly I say to you, there is no one who has left

house or spouse or brothers or parents or children, for the sake of the Kingdom of God, [30]who will not receive manifold more in this time, and in the age to come eternal life."

The call to establish a close personal relationship with him is issued by Jesus in Luke 18:22 with the same words he used in 5:27 and 9:59, "Follow me" (ἀκολούθει μοι). The ruler is also told to "sell all" that he has and "distribute to the poor."[54] Unlike the case of Levi, in this instance the invitation of Jesus is not accepted. But, since Luke does not tell the reader that this individual "went away sorrowful" (cf. Mk. 10:22), neither is the invitation clearly rejected.[55] The indecision of the ruler when invited to "sell all" that he had and follow Jesus (Lk. 18:22), leads Jesus to add that, without God's help, it is impossible for a rich person to enter the Kingdom (18:24-25). These words are spoken by Jesus while he is "looking at" the ruler (Lk. 18:24), unlike Mark 10:23 where "Jesus looked around and said [these words] to his disciples." Perhaps Luke is intentionally leaving the story open-ended because it fits the situation of many in his audience and it is more challenging if the rich reader has to make the decision, write the ending, him/herself.[56] In any event, it is clear that riches, which in the Hebrew Scriptures are frequently seen as a sign of God's blessing (e.g., Gen. 13:2; 26:13; 30:43; 1 Kings 3:13), are viewed by Jesus as a potential obstacle to salvation.

A comparison between the rich ruler and Jesus' disciples is invited when, in Luke 18:29, Peter says that he and the others have fulfilled the conditions that Jesus presented to the rich ruler.[57] Jesus responds by noting that those who have preferred nothing to the Kingdom of God will "receive manifold more in this time, and in the age to come eternal life" (Lk. 18:30). Although he has substantially altered his Markan source here (cf. Mk. 10:30), Luke seems to agree with Mark that the "more" which one will receive in this life means association with the new family of Jesus, i.e. the church.[58]

Several of the themes we have pointed out previously as important also appear in this pericope. (1) Jesus calls the ruler to follow him only after this individual has heard Jesus' words. Although the ruler is mentioned for the first time in Luke 18:18, it appears that he has heard Jesus' words about the coming of the Kingdom (Lk. 17:20-37), the widow and the judge (18:1-8), the Pharisee and the publican (18:9-14), and the little children (18:16-17). Since there is no mention of a change in location or audience after 17:11-12, this ruler may even have witnessed the healing of the ten lepers (17:11-19).[59] (2) Jesus invites sinners to become his disciples. Scholars recognize that there is a close connection between the story of the rich ruler and the preceding two pericopes. "The children, like the publican, are nearer the Kingdom than they could suppose themselves to be; the rich young man, like the Pharisee, is farther from it than he supposed himself to be."[60] Both the Pharisee and the rich man are exposed as idolaters,[61] yet Jesus invites the latter to repent (i.e. abandon his false god) and become his follower. Luke is using these three stories to teach the reader that the entry of anyone "into eternal life or into the Kingdom is a miracle of God's grace, which cannot be earned but only accepted with humility and faith."[62] Of course this acceptance involves showing concretely one's love for God and one's neighbor by obedience to the commandments and limitless charity.[63] (3) Discipleship is expressed in terms of following Jesus. This motif is seen clearly when Jesus says to the rich ruler "Follow me" ($\dot{\alpha}\kappa o\lambda o\acute{v}\theta\epsilon\iota\ \mu o\iota$). (4) Luke's teaching that the disciple of Jesus must take a radical stance toward possessions is obviously present in 18:22ff. This is seen especially in Jesus' words about the camel and the eye of the needle and in Luke's addition of "all" ($\pi\acute{\alpha}\nu\tau\alpha$) to Jesus' admonition in Mark, "sell what you have" (Mk. 10:21). While Mark implies that this individual must leave all behind, Luke specifies that Jesus meant everything. Frequently Luke presents almsgiving as a response to conversion in the Gospel.[64] Is this what he has in mind here? Or, when Jesus demands that the rich ruler abandon all his possessions, as did Peter, James, John (Lk. 5:11), and Levi (5:28), does this mean that *total* abandonment of *all* one's possessions is an *absolute* requirement for entry into the Kingdom of God? This important issue will be examined more closely below.

The Great Commission (Lk. 24:44-49)

No discussion of the call and commissioning stories in Luke's

Gospel would be complete without an examination of the
Great Commission which the risen Lord gives to his disciples
in Luke 24.[65] In the evening of the day on which the empty
tomb is discovered, Jesus appears to Cleopas and an unnamed
disciple on the road to Emmaus. Once these disciples discover
the identity of their companion, in the breaking of the bread
(Lk. 24:30-31, 35), Jesus vanishes. The two disciples promptly
return to Jerusalem where they tell their story to the "eleven
and those who were with them" (24:33). Quite unexpectedly,
Jesus suddenly appears among this group of disciples. After
responding to their fear and astonishment by identifying himself, Jesus commissions them to be his witnesses.[66]

> 24[44]Then he said to them, "These are my words which I
> spoke to you, while I was still with you, that everything
> written about me in the law of Moses and the prophets and
> the psalms must be fulfilled." [45] Then he opened their minds
> to understand the scriptures, [46] and said to them, "Thus it is
> written that the Christ should suffer and on the third day
> rise from the dead, [47] and that repentance and forgiveness
> of sins should be preached in his name to all nations,
> beginning from Jerusalem. [48] You are witnesses of these
> things. [49] And behold, I send the promise of my Father
> upon you; but stay in the city, until you are clothed with
> power from on high."

These last words which Jesus, the risen Lord, speaks to his
disciples in Luke's Gospel stress several of the themes we have
been discussing throughout this chapter. The eleven and "those
who were with them" are the disciples of Jesus who accompanied him during most of his ministry.[67] (1) These are the
followers of Jesus who joined him on the journey only after
they had heard his words and observed his powerful deeds. In
this pericope, proclamation and miracle are found together.
Before they set out (3) on their missionary travels, which will
take them from Jerusalem to all the nations (Lk. 24:47), these
disciples see the resurrected Jesus and hear him speak.
(2) When the risen Lord speaks, he commissions these disciples
to go forth and preach "repentance and forgiveness of sins in
his name" (24:47). Like the Master himself, the disciples of

Jesus must associate with sinners in order to bring them the offer of God's salvation.

While it is true that (5) these disciples have left behind their possessions in order (4) to follow Jesus (cf. Lk. 18:28),[68] the message they are commissioned to bring to the nations mentions explicitly neither possessions nor "following." There is a connection made, however, between repentance and possessions in Luke's Gospel. Jesus, who has come to call sinners to repentance (5:32), teaches that the forgiven sinner must bear fruit that befits repentance (13:1-9; cf. 3:8; Acts 26:20). Perhaps the best example of this is when the repentant sinner Zacchaeus[69] provides restitution to those he has defrauded and gives half of his goods to the poor (Lk. 19:1-10). Luke may intend the reader to understand that a radical shift in one's attitude toward possessions is required when one responds positively to the preaching of repentance and forgiveness in Jesus' name.

In the Great Commission, a change in discipleship vocabulary is signaled when the disciples of Jesus are referred to as his witnesses. "To follow" (ἀκολουθεῖν) does not occur as frequently in Acts as in the Gospel and is not used to indicate discipleship in Luke's second volume.[70] On the other hand, Jesus' disciples who are only called witnesses (μάρτυς) once in the Gospel (Lk. 24:48) are designated as such nearly a dozen times in Acts.[71] These changes will be examined more closely in the next chapter.

Conclusion

In the Gospel, Luke portrays the life of the Christian disciple as a journey. Those who would be followers of Jesus must leave their own way and join Jesus as he travels toward resurrection, ascension, and exaltation. The seeds of discipleship are sown when one sees the marvelous deeds of Jesus or his disciples (e.g. the Twelve or the Seventy) and listens to his, or their, words about salvation and the Kingdom of God. In the post-resurrection period this usually means listening to the preaching of Christian missionaries about Jesus and the Kingdom of God. A disciple is one who responds positively to the message of Jesus and his followers about forgiveness and reconciliation by repenting, converting, and joyfully praising God. The life of the Christian disciple is characterized by prayer, radical renunciation of possessions, and cooperation with other members of this new community to carry on the mission of Jesus by preaching the Kingdom of God with its message of salvation. These same themes are included and developed further in Luke's second volume, the Acts of the Apostles.

3

Call and Commissioning Stories: Acts

It is generally assumed that Luke exercised a much freer hand in creating the Acts of the Apostles than he did in writing his Gospel. For this reason one should pay close attention to Luke's story about the early church and its missionary activities. The reader of Luke's two-volume work must ask whether or not the initial followers of Jesus obeyed the command of the risen Lord, to preach repentance and forgiveness of sins in his name to all nations (Lk. 24:47), as they served as his "witnesses in Jerusalem and in all Judea and Samaria and to the end of the earth" (Acts 1:8). The reader must also seek to discover what differences, if any, exist between the pre- and post-resurrection demands of Christian discipleship.

We began our discussion of what it means to be a disciple of Jesus by examining those pericopes in the Gospel in which Jesus himself invited individuals to follow him or commissioned them to perform some specific task. In the course of our investigation we saw that the Twelve (Lk. 9:1-6) and the Seventy (10:1ff.) carried on the ministry of Jesus while away from him as they preached the Kingdom, exorcized, and healed. The missionary journeys of these disciples during the ministry of Jesus foreshadow the activity of the numerous Christian missionaries mentioned in Acts. Since the risen Lord issues the call to discipleship in the post-resurrection period through these intermediaries, it seems appropriate to focus in this chapter on the invitations to discipleship found in the missionary sermons in Acts 1-17.[1] This decision is supported by the fact that most scholars believe Martin Dibelius was correct when he claimed that the speeches in Acts were composed by the author of Acts and reveal Luke's theological outlook.[2] Before focusing on these missionary sermons, however, two of the more significant transitional passages between the Gospel and Acts deserve attention: the commissioning scene at the outset of Acts (Acts 1:1-14) and the selection of Matthias (1:15-26).

The Universal Mission (Acts 1:1-14)

As was common in the ancient world, Luke begins his second volume by briefly summarizing the contents of the first.[3] The reader is reminded: (1) that in the Gospel Luke dealt with all that Jesus began to do and teach, (2) that Jesus ascended only after having given instructions to the apostles, and (3) that this instruction took place over a 40 day period (Acts 1:1-3). Jesus, the risen Lord, is alive and continues his teaching and activity in the world through his disciples, whom he has carefully instructed. The continuity between the ministry and message of Jesus and that of his disciples is thus established. This is seen further when Luke elaborates on the commands which the risen Lord gave to his disciples (cf. Lk. 24:44-49).

> 1[4] And while staying with them he charged them not to depart from Jerusalem, but to wait for the promise of the Father, which, he said, "you heard from me, [5]for John baptized with water, but before many days you shall be baptized with the Holy Spirit." [6]So when they had come together, they asked him, "Lord will you at this time restore the Kingdom to Israel?" [7]He said to them, "It is not for you to know times or seasons which the Father has fixed by his own authority. [8]But you shall receive power when the Holy Spirit has come upon you; and you shall be my witnesses in Jerusalem and in all Judea and Samaria and to the end of the earth."

After they learn that being "clothed with power from on high" (Lk. 24:49) means being "baptized with the Holy Spirit" (Acts 1:5), the disciples discover the full extent of their missionary preaching. "Through the death and exaltation of the Messiah, the Spirit which operated in him has come to be imparted to his followers."[4] The Holy Spirit unites the risen Lord and his disciples. It is in the Spirit's power and under its guidance that the Christian missionaries preach the gospel. "Beginning from Jerusalem" (Lk. 24:47; Acts 1:8), they must function as Jesus' witnesses "to the end of the earth" (Acts 1:8). The universal scope of the mission, foreshadowed in the Gospel, is now stated clearly.

While the mission theme is paramount here, it should be noted that once again the disciples have seen the resurrected Lord and heard his words. Implicit in the witness motif, as previously stated, is the preaching to sinners of repentance and the forgiveness of sins. This will become explicit in the missionary speeches of Acts. In the final verses of this section (Acts 1:1-14) the reader encounters the familiar themes of prayer and community. After Jesus has ascended, his male and female disciples returned to Jerusalem, to the upper room, and "with one accord devoted themselves to prayer" (1:14).

The Selection of Matthias (Acts 1:15-26)

One day when this community was gathered together, Peter stood up and reminded them that both the defection of Judas and his replacement by another were foreshadowed in Scripture (Acts 1:16-20). Since the former has already taken place, what remains is to fill the vacancy left by Judas' betrayal (cf. Psalm 109:8).

> 1[21] "So one of those who have accompanied us during all the time that the Lord Jesus went in and out among us, [22]beginning from the baptism of John until the day when he was taken up from us—one of these must become with us a witness to his resurrection." [23]And they put forward two, Joseph called Barsabbas, who was surnamed Justus, and Matthias. [24]And they prayed and said, "Lord, who knowest the hearts of all people, show which

one of these two thou hast chosen [25]to take the place in this ministry and apostleship from which Judas turned aside, to go to his own place." [26]And they cast lots for them, and the lot fell on Matthias; and he was enrolled with the eleven apostles.

The fact that Luke reports at such length the selection of Matthias to replace Judas indicates that the Twelve are important for him. It is usually suggested that in their role as witnesses the Twelve serve as a vital link between Jesus and the early church. They guarantee the truth of the church's message as they bear witness to the risen Lord. It can also be argued that the Twelve constitute the "twelve-tribe" framework upon which the new Israel is to be formed.[5] The parenthetical remark (Acts 1:15) that the Christian community was composed of 120 persons may have reminded the reader of Acts that according to Jewish law 120 men were required to establish a community with its own council. Luke may be symbolically portraying the disciples of Jesus as sufficient in numbers to form their own community.

After they serve this function as a link between Jesus and the early church, however, the Twelve become unimportant for Luke, at least until the final judgement. Although not stated as clearly as in Matthew 19:28, Luke intends the reader to understand that the Twelve will be seated upon twelve thrones "judging the twelve tribes of Israel" (Lk. 22:30). Any discussion of hierarchy and leadership in the Christian community according to Luke-Acts, therefore, will have to take into consideration the fact that this group, the Twelve, ceases to be important after the first chapters of Acts.

The Pentecost Sermon (Acts 2:14ff.)

Peter's Pentecost speech in Acts 2 has been called the "keynote address" of Acts, "a summary statement of the theological viewpoint of the author from which the subsequent unfolding of the book is to be understood."[6] It is the first example in Acts, after the Pentecost event (Acts 2:11), of the Spirit-inspired preaching of the word and deeds of God promised in the prophecy of Joel (Acts 2:16-21). In this Pentecostal sermon we find many of the same themes mentioned in the preceding chapter. (1) Individuals hear the word of God in the preaching of Jesus and/or observe his miracles before becoming Christian disciples.[7] In the Gospel stories which were examined above, individuals listened to the preaching of the historical Jesus himself. However, Luke also indicates in the Gospel that the preaching of the Kingdom was delivered to some either by the Twelve (Lk. 9:1-6) or by the Seventy (10:1ff.). In the speech at hand, Peter appeals for the attention of the audience by saying, "give ear to my words ($\dot{\rho}\hat{\eta}\mu\alpha$)" (Acts 2:14). Before he speaks directly about God's activity in Jesus of Nazareth. Peter says "Hear these words ($\lambda\acute{o}\gamma o\varsigma$)" (2:22).[8] Luke also informs the reader that Peter testified "with many other words" (2:40) and adds that "those who received his word were baptized" (2:41). Just as the preaching of the good news by Jesus was an important feature in the Gospel, so in Acts a central place is occupied by the preaching of his disciples. Without the preaching of the disciples, the message of salvation would not have been heard. The word of God preached by the disciples is:

> the message concerning Jesus, belief in whom brings forgiveness of sins and deliverance in the judgement. Here then is the clamp which fastens the two eras together and justifies, indeed demands, the continuation of the first book (depicting the life of Jesus as a time of salvation) in a second; for the salvation which has appeared must be preached to all peoples, and the very portrayal of this mission will serve the awakening of belief, and hence the attainment of that salvation.[9]

As was stated above, and will be examined more fully below, when Luke talks about future disciples hearing the words of Jesus and his disciples he is not merely concerned with passive listening. Along with hearing must come understanding;[10] and along with hearing and understanding must come action, faithful obedience. These responses to the word are already indicated in the Gospel: (a) The risen Lord interprets to the Emmaus travelers (Lk. 24:27) and to his other disciples (24:44f.)

everything in the law of Moses, the prophets and the psalms which refers to him and which has to be fulfilled. The speeches in Acts usually include references to the Jewish Scriptures and a comment that this promise of God has been fulfilled in the life, death, and resurrection of Jesus. In Peter's Pentecost sermon, the words of numerous passages from the Hebrew Scriptures (e.g., Joel 3:1-5, Ps. 16:8-11, 2 Sam. 7:12; Ps. 132:11; Ps. 110:1) are said to have been fulfilled in the ministry of Jesus and the early church. (b) John the Baptist warns that one will not be saved merely by belonging to the people of God or coming to be baptized (Lk. 3:7ff.). Those who wish to flee from the wrath to come must "bear fruits that befit repentance" (3:8).

Peter's post-resurrection audience did not witness any new miracles of the historical Jesus, but they were present when the disciples of Jesus "were all filled with the Holy Spirit, and began to speak with other tongues, as the Spirit gave them utterance" (Acts 2:4). In fact, the tongues phenomenon is the occasion which prompts the discourse. There is obviously an intrinsic connection between the first part of the discourse and the preceding sign. The Holy Spirit, which came down upon Jesus at his baptism and empowered him during his ministry (Lk. 3:22; 4:18), comes down upon the assembled Christian community at Pentecost and empowers Jesus' followers as they speak and act in his name (Acts 2).

The marvelous deeds of Jesus are also referred to in Peter's speech. Before he invites them to become disciples Peter speaks about Jesus as "a man attested to you by God with mighty works and wonders *(τέρατα)* and signs *(σημεῖα)* which God did through him in your midst, as you yourselves know" (Acts 2:22). Immediately following Peter's sermon, Luke mentions that "many wonders *(τέρατα)* and signs *(σημεῖα)* were done through the apostles" (Acts 2:43). Instead of witnessing the words and works of the historical Jesus himself, therefore, future disciples will be confronted with the authoritative words and powerful works of the Christian missionary before being invited to Christian discipleship.[11] "At every point where the Gospel was first established among a certain people, the foundation was made in a miraculous context, with manifest showing of signs and powers worked by the hands of the

Apostles."[72] Acts, therefore, is about what Jesus continues to do and teach through his disciples as a result of the activity of the Holy Spirit.[13]

(2) Jesus and his disciples associate with outcasts and sinners. We are reminded of this motif when we learn that after the crowd heard the words of Peter at Pentecost they asked him and the rest of the apostles, "Brethren, what shall we do?" And Peter said to them 'Repent and be baptized every one of you in the name of Jesus Christ for the forgiveness of your sins; and you shall receive the gift of the Holy Spirit.'" (Acts 2:38). Luke emphasizes the association of Jesus and his disciples with outcasts and sinners because "there is genuine hope for conversion only in the case of persons who have a *sense of their sinfulness* before God and are anxious to obtain God's forgiveness."[14] Peter is an excellent example of this when, in the initial call story in the Gospel, he says to Jesus, "Depart from me, for I am a sinful man, O Lord" (Lk. 5:8). When Peter calls the members of his audience to repentance, here in Acts 2:38, he echoes the similar calls of John the Baptist (Lk. 3:8) and Jesus (e.g. 5:32; 13:3,5; 15:7,10; 16:30; 17:3-4) and reminds the reader of Jesus' command "that repentance and forgiveness of sins should be preached in his name to all nations" (24:47). Such an exhortation to repentance is frequently found in the speeches in Acts (3:17-20; 5:31; 10:42f.; 13:38-41).

Although the importance of baptism will be discussed more thoroughly below, it should be mentioned here that Luke understands baptism as an indispensable, outward indication of the existence of faith. It is a sign of the personal bond the individual has with Jesus and with his disciples who compose the spiritual family of Jesus, the church.[15]

It is too early in Luke's story for Peter to be evangelizing among the Gentiles, but the audience he is addressing seems to foreshadow this later activity. Just as the sending of the Seventy (Lk. 10:1ff.) looks forward to the future Gentile mission of the church, so does Peter's speech to a crowd composed of "Jews and proselytes" (Acts 2:10) and of "devout individuals from all nations under heaven" (2:5; cf. 2:39).

(3) The missionary theme, so crucial to Luke's understanding of Christian discipleship,[16] is also found in this pericope.

One of the obvious results of the empowering of the Holy
Spirit is Peter's missionary speech itself (cf. Acts 2:37-41,47b).
The connection with the earlier missionary texts (Lk. 24:46-49;
Acts 1:8) is provided when Peter proclaims that he and the
other disciples are "witnesses" (Acts 2:33) to the fact that God
has fulfilled his promises, found in the Jewish Scriptures, in
the ministry and resurrection of Jesus. Peter has been clothed
with power from on high (2:2ff.; cf. Lk. 24:49; Acts 1:8) and is
beginning to bring the message of salvation to all nations (cf.
Lk. 24:47; Acts 1:8). He has been very successful thus far, as
his first fishing trip (cf. Lk. 5:10) has resulted in about three
thousand converts (Acts 2:41).

The main task of Peter and the other witnesses is to affirm
the reality of the resurrection of Jesus (Acts 2:32; 3:15; 4:33;
5:32; 10:41; 13:31; cf. Lk. 24:48).[17] In order for the disciples to
serve as effective witnesses they must testify publicly, in both
word and deed, about what they have seen and heard.[18] It
should come as no surprise, therefore, to learn: (a) that the
themes of bearing witness and preaching are intimately related
and (b) that Luke represents the Twelve as devoted "to prayer
and to the ministry of the word" (Acts 6:2,4). The speeches in
Acts are important not only because of the amount of space
devoted to them, about one fifth of the book,[19] but because of
their association with the theological motif of witness.

The witness motif is important in Luke-Acts as the author
suggests that discipleship involves giving witness to the risen
Christ.[20] This is seen clearly when the risen Jesus says to his
apostles "you shall be my witnesses in Jerusalem and in all
Judea and Samaria and to the end of the earth" (Acts 1:8).
Several verses later, Luke defines an apostle as someone who
was present during Jesus' Galilean ministry, followed Jesus on
the trip to Jerusalem, and witnessed the ascension (1:21-22).
The witnesses guarantee the accuracy of the church's message
about the entire career of Jesus, from his baptism to his
ascension. It is important to note, however, that the title of
"witness" is not limited to the Twelve. Although neither one
was a follower of the earthly Jesus "from his baptism to his
ascension," both Paul (22:15; 26:16) and Stephen (22:20) are
described as witnesses to the risen Christ. The theme of
authentic witness, which permeates Acts and focuses especially

on the resurrection (2:32; 3:15; 4:33; 10:39-41; 13:31; cf. Lk. 24:48), is intimately related to the journey motif because what is to begin in Jerusalem is to be carried to all nations (cf. Acts 1:8). The suggestion that "Christian witness is basically communal"[21] will be discussed below when we examine the communal dimension of Christian discipleship.

Two other motifs mentioned in Chapter 2 appear in a slightly different way in Acts 2:37-47. This passage, which follows immediately after Peter's speech and presents the response of his listeners, is said to form "the climax of the first stage of the Acts narrative":[22] (4) Discipleship expressed in terms of following Jesus, and (5) Discipleship involving a radical stance toward possessions.

> 2[37]Now when they heard this they were cut to the heart, and said to Peter and the rest of the apostles, "Brethren, what shall we do?" [38]And Peter said to them, "Repent, and be baptized every one of you in the name of Jesus Christ for the forgiveness of your sins; and you shall receive the gift of the Holy Spirit. [39]For the promise is to you and to your children and to all that are far off, every one whom the Lord our God calls to him." [40]And he testified with many other words and exhorted them, saying, "Save yourselves from this crooked generation." [41]So those who received his word were baptized, and there were added that day about three thousand souls. [42]And they devoted themselves to the apostles' teaching and fellowship, to the breaking of bread and the prayers.
>
> [43]And fear came upon every soul; and many wonders and signs were done through the apostles. [44]And all who believed were together and had all things in common; [45]and they sold their possessions and goods and distributed them to all, as any had need. [46]And day by day, attending the temple together and breaking bread in their homes, they partook of food with glad and generous hearts, [47]praising God and having favor with all people. And the Lord added to their number day by day those who were being saved.

Discipleship is not expressed in Acts explicitly in terms of following Jesus. One notices that in Acts ἀκολουθεῖν (to follow) does not occur as frequently as in the Gospel and is not used to indicate discipleship.[23] Since ἀκολουθεῖν can also be understood literally as "to accompany, go after, or go along with a person in time and place,"[24] perhaps Luke chose to avoid any possible misunderstanding by not using this verb to refer to discipleship after the death of Jesus. Luke does not want the resurrection of Jesus, so central to his theology, to be understood simply as the resuscitation of a dead body. In the post-resurrection period one cannot follow the earthly Jesus to Jerusalem. One can continue to speak of discipleship as a journey, however, because the ultimate goal of Jesus' journey is God, not Jerusalem.

In this passage we see that the element of intimacy associated with following Jesus is now associated with receiving the Spirit. In Acts 2:38-39 this is expressed in terms of "the promise" (cf. Lk. 24:49; Acts 1:4-5) for Jews, Gentiles, and all whom God calls to himself. Receiving the Spirit functions in Acts as following Jesus did in the Gospel—both have the two-fold role of fostering intimacy and empowering mission. The visible fruit of the Spirit's activity within the church is κοινωνία (Acts 2:42), the unity and harmony of the Christian community, marked by the institution of the common fund, mutual sharing, and joy.[25]

Luke's use of "to follow" (ἀκολουθεῖν) in a figurative sense indicates that the journey motif was never meant to be understood merely in physical terms. He portrays Christian discipleship "as the identification of oneself with the master's way of life and destiny in an intimate, personal following of him."[26] There is a connection, therefore, between the journey motif and the life of faith. Luke presents a developmental picture of both the earthly life of Jesus[27] and the life of the church.[28] Within this larger picture, Luke suggests that following Jesus on the journey to God means making progress in the life of faith. One's faith may be smaller than a mustard seed, but it can be increased (Lk. 17:5-6). And after hearing the word of God, one needs to hold fast to it, and to bring forth fruit with patience (8:15).[29] The journeys of Jesus and his followers in Luke-Acts suggest that the third evangelist wants his readers to understand the life of faith as active, not static. Following Jesus involves belief in the Lord Jesus (cf. Acts 4:12; 10:43;

16:31) and hearing and doing the will of God (cf. Lk. 6:46-49; 8:21). According to Acts 2:44-45 discipleship involves a radical stance toward possessions. Unlike some of the Gospel call stories, however, there is no mention of the disciple having to leave "everything" in order to follow Jesus. New disciples apparently take along their possessions as they join the Christian community; they do not rid themselves of their worldly goods by leaving them (e.g., Lk. 5:11,28) or distributing them to the poor in general (18:22). When Luke informs the reader that the members of the Jerusalem church "had all things in common; and they sold their possessions and goods and distributed them to all, as any had need" (Acts 2:45), he is suggesting that there is a renunciation of wealth and a general pooling of resources in a common fund. Later in Acts (4:32-5:11), however, Luke seems to suggest that it is permissible for Christians to retain their private property as long as they are willing to dispose of it as need arises within the community.[30] This later attitude toward possessions is still radical, but it can be described more accurately as detachment than abandonment. When we explore this difference in greater detail below, we will also have to discuss the possibility that Luke understands one's relationship to possessions as a symbol of one's relationship to God. Does Luke represent an individual's acceptance or rejection of God's presence in his/her life by his presentation of that person's attitude toward and actual use of possessions?[31]

Although they will be discussed in more detail below, several other themes must be mentioned at this point. (a) What was said previously about the miraculous activity of Jesus and his disciples can also be applied to prayer. "Prayer marks not only the ministry of Jesus and his first disciples, but also every stage in the outreach of the gospel to the Gentile world."[32] (b) In this pericope the reader also encounters joy (Acts 2:46), one of the important themes found in the Gospel. The Christian disciple is pictured as one who responds to the apostles' message of salvation with joy, wonder, praise, and blessing (8:8,39; 13:48,52; 16:34), and who delights in helping to bring this message of the Kingdom of God to others (5:41; 11:23; 12:14; 15:3,31).[33] (c) The importance of the Eucharist for the Christian discipleship is seen in the mention of the breaking of bread in Acts 2:46. Jesus himself breaks bread at the Lord's Supper (Lk. 22:19) and at Emmaus (24:30-31,35), while the Christian community gathers to break bread at Troas (Acts 20:7; cf. 27:33-38).

The Sermon in the Temple Area (Acts 3:12ff.)

Peter's second speech in Acts is delivered to a group of people who gathered around him and John after the healing of the lame man at the Beautiful Gate (Acts 3:1-10). The pattern here is reminiscent of the Pentecost event and speech. In both Acts 2 and 3 an unusual event is followed by a speech in which Peter begins by explaining what has just happened to an astonished crowd. In all likelihood Luke expects the reader to understand this healing as one of the signs performed by the apostles (2:43; cf. 2:22) in fulfillment of the prophecy of Joel (3:18). The fact that Peter is able to do the kind of thing that Jesus did, by acting in the name of Jesus (3:6), points once again to the continuity between the ministry of Jesus and that of his disciples. This address also includes several of the themes Luke appears to be interested in developing. (1) The audience is familiar with the words and/or deeds of Jesus and his disciples. It is obvious that the people whom Peter is addressing are aware that the lame man has been healed. These are the same people who "were filled with wonder and amazement at what had happened to him" (3:10) and who surround Peter, John, and the healed man in Solomon's Portico (3:11). Peter begins his speech by asking, "Why do you wonder at this, or why do you stare at us, as though by our own power or piety we had made him walk?" (3:12). Luke, in a summary statement after Peter's speech, tells the reader that "many of those who heard the word (λόγος) believed" (4:4). The importance of listening to the word of the Christian missionary is emphasized by Peter's reference to Deuteronomy 18:15,18.

> 3:22Moses said, 'The Lord God will raise up for you a prophet from your brethren as he raised me up. You shall listen to him in whatever he tells you. 23And it shall be that

every soul that does not listen to that prophet shall be destroyed from the people.'

The reader of Luke's two-volume work knows that Jesus has said to his disciples, "whoever hears you hears me, and whoever rejects you rejects me, and whoever rejects me rejects the one who sent me" (Lk. 10:16; cf. 9:48). Thus whoever refuses to listen to Peter has not listened to the prophet Jesus and will be cut off from the people of God (cf. 21:15; Acts 3:22-23; 26:23). This is because Luke clearly understands the "word" (both ῥῆμα and λόγος) as the message of Jesus and his disciples about salvation.[34] Luke presents the possibility of acceptance and rejection as a present reality, because Jesus is alive and at work through the words and deeds of his witnesses.[35]

The importance of prayer in the life of the Christian disciple is suggested when Luke reports that "Peter and John were going up to the temple at the hour of prayer" (Acts 3:1). Closely connected with the praise of God is joy, mentioned above as a characteristic of discipleship. In the Gospel, Luke frequently ends a story by noting that the people involved and/or the spectators praised God.[36] In the story of the healing of the lame man by Peter (3:1-10) we find both the recipient of the miracle and "all the people" praising God (3:8-10). Luke informs the reader that the Gentiles "glorified the word of God" when they heard the message of salvation addressed to them (13:48). Members of the Jerusalem community also glorified God when they heard that he had granted repentance to the Gentiles (11:18; cf. 21:20). Luke seems to use the verb "to praise or glorify" (δοξάζειν) in a special sense in his two-volume work. Individuals give glory and praise to God when he manifests his salvific activity in Jesus the Savior.[37]

(2) It is clear that these words of Peter are addressed to individuals considered to be sinners. During the course of this address, Peter urges his listeners to "repent therefore, and turn again, that your sins may be blotted out" (Acts 3:19). The speech ends with Peter noting that "God, having raised up his servant, sent him to you first, to bless you in turning every one of you from your wickedness" (3:26).[38]

(3) Although Peter is engaged in the missionary work de-

manded of a disciple, he does not mention this requirement to his audience. As in his earlier speech, however, Peter does note that he and his companions are "witnesses" to the fact that God has fulfilled his promises in the life, death, and resurrection of Jesus (Acts 3:15).

(4) "Following Jesus" by becoming a member of the Christian community is not referred to explicitly in the speech itself; but, shortly after Peter finishes Luke reports that "many of those who heard the word believed; and the number of the men came to about five thousand" (Acts 4:4). Once again, see above, Luke emphasizes that individuals "heard the word" that was preached to them. Movement is also suggested by Luke's word play on ἐπιστρέφειν (to turn toward) and ἀποστρέφειν (to turn away) in Acts 3:19,26.[39] The verb translated in Acts 3:19 as "to turn again" (ἐπιστρέφειν) supposes both a change of direction and a movement. The individual does not just "turn toward" God, but must reverse direction. The person who has been walking away from God must now walk toward him. What this means in practice is the reorientation of one's entire life.[40] As we shall see below, this means turning away from wickedness (Acts 3:26) and performing deeds worthy of repentance (26:20).

(5) Peter does not inform his audience during the speech that discipleship requires a radical stance toward possessions. But the reader soon learns that "the company of those who believed," including, one assumes, those who came to believe as a result of Peter's speech,

> 4 32b were of one heart and soul, and no one said that any of the things which he/she possessed was his/her own, but they had everything in common. 33And with great power the apostles gave their testimony to the resurrection of the Lord Jesus, and great grace was upon them all. 34There was not a needy person among them, for as many as were possessors of lands or houses sold them, and brought the proceeds of what was sold 35and laid it at the apostles' feet; and distribution was made to each as any had need.

The reader of Acts 3-4 is thus reminded that the Christian disciple must adopt a radical stance toward possessions. This, of course, is consistent with the words and actions of Jesus and his disciples in the Gospel and in the initial chapters of Acts.

Peter's Defense Before the Sanhedrin (Acts 4:8-12)

After Peter's sermon in the temple area, he and John were arrested and held overnight by the Jewish authorities (Acts 4:1-4). The following day they were brought before the High Council and asked by what power or by what name they had healed the lame man (4:7). During his earthly ministry, Jesus had warned his disciples that they would be persecuted and delivered up to the synagogues and prisons, and brought before kings and governors for his name's sake (Lk. 21:12). He urged them not to be anxious in such moments, however, because "the Holy Spirit will teach you in that very hour what you ought to say" (12:11-12). The promise of Jesus is fulfilled when Peter, "filled with the Holy Spirit" (Acts 4:8a), answers the members of the Jewish Council[41]

> 4[8b] "Rulers of the people and elders, [9]if we are being examined today concerning a good deed done to a cripple, by what means this man has been healed, [10]be it known to you all, and to all the people of Israel, that by the name of Jesus Christ of Nazareth, whom you crucified, whom God raised from the dead, by him this man is standing before you well. [11]This is the stone which was rejected by you builders, but which has become the head of the corner. [12]And there is salvation in no one else, for there is no other name under heaven given among human beings by which we must be saved."

Peter and John were arrested and brought before the Sanhedrin because of the mighty work they had done in the name of Jesus Christ of Nazareth and because of Peter's powerful words following this healing. Once again Luke has demonstrated by example that the Christian disciple must publicly and unashamedly (cf. Lk. 9:26) profess the words of and about Jesus. Although repentance is not specifically called for, it is clear that sinners are being addressed with this word of salvation. Referring to Psalm 118:22 and Isaiah 28:16, Peter tells his audience that Jesus is the one "whom you crucified" (Acts 4:10), "the stone which was rejected by you builders" (4:11). He then says that "there is salvation in no one else, for there is no other name under heaven given among human beings by which we must be saved" (4:12). This is an obvious reference to the prophecy of Joel mentioned in Peter's Pentecost speech: "whoever calls on the name of the Lord shall be saved" (2:21). Luke's reference to the "name" in Acts 4:12 suggests baptism in the name of Jesus Christ and serves to link these words of Peter with his earlier statements: (a) "Repent, and be baptized every one of you in the name of Jesus Christ for the forgiveness of your sins" (2:38) and (b) "Repent therefore, and turn again, that your sins may be blotted out" (3:19). It is generally assumed that sins will be blotted out in baptism.[42] Peter's sermon is followed shortly by the verses cited above concerning the Jerusalem community and its use of possessions (4:32ff.).

The power and authority found in the words and deeds of the disciples is acknowledged by the High Council. These important officials cannot deny that the disciples performed this mighty act (Acts 4:16). Even though they have nothing to say in opposition,[43] however, these officials still seek to stop the equally powerful words of the disciples by prohibiting them "to speak or teach at all in the name of Jesus" (4:18). Peter and John, obedient to Jesus' directive to render to God the things that are God's (Lk. 20:25),[44] resist and are finally released. Luke tells the reader that prayer marked the release of these two disciples as "everyone praised God for what had happened" (Acts 4:22; cf. 4:31). "As it stands, the prayer indicates that the early church turned to God in time of persecution, found comfort in the fact that he knew beforehand what would happen, and claimed strength to carry on its witness."[45]

The "word of God," an expression used in the Gospel to describe the preaching of Jesus (Lk. 5:1; 8:11; 11:28), is employed here to designate the content of the apostolic preaching (Acts 4:29,31). Luke continues to emphasize the close relationship between the message of Jesus and that of the early Christian missionary. The good news of salvation continues to be offered to all through the Spirit-directed ("they were all filled with the Holy Spirit and spoke the word of God with boldness," 4:31b; cf. 4:8) missionary efforts of the early church.

Before we examine Peter's next speech, it is important to note both the distinctiveness of the setting for this speech in Acts 4 and the influence this has on the form of the address. Peter's primary intention here is not to convert the audience, but to explain by what authority the apostles had healed the lame man. The law court setting causes Peter to issue a defense of his actions. We are now moving into a new phase of discipleship, which will include persecution. The witness function is somewhat different here than it was in Peter's earlier speeches, more in keeping with Luke 21:12-13, where Jesus discusses testimony before hostile authorities, than with the missionary focus of Luke 24:47-48 and Acts 1:8.

The Second Trial Before the Sanhedrin (Acts 5:29-32)

According to the narrative in Acts 5:12-16, the apostles perform signs and wonders among the people (the fulfillment of their prayer in Acts 4:30) and continue to meet together in Solomon's Portico. Luke also reports that "more than ever believers were added to the Lord, multitudes both of men and women" (5:14). The high priest and the Sadducees were outraged at this activity of the disciples and, reminiscent of Acts 4:1ff.,[46] had the apostles arrested and imprisoned. When they were brought before the Council the high priest questioned them, saying, "We strictly charged you not to teach in this name, yet here you have filled Jerusalem with your teaching and you intend to bring this man's blood upon us" (5:28). Peter and the apostles respond by saying,

> 5²⁹ᵇ "We must obey God rather than human beings. ³⁰The God of our ancestors raised Jesus whom you killed by hanging him on a tree. ³¹God exalted him at his right hand as Leader and Savior, to give repentance to Israel and forgiveness of sins. ³²And we are witnesses to these things, and so is the Holy Spirit whom God has given to those who obey him."

It is obvious to the reader of Acts 4-5 that the Jewish authorities are well aware of the preaching and miracle-working ministry of the disciples of Jesus. These officials, who previously had sought to stop the public preaching of the apostles (Acts 4:18), attempt once more to silence these disciples. The reader soon learns that they "called in the apostles, they beat them and charged them not to speak in the name of Jesus, and let them go" (5:40). The Jewish authorities are no more successful in stopping the missionary activity of the apostles this time than they were before. In fact, Luke tells the reader, in words reminiscent of his fourth beatitude (Lk. 6:22-23), that the apostles "left the presence of the council, rejoicing that they were counted worthy to suffer dishonor for the name" (Acts 5:41). The third evangelist ends this episode by reporting that "every day in the temple and at home they did not cease teaching and preaching Jesus as the Christ" (5:42). The apostles' preaching, literally "proclaiming good news" (εὐαγ-γελίζεσθαι) is described here in terms reminiscent of the message of Jesus, who said, "I must preach the good news (εὐαγγελίζεσθαι) of the Kingdom of God ... for I was sent for this purpose" (Lk. 4:43; cf. 4:18; 7:22; 8:1; 16:16; 20:1). It also serves to remind the reader of Luke's report that during the ministry of Jesus the Twelve "went through the villages, preaching the gospel (εὐαγγελίζεσθαι) and healing everywhere" (9:6).

Although the high priest is extremely upset at the accusation that he and the other Jewish officials are responsible for the death of Jesus, Peter continues to assert that they are guilty of sinful behavior in the death of Jesus "whom you killed by hanging him on a tree" (Acts 5:30). Of course, the identification of someone as a sinner is not an end but a beginning. Jesus and his disciples associate with outcasts and sinners in order to bring them the message of salvation. A connection between the word of God and salvation is made when the angel says to the apostles, "Go and stand in the temple and speak to the people all the words (ῥῆμα) of this Life" (5:20).[47] The proclamation of salvation, which has appeared in each of the speeches examined thus far, is connected in Acts 5:29-32 with the call to repentance. In this speech, Jesus is specifically referred to as "Savior" (σωτήρ) and his exaltation is said to be for the purpose of giving "repentance (μετάνοια) to Israel and forgiveness of sins" (5:31). This same connection is made in Peter's earlier speeches in Acts[48] when he urges his listeners to repent (μετανοεῖν; Acts 2:38; 3:19) and promises that "whoever calls on the name of the Lord shall be saved" (2:22; cf. 4:12).[49] Ultimately, of course, this theme finds its roots in the statement of the Savior (σωτήρ; cf. Lk. 2:11) himself, "I have not come to call the righteous, but sinners to repentance (μετάνοια)" (Lk. 5:32). The concluding verse of the apostles' speech also touches on another theme we have mentioned previously. Passive listening/hearing is not sufficient for the Christian disciple; God gives the Holy Spirit only to those who obey (Acts 5:32).

The emphasis placed on the association with the Spirit as co-witness in this speech (Acts 5:32) reminds the reader of the witness theme mentioned by Peter in his first two sermons (2:32; 3:15); the disciples of Jesus function as his witnesses (μάρτυρες). The missionary aspect of Christian discipleship is thus highlighted as one recalls the words of the risen Lord to his disciples, "You shall be my witnesses (μάρτυρες) in Jerusalem and in all Judea and Samaria and to the end of the earth" (Acts 1:8; cf. Lk. 24:48; Acts 1:22).

While clearly related to Peter's earlier sermons, this address is even more similar to Peter's third speech, his defense before the Jewish Council (Acts 4:8-12). In this second pair of speeches the imprisoned apostle is bearing witness to the risen Lord before a hostile audience. The implications of "witness" are being developed in the direction of persecution, as can be seen in the next two chapters which chronicle Stephen's arrest (Acts 6), his speech, and his martyrdom (7).[50]

Peter's Sermon to Cornelius (Acts 10:34-43)

As Acts 10 opens, the reader is introduced to the Roman centurion Cornelius, "a devout man who feared God with all his household, gave alms liberally to the people, and prayed constantly to God" (Acts 10:2; cf. 10:4,30-31). We soon learn that this same Cornelius is the recipient of a vision in which he is commanded to send for "Simon who is called Peter" (10:5).

Peter has had a vision as well and, as a result, he goes to Cornelius' house with the messengers the centurion has sent. When he arrives, Peter speaks to Cornelius. This is the first speech in Acts directed specifically to Gentiles. As one might expect, therefore, a note of universalism is sounded at the outset when Peter says, "'Truly I perceive that God shows no partiality, but in every nation any one who fears him and does what is right is acceptable to him" (10:34-35). Peter then continues:

> 10³⁶You know the word which he sent to Israel, preaching good news of peace by Jesus Christ (he is Lord of all), ³⁷the word which was proclaimed throughout all Judea, beginning from Galilee after the baptism which John preached: ³⁸how God anointed Jesus of Nazareth with the Holy Spirit and with power; how he went about doing good and healing all that were oppressed by the devil, for God was with him. ³⁹And we are witnesses to all that he did both in the country of the Jews and in Jerusalem. They put him to death by hanging him on a tree; ⁴⁰but God raised him on the third day and made him manifest; ⁴¹not to all the people but to us who were chosen by God as witnesses, who ate and drank with him after he rose from the dead. ⁴²And he commanded us to preach to the people, and to testify that he is the one ordained by God to be judge of the living and the dead. ⁴³To him all the prophets bear witness that every one who believes in him receives forgiveness of sins through his name.

It should come as no surprise to learn that virtually all of the themes we have discussed previously as important to Christian discipleship in Luke-Acts are found in this speech. (1) Both the words and deeds of Jesus are referred to here. Peter says, "You know the word (λόγος) which he sent to Israel, preaching good news of peace by Jesus Christ (he is Lord of all), the word (ῥῆμα) which was proclaimed throughout all Judea" (Acts 10:36-37). Luke's use of "the word" in the speeches and early chapters of Acts was discussed above, as was his constant emphasis on the fact that those addressed by the apostles actually "hear" what is said (10:33; cf. 10:22; 11:14). Since seeing is frequently mentioned alongside hearing in Luke-Acts, one should not be surprised to find Peter noting here that Jesus "went about doing good and healing all that were oppressed by the devil" (10:38).[51] And the missionary preaching of the disciples is referred to by Peter when he says that Jesus "commanded us to preach to the people, and to testify that he is the one ordained by God to be judge of the living and the dead" (10:42). As in Peter's first speech, those who hear the word (λόγος; cf. Acts 2:41; 10:44) respond by being baptized (2:38; 10:47-48). Although the miracle working of the disciples is not specifically mentioned in this speech, Luke does remind the attentive reader of this activity of the apostles. The pericope immediately preceding the Cornelius episode relates how the dead Tabitha was brought back to life by Peter (9:36-43).

(2) The disciples of Jesus follow his command as they offer outcasts and sinners the gift of salvation. The risen Lord told his followers that "repentance and forgiveness of sins should be preached in his name to all nations" (Lk. 24:47). In his sermon to Cornelius, Peter is obedient to this charge as he notes that every one who believes in Jesus "receives forgiveness of sins through his name" (Acts 10:43). As the narrative continues, Luke informs the reader that these Gentile converts received the Holy Spirit (10:45-47) and he indicates that those who believed were baptized in the name of Jesus Christ (10:47-48). This is exactly what Peter had said in his Pentecostal sermon: "Repent, and be baptized every one of you in the name of Jesus Christ for the forgiveness of your sins; and you shall receive the gift of the Holy Spirit" (2:38). Peter admits this similarity exists when he reports about this episode to the Jerusalem Christians: "As I began to speak, the Holy Spirit fell on them just as on us at the beginning" (11:15). Those in the Jerusalem community acknowledge that repentance has also been involved in the conversion and baptism of the Gentiles, a point not made explicit in Peter's speech, when they say, "Then to the Gentiles also God has granted repentance (μετάνοια) unto life" (11:18). In the speech before the Sanhedrin, discussed above, Peter and the apostles declare that God has given "repentance (μετάνοια) to Israel and forgiveness of sins" (5:31). Now it is admitted that the same gift has been given to the Gentiles (cf. 17:30; 20:21; 26:20). Whether Jew or Greek, one must believe in Christ in order to be saved (10:43; cf. 15:9,11).

(3) Although Peter does not speak about the missionary dimension of Christian discipleship to Cornelius, his own activity suggests that this is in fact the responsibility of at least some members of the Christian community. Of course, the reader of Acts 10 is already aware of the missionary activity of Philip (Acts 8) and Paul (9). After hearing Philip's authoritative words and observing his powerful deeds (8:6, 12-13), many in Samaria, including Simon the sorcerer, believed and were baptized. Philip also baptizes an Ethiopian whom he met on the road from Jerusalem to Gaza. This individual was reading Isaiah 53:7f., but needed Philip to guide him to a proper interpretation of the text. In Acts 9 it is Saul/Paul who is baptized after hearing the words of the risen Lord. He then conducts a preaching ministry of his own both in Damascus and in Jerusalem.

Luke's report in Acts 10 of the beginning of the Gentile mission, preceded by the stories about Philip and Paul, is followed immediately by other missionary success stories. First, Luke informs the reader that "those who were scattered because of the persecution that arose over Stephen traveled as far as Phoenicia and Cyprus and Antioch, speaking the word to none except Jews" (Acts 11:19). Then he reports the success of missionaries from Cyprus and Cyrene who were "preaching the Lord Jesus" among the Gentiles at Antioch where "a great number that believed turned to the Lord" (11:20-21). Finally, Luke discusses the missionary activity of Barnabas and Saul at Antioch, mentioning in passing that it was in Antioch that "the disciples were for the first time called Christians" (11:26).

During the speech itself, Peter mentions that he and the others function as witnesses (μάρτυρες; Acts 10:39, 41) to the life, death, and resurrection of Jesus (10:36-41). This same theme is found in the earlier missionary speeches (e.g., 2:32; 3:15; 5:32) and, as mentioned above, ultimately has its roots in the words of the Risen Lord to his disciples, "You shall be my witnesses (μάρτυρες) in Jerusalem and in all Judea and Samaria and to the end of the earth" (1:8; cf. Lk. 24:48).

It is obvious that the Christian community in general has a missionary responsibility. Barnabas, for example, is sent to Antioch by the Jerusalem church (Acts 11:22). This issue will be discussed further below as we seek to answer the following questions: (a) Does each Christian have a missionary responsibility? Or, is it only an obligation of the community as a whole? (b) If each Christian does have a missionary responsibility, how can this obligation be discharged? Can one fulfill this demand of discipleship by supporting (e.g., financially or with prayers) others who are engaged in missionary work? Or, must every Christian be more personally active in the missionary effort?

(4) As in several other speeches in Acts, the convert is not told explicitly to "follow Jesus" but is pictured as being baptized. It has already been pointed out that Peter commanded all those who heard his words and believed to be baptized (Acts 10:44-48). While incorporation into the church is not mentioned directly, these believers do receive the agent of κοινωνία, the Holy Spirit. The continued reference to the role of the Spirit in this story (10:44,45,47; 11:15,16) creates an explicit parallel with the foundation of the Jerusalem community (10:47; 11:15,17; cf. 2:4) and is also tied in with Jesus' own empowerment by the Spirit at his baptism (10:38). The Spirit comes upon Jesus at the beginning of his ministry (Lk. 3:22) and upon the church at the beginning of its mission to the Jews (Acts 2) and its mission to the Gentiles (Acts 10-11). Jesus bestows upon his followers the gift of the Holy Spirit who will allow them to speak the word of God with boldness (4:31) and will guide the mission according to God's design (1:8). The mission theme, implicit in "following Jesus," is present in this passage when the Holy Spirit instructs Peter about the rightness of the Gentile mission (10:19-20; 11-12).

It was pointed out in the preceding chapter that in the Gospel Luke portrays Jesus as one who prays. The baptism (Lk. 3:21), the choosing of the Twelve (6:12), the confession of Peter (9:18), the transfiguration (9:28,29), and the betrayal (22:39-46) are all preceded by a comment that Jesus was praying (cf. 5:16; 11:1; 23:34,46). Jesus teaches his disciples a prayer (11:2-4) and urges them to pray always and not lose heart (11:5-8; 18:1-8; cf. 22:40). In Acts the early church is pictured as following Jesus' teaching and example concerning faithfulness in prayer (e.g. Acts 1:14,24; 2:42,46,47; 4:24-31; 12:5,12; 20:36; 21:5).[52] In this story of the initial proclamation of the good news to the Gentiles, it is specifically stated that both Cornelius (10:2,4,30) and Peter (10:9; 11:5) are engaged in prayer at the time the divine commission is received (this same theme is found in the preceding story when Peter prays before commanding, "Tabitha, rise" [9:40]).[53]

(5) The attitude toward possessions demanded of the Christian disciple is alluded to both in the Cornelius story and in the pericope which immediately precedes it. Luke introduces Cornelius to the reader as a man who "gave alms (ἐλεημοσύνη) liberally to the people" (Acts 10:2). Later, the angel of God who appears to Cornelius in a vision assures him with these words, "Your prayers and your alms (ἐλεημοσύνη) have ascended as a memorial before God" (10:4; cf. 10:31). While it is true that Cornelius' almsgiving characterizes his pre-Christian life, not the period of discipleship, elsewhere in Luke-Acts almsgiving is seen as appropriate behavior for Christians. In the Gospel, Jesus says to those who are already his disciples (Lk. 12:22), "Sell your possessions, and give alms" (12:33). In Acts, Paul reports that "after some years I came to bring to my nation alms and offerings" (Acts 24:17).[54] Immediately prior to the Cornelius story itself, a disciple named Tabitha is identified as someone who "was full of good works and acts of charity (ἐλεημοσύνη)" (9:36).

The Conversion of Saul/Paul

Thus far we have been examining the speeches in Acts which contain the missionary proclamation of the apostles to Jews and Gentiles. Although each of the five speeches discussed thus far involved Peter, the final three speeches do not. The sixth missionary speech is the first one delivered by Paul and is, therefore, extremely important in the overall framework of Acts. Before we examine this speech, however, it is necessary to look at the call of Saul/Paul himself.

On three separate occasions (Acts 9:1-19; 22:3-21; 26:9-18) Luke reports the call of the Jew named Saul who had been persecuting Christians.[55] Since the call is issued by the risen Lord himself it is important that we look at these passages and compare what is said in them to what we have learned about discipleship from the call stories in the Gospel and from the call to discipleship issued by Peter and the apostles in the speeches we have already examined.

Acts 9:1-19

The communal dimension of Christianity is signaled at the outset of this pericope when Luke refers to the Christian community as "the Way" *(ἡ ὁδός)*. [56] The reader learns that Saul, a well known persecutor of the "church" *(ἐκκλησία)* in Jerusalem (Acts 8:1,3), is prepared to bring bound to Jerusalem any he found "belonging to the Way, men or women" (9:2). Important themes which we have discussed previously are also present here: (1) As he journeys toward Damascus, Saul hears the words of the risen Lord, "Saul, Saul, why do you persecute me?" (9:4). In response to Saul's question, "Who are you, Lord?" the risen Christ answers, "I am Jesus, whom you are persecuting; but rise and enter the city, and you will be told what you are to do" (9:6). A Christian disciple named Ananias also receives a vision in which he hears the words of the risen Lord. It so happened that Saul was blind after his vision and Ananias was instructed to "lay his hands on him so that he might regain his sight" (9:12). After Ananias found Saul, who had been praying (9:11), the miraculous cure took place as the Lord had promised (9:17-18). Both Saul and Ananias, therefore, heard the words of the risen Lord and were witnesses to a miraculous healing.

(2) Saul is obviously viewed as a sinner by both Ananias and the risen Jesus. The close connection between Jesus and his disciples, seen earlier, is found in the opening words of Jesus to Saul, "Saul, Saul, why do you persecute me?" (Acts 9:4), "I am Jesus, whom you are persecuting" (9:5). Ananias also seems to be referring to Saul's sin as persecution (of Jesus, the church, or the Way), when he says, "I have heard from many about this man, how much evil he has done to thy saints at Jerusalem; and here he has authority from the chief priests to bind all who call upon thy name" (9:13-14). Repentance, although not specifically mentioned, is implied when Luke notes that after Saul received his sight he was baptized and filled with the Holy Spirit (9:17-18). The necessity of repentance

as a prerequisite for baptism and receiving the Spirit was discussed above in relation to the speeches of Peter (cf. Acts 2:38). It should also be noted that Ananias is told that Saul is praying as he awaits the former's arrival, a typically Lukan detail which would seem here to imply repentance.

(3) Unlike the speeches in Acts we have discussed, but similar to the call stories in the Gospel, there is an explicit reference to the missionary dimension of discipleship in this pericope. The risen Lord commissions (ἀποστέλλειν) Ananias to bring the saving message to Paul (Acts 9:17). Speaking to Ananias about Saul, the risen Jesus says, "he is a chosen instrument of mine to carry my name before the Gentiles and kings and the sons of Israel; for I will show him how much he must suffer for the sake of my name" (Acts 9:15-16). Immediately after his conversion, Paul begins to fulfill his commission, associating with the disciples at Damascus and preaching in the Jewish synagogues (9:19-22). Throughout the rest of Acts, Luke reports the numerous exploits of Paul as he fulfills the missionary task assigned to him by the risen Jesus. The difficulties of discipleship are referred to here when the Lord tells Ananias that Paul "must suffer for the sake of my name."

Acts 22:3-21

Luke has Paul speak about his conversion experience as part of his defense before the tribune in Acts 22. This version of the story begins like the report in Acts 9, with Paul admitting:

> 22⁴I persecuted this Way to the death, binding and delivering to prison both men and women, ⁵as the high priest and the whole council of elders bear me witness. From them I received letters to the brethren, and I journeyed to Damascus to take those also who were there and bring them in bonds to Jerusalem to be punished.

(1) As in the earlier version, Paul hears the words of the risen Lord, "Saul, Saul, why do you persecute me?" (Acts

22:7), "I am Jesus of Nazareth whom you are persecuting" (22:8). He also reports his experience of the miraculous cure. He was unable to see after the vision (22:11), but when Ananias spoke to him he received his sight (22:13). The involvement of Jesus in this healing is suggested when Ananias says, "The God of our ancestors appointed you to know his will, to see the Just One and to hear a voice from his mouth; for you will be a witness for him to all people of what you have seen and heard" (22:14-15). Paul, like many before him, becomes a Christian disciple after hearing the words of Jesus and his disciples and seeing their powerful deeds. As a result of his conversion, Paul joins with many others as a witness (μάρτυς) to the risen Lord. He receives his commission to go among the Gentiles (22:21) while at prayer (22:17), reminiscent of the story about Peter (10:9; 11:5) and Cornelius (10:2,4,30).

(2) The sinfulness of Paul is mentioned even more explicitly here, in Paul's personal account, than in the earlier presentation of his conversion. Paul admits to having been a persecutor (Acts 22:4-5) and claims that this behavior is public knowledge (22:19-20). Jesus identifies him as a persecutor (22:7-8) and Ananias urges him, "Rise and be baptized, and wash away your sins, calling on his name" (22:16). The call to faith here (22:16) implies the awareness of sin and the desire for pardon, the same pattern for conversion suggested in Peter's speech to Cornelius (10:43), in Paul's sermon at Pisidian Antioch (13:38), and in Paul's speech before King Agrippa II (26:17-18).

(3) The missionary dimension of discipleship is seen both in the words of Ananias, "you will be a witness for him to all people of what you have seen and heard" (Acts 22:15), and in the words of the risen Lord, "Make haste and get quickly out of Jerusalem.... Depart; for I will send (ἀποστέλλειν) you far away to the Gentiles" (22:18,21). In addition to Paul (22:21; 26:17) Jesus sends (ἀποστέλλειν) the Twelve (Lk. 9:2; 22:35) and the disciples (Lk. 10:1,16; 22:35). Luke reports that a day or so after Paul delivered this defense the Lord appeared to him again and said, "Take courage, for as you have testified about me at Jerusalem, so you must bear witness also at Rome" (Acts 23:11). This, of course, confirms his call to be a missionary and reminds the reader of the programmatic words of Jesus in Acts 1:8: "You shall be my witnesses in Jerusalem

and in all Judea and Samaria and to the end of the earth." The universal character of the mission entrusted to Paul is underscored here, just as it was in the first report of his conversion (cf. 9:15).

(4) Mention of the Way (ἡ ὁδός) and baptism agree with what we have seen thus far in Acts. Following Jesus is now expressed in terms of being baptized in his name, thereby becoming a member of the Christian community. In the preceding chapter we concluded that the acceptance of Jesus' message implied the establishment of a personal relationship with him. In Acts, acceptance of the message about Jesus likewise implies a personal commitment to him. This is seen in Luke's use of the expression "those who believed in (πιστεύειν ἐπί)" the Lord (Acts 22:19; cf. 9:42; 11:17; 16:31).[57]

Acts 26:9-18

The third and final mention of Paul's conversion experience along the Damascus road is found as part of his speech to King Agrippa II. This defense comes at the end of a series of appearances of Paul before various Jewish and Roman authorities. Paul is seen here obeying the words of Jesus in Luke 21:12-13[58] and fulfilling the commission he was given in Acts 9:15:

> Luke 21[12]"But before all this they will lay their hands on you and persecute you, delivering you up to the synagogues and *prisons*, and you will be brought *before kings and governors* for my name's sake. [13]This will be a time for you to bear testimony."
>
> Acts 9[15b]"to carry my name before the Gentiles and *kings* and the children of Israel."

In Luke-Acts, only Paul is led before both a king (Agrippa II) and a governor (Festus).

After Paul defends himself against the charges leveled against him by the Jews (Acts 21:38), in a speech which includes the account of his conversion just discussed, he is taken into custody by the tribune, Claudius Lysias, and then brought before the Sanhedrin. When Paul's life appears to be in danger, the tribune rescues him and places him in protective custody (23:10). Claudius Lysias then sends Paul to the governor, Felix, in Caesarea (23:23ff.). Felix had "rather accurate knowledge of the Way (ἡ ὁδός)" (24:22), but wanting to please the Jews, he left Paul in prison for two years, refusing to release him even when he was replaced as governor by Porcius Festus (24:27). During the trial conducted by the new governor, Paul made an appeal to the emperor (25:11). Festus accedes to Paul's request, "You have appealed to Caesar; to Caesar you shall go" (22:12). Before this takes place, however, King Agrippa II arrives at Caesarea to welcome Festus. He is informed about Paul's case and says to Festus, "I should like to hear the man myself" (25:22). The next day Paul is brought before Agrippa and delivers the speech in which he describes his conversion.

Once again Paul openly admits to having persecuted Christians:

> 26⁹"I myself was convinced that I ought to do many things in opposing the name of Jesus of Nazareth. ¹⁰And I did so in Jerusalem; I not only shut up many of the saints in prison, by authority from the chief priests, but when they were put to death I cast my vote against them. ¹¹And I punished them often in all the synagogues and tried to make them blaspheme; and in raging fury against them, I persecuted them even to foreign cities."

The sinfulness of his behavior is confirmed by the words of the risen Lord: "Saul, Saul, why do you persecute me?" (Acts 26:14) and "I am Jesus whom you are persecuting" (26:15). Paul himself will encounter sinners as he goes about the missionary task assigned to him by the Lord, "to open their eyes, that they may turn from darkness to light and from the power of Satan to God, that they may receive forgiveness of sins and a place among those who are sanctified by faith in me" (26:18). Paul "was not disobedient to the heavenly vision," he tells King Agrippa, "but declared first to those at Damascus, then at Jerusalem and throughout all the country of Judea, and also to the Gentiles, that they should repent and turn to God and perform deeds worthy of their repentance" (26:19-20). In urging his audience to demonstrate their conversion concretely, Paul is echoing the same idea John the Baptist expressed metaphorically in the Gospel: "Bear fruits that befit repentance" (Lk. 3:8). Another Lukan interest, the universal character of Paul's mission, is also apparent in this third account of Paul's conversion (cf. Acts 9:15; 22:15), when he announces to Agrippa that he has preached repentance to the Gentiles (26:20).

Paul, like the other disciples of Jesus, hears the powerful word of the Lord before he converts. That "seeing" is also involved is suggested when the risen Christ says that Paul must bear witness "to the things in which you have seen me and to those in which I will appear to you" (Acts 26:16).[59] It is obvious that more than passive listening is required of the would-be disciple when Paul says that people should "repent and turn to God and perform deeds worthy of their repentance" (26:20). One turns to God by accepting and having faith in Christ (26:18). That discipleship involves service of one sort or another is clear from Paul's words here and from the words of the risen Lord to Paul, "I have appeared to you for this purpose, to appoint you to serve and bear witness" (26:16). The parallels between Jesus and Paul in Luke-Acts will be examined more closely below. It is enough here to state that the task of the Suffering Servant, begun by Jesus, is carried on by Paul.[60]

At the end of this speech before King Agrippa, Paul formulates a definition of his own preaching. He tells his audience that his purpose in preaching is to demonstrate, with the help of the Jewish Scriptures, "that the Christ must suffer, and that, by being the first to rise from the dead, he would proclaim light both to the people and to the Gentiles" (Acts 26:23). This is remarkably similar to what Jesus said in Luke 24:46-47: "Thus it is written, that the Christ should suffer and on the third day rise from the dead, and that repentance and forgiveness of sins should be preached in his name to all nations, beginning from Jerusalem." The death and resurrection of Jesus have already taken place, while the mission to the

Gentiles will be fulfilled in the ministry of Paul. Through him and the other missionaries the work of the risen Lord is carried on.[61]

These three reports of the conversion of Paul contain many of the same elements that we have already seen in the Gospel call stories and the call stories in Acts. What remains for us to do here is examine the actual origin of Paul's missionary enterprise and the three most famous speeches delivered by Paul in an effort to see what, if anything, these passages add to our understanding of the requirements of Christian discipleship.

The Commissioning of the Antioch Community (Acts 13:1-12)

After receiving his commission from the risen Lord, Paul spends several days with the Christian community at Damascus. During this time he proclaims in the synagogues that Jesus is the Son of God (Acts 9:19b-20). Before long, however, he encounters serious opposition. When Paul learns that the Jews are plotting to kill him, he arranges a nighttime escape from Damascus (9:23-25). Upon his arrival in Jerusalem, Paul attempts to join the Christians there, "but they were all afraid of him, for they did not believe that he was a disciple" (9:26). The situation improves once Barnabas speaks out in Paul's defense and introduces him to the apostles. Now accepted, Paul joins with the Jerusalem community in its disputes against the Hellenists. When the Christians learn that these Diaspora Jews who are living in Jerusalem intend to kill Paul, they help him escape to Tarsus (9:27-31).

Paul seems to have remained in Tarsus until his old friend Barnabas persuaded him to come to Antioch. When news of the great growth in the number of believers at Antioch reached the Jerusalem community they responded by sending Barnabas to Antioch. Barnabas soon realized that he needed some help so he went to Tarsus and convinced Paul to join him at Antioch. "For a whole year they met with the church, and taught a large company of people" (Acts 11:26). In addition to serving as teachers, Barnabas and Saul were entrusted by the Antioch community to bring the proceeds of the famine relief collection to the brethren who live in Judea (11:29-30).

After they return from Jerusalem, Paul and Barnabas are commissioned to conduct a missionary campaign on behalf of the Antioch community.

13¹Now in the church at Antioch there were prophets and teachers, Barnabas, Symeon who was called Niger, Lucius of Cyrene, Manaen a member of the court of Herod the tetrach, and Saul. ²While they were worshiping the Lord and fasting, the Holy Spirit said, "Set apart for me Barnabas and Saul for the work to which I have called them." ³Then after fasting and praying they laid their hands on them and sent them off.

⁴So, being sent out by the Holy Spirit, they went down to Seleucia; and from there they sailed to Cyprus.

The initial verses of this episode support the claim, made earlier, that prayer marks not only the ministry of Jesus and his first disciples, but also every stage in the outreach of the gospel to the Gentile world. While the Antioch community is "worshiping the Lord and fasting," the Holy Spirit announces that Paul and Barnabas have been chosen "for the work to which I have called them." While the exact "work" that the Spirit has in mind is not mentioned, the close connection between the Spirit and the missionary enterprise elsewhere suggests that this will be missionary work.[62] The community responds to the words of the Holy Spirit by "praying," laying their hands on Barnabas and Saul, and sending them off.

13⁵When they arrived at Salamis, they proclaimed the word of God in the synagogues of the Jews. And they had John to assist them. ⁶When they had gone through the whole island as far as Paphos, they came upon a certain magician, a Jewish false prophet, named Bar-Jesus. ⁷He was with the proconsul, Sergius Paulus, a man of intelligence, who summoned Barnabas and Saul and sought to hear the word of God. ⁸But Elymas the magician (for that is the meaning of his name) withstood them, seeking to turn away the proconsul from the faith. [9]But Saul, who is also called Paul, filled with the Holy Spirit, looked intently at him [10]and said, "You son of the devil, you enemy of all righteousness, full of all deceit and villainy, will you not stop making crooked the straight paths of the Lord? [11]And now, behold, the hand of the Lord is upon you, and you shall be blind and unable to see the sun for a time." Immediately mist and darkness fell upon him and he went about seeking people to lead him by the hand. [12]Then the proconsul believed, when he saw what had occurred, for he was astonished at the teaching of the Lord.

It should come as no surprise to learn that several of the themes we have discussed previously as important to Christian discipleship in Luke-Acts are found in this passage. (1) Both the words and deeds of Jesus are referred to here. The risen Lord continues to do and teach through his disciples by means of the activity of the Holy Spirit. Paul and Barnabas, already identified as teachers (Acts 11:26; cf. 13:1), "proclaimed the word of God in the synagogues of the Jews" (13:5) when they arrived at Salamis. And Luke informs the reader that Sergius Paulus wants "to hear the word of God" (13:7), the message of Jesus and his disciples about salvation.

The miracle which evokes faith in this episode is the temporary blinding of Elymas the magician. This is reminiscent of the story about the conversion of Paul, although in the present pericope it is Sergius Paulus and not Elymas who converts. Because Paul obeys the words of the risen Lord (Acts 9:6) and enters the city of Damascus after he has been blinded, one could argue that the blinding, rather than the subsequent healing (9:18), is the miracle that evokes faith. In any case, the combination of word and work in Acts 13:5-12 climaxes in the belief of Sergius Paulus at the "teaching ($\delta\iota\delta\alpha\chi\acute{\eta}$) of the Lord" as presented by Paul and Barnabas. Sergius Paulus, like Paul and many before him, becomes a Christian after hearing the words of Jesus/his disciples and seeing his/their powerful deeds.

The missionary theme (3), so crucial to Luke's understanding of Christian discipleship, is clearly present in this pericope. The good news of salvation is offered to all through the Spirit directed missionary efforts of the early church. Paul and Barnabas, chosen by the Spirit for the missionary enterprise (Acts 13:2), are sent out both by the Antioch communiity (13:3) and by the Holy Spirit (13:4). And Luke reports that Paul is "filled with the Holy Spirit" (13:9) when he addresses his powerful words to Elymas the magician.

The theme of "following Jesus" (4) is present in this pericope in the Spirit-directed activity of Paul and Barnabas. It was pointed out earlier that receiving the Spirit functions in Acts as following Jesus did in the Gospel—both have the two-fold role of fostering intimacy and empowering mission. In the Gospel, Jesus receives the Holy Spirit (Lk. 3:22; cf. 4:1,14,18-21) and promises that the "heavenly Father" will give the Holy Spirit to those who ask him" (11:13; cf. 12:12). In Acts, however, it is the exalted Jesus who pours out the Holy Spirit (2:33; cf. 2:38) upon those who believe. The risen Jesus continues to work and to teach through the earthly activity of his disciples upon whom he has bestowed the gift of the Holy Spirit.

Paul at Antioch of Pisidia (Acts 13:16-41)

After the conversion of Sergius Paulus, Paul and his company set sail from Paphos and arrive at Perga in Pamphylia. From Perga they travel to Antioch of Pisidia where Paul delivers a speech in the local synagogue. The first speech given by Paul in Acts is generally thought to represent Luke's idealized version of how Paul preached to the Jews. It contains the same basic elements that make up the speeches of Peter and includes several words familiar to us from previous speeches: "to hear" (ἀκούειν; Acts 13:16, 44), "word" (λόγος, Acts 13:15, 26, 44, 48, 49), and "salvation" (σωτηρία; Acts 13:23, 26, 47).[63] Here the reader finds Paul fulfilling the demands of his conversion (22:15; 26:16) as he includes himself among the disciples who function as witnesses (μάρτυρες) to the resurrection (13:31; cf. Lk. 24:49; Acts 1:8, 22; 2:32; 3:15; 5:32; 22:20), carrying Jesus' name before the children of Israel (cf. Acts 9:15).

As in many of the speeches of Peter, Paul includes several references to the Jewish Scriptures which he then interprets as having been fulfilled in the life, death, and resurrection of Jesus. John's baptism of repentance is mentioned (Acts 13:24), as is the fact that God has sent the message of salvation to his people (13:26ff.) in the person of Jesus, through whom "forgiveness of sins is proclaimed" to the people (13:38). Like Peter before him (Acts 5:31), Paul identifies Jesus as a Savior (13:24).[64]

It is clear that the message of Paul, like that of Peter and Jesus himself, was delivered to sinners. The audience heard Paul speak the "word" of salvation which includes the invitation to have one's sins forgiven (Acts 13:38; cf. 2:38; 5:31; 10:43; 20:21; 28:27; Lk. 24:47), i.e. to believe and be "freed from everything from which you could not be freed by the law of Moses" (Acts 13:39). These same points are made in the next pericope when Luke reports that "almost the whole city gathered together to hear the word of God ... spoken by Paul" (13:44f.). As has been mentioned previously in this chapter, Luke understands the content of the apostolic preaching to be the "word of God" and wants to emphasize that the audience actually "heard" the preaching of these Christian missionaries. Paul is exercising his missionary responsibility simply in giving this speech, but specific mention of the mission occurs in the next pericope when Paul talks about turning to the Gentiles in order to fulfill the command of the Lord, "I have set you to be a light for the Gentiles, that you may bring salvation to the uttermost parts of the earth" (13:47).

The intimate connection between the ministry of Jesus and that of his disciples is apparent when one realizes that Isaiah 49:6 (a suffering Servant text) is seen here as fulfilled by Paul and the early Christian missionaries (Acts 13:47) and is said by Simeon to have been fulfilled in Jesus (Lk. 2:32). Mention that Paul and Barnabas "shook off the dust from their feet" against those who persecuted them and drove them out of the district (Acts 13:50) serves to recall Jesus' similar charge both to the Twelve (Lk. 9:5) and to the Seventy (10:10-11). The pericope concludes on a positive note, however, as one learns that "the disciples were filled with joy and with the Holy Spirit" (Acts 13:52). This is reminiscent of Luke's observation that the

Seventy returned from their mission with joy"(Lk. 10:17) and in that same hour Jesus "rejoiced in the Holy Spirit" (10:21).

Paul at Athens (Acts 17:22-31)

Following the divine call to preach the gospel in Macedonia (Acts 16:6-10), Paul visits Philippi (16:11-40), Thessalonica (17:1-9), Beroea (17:10-15), and now Athens (17:16-34). Next he will go to Corinth (18:1-18). While at Athens, he argues in the synagogue with Jews and God-fearers (17:17) and delivers an important speech on the Areopagus, a famous hill overlooking the city. Corresponding to Luke's version of a typical missionary speech to the Jews (13:16-41) is this idealized presentation of a similar missionary address to the Gentiles. This sermon, apart from the few sentences spoken in Lystra (14:15-17), is the only one in Acts which Paul preaches to the Gentiles.[65]

In both the chapter 13 speech and the chapter 17 speech Paul's preaching is successful (cf. Acts 13:43, 48; 17:34). Luke's purpose in these passages is to show the reader that God's plan includes both Jews and Gentiles. The chapter 17 speech is often seen as a model for Gentile preaching as it combines Old Testament references (see 17:24 and Isa. 42:5), Greek religious and philosophical thought (e.g., Acts 17:27-28), and Christian revelation (17:30-31).

Paul's activity in Athens, and the speech he delivers as he stands in the middle of the Areopagus, should remind the reader of the themes we have examined previously. In this pericope, Paul fulfills (3) the missionary demands of his conversion (cf. Acts 22:15; 26:16) as he continues to function as a witness by publicly preaching Jesus and the resurrection (17:18, 31-32). Luke emphasizes (1) the importance of hearing the word of and about Jesus as writes that when the crowd "heard *(ἀκούειν)* of the resurrection of the dead, some mocked; but others said, 'We will hear *(ἀκούειν)* you again about this.'" (17:32). When Paul informs his audience that God commands all people, wherever they live, to repent (17:30), he is implying that his powerful words are addressed (2) to sinners. This word of salvation addressed to sinners in the missionary enterprise has the desired effect as the reader learns that "some people joined him and believed, among them Dionysius the Areopagite and a woman named Damaris and others with them" (17:34). Thus the reader is reminded that both Jews (2:37; 3:19; 5:31) and Gentiles (11:18; 20:21; 26:20) have been summoned by God to repent.

Paul's Farewell Address at Miletus (Acts 20:17-38)

Before he sets off for Jerusalem Paul takes the opportunity to address the leaders of the Ephesian community. Well aware that arrest and imprisonment (Acts 20:22-23) probably await him in Jerusalem, Paul sums up his missionary and pastoral experience in this farewell address, the only speech in Acts he delivers exclusively to Christians.

In this speech Paul uses himself as an example when he sets forth instructions for those who will lead the Christian community after he has departed. Luke has already demonstrated how the example of Jesus, presented in the Gospel, has been embodied in the careers of his disciples. Now he is showing the reader how these disciples serve as an example for the next generation of Christians.[66] Many of the themes important to Luke appear in this sermon as they have in the other speeches in Acts. (1) Paul urges the elders to remember "the words (λόγος") of the Lord Jesus, how he said, 'It is more blessed to give than to receive'"(Acts 20:35). Luke probably intends the reader to see a reference to the deeds of Jesus in Paul's remarks about how complete his instruction has been: "I did not shrink from declaring to you anything that was profitable"(20:20). "I did not shrink from declaring to you the whole counsel of God"(20:27). "I did not cease night or day to admonish every one with tears"(20:31; cf. 20:7-12). The words and deeds both of Jesus and of his missionary, Paul, are referred to in this speech. When Luke informs the reader that Paul has been "preaching the kingdom"(20:25; cf. 19:8; 28:23, 31) he is clearly connecting the message of Paul with that of Jesus (Lk. 4:43-44; 8:1; cf. 4:18-19), the Twelve (9:2; cf. 24:47), and other Christian missionaries (Acts 8:12; 14:22). One can conclude, therefore, that Luke wants to ground the disciples' acts in the deeds of Jesus and their teaching in the instruction of Jesus.[67]

(2) Despite numerous sufferings, Paul testified publicly both to Jews and to Gentiles of "repentance (μετάνοια) to God and of faith *(πίστις")* in our Lord Jesus Christ" (Acts 20:20-21). All these themes (suffering, public testimony, bearing witness both to Jews and to Gentiles, repentance, and faith) have been mentioned previously as important aspects of Christian discipleship for Luke. In this passage one reads that the Holy Spirit continually warns Paul of the persecutions awaiting him (20:23). Luke is clearly presenting this as another facet of bearing witness to the gospel (20:24). The picture of Paul and the elders praying together after the speech (20:36) should serve to recall our earlier discussions about the importance of prayer for Christian discipleship.

(3) While Paul himself is a model for missionary activity,[68] his instructions to the Ephesian elders focus more on their duties as leaders of the Christian community than on any missionary responsibility they might have. Some have concluded, however, that since it is not free from internal trouble the church itself should be seen as an appropriate location for missionary activity.[69] The communal dimension of Christianity appears to be taken for granted here as Paul instructs "the elders of the church" on being "guardians" of "the flock." Luke indicates that the Holy Spirit has an important role to play in guiding the community, since it is the Holy Spirit who puts people in positions of authority and responsibility.

> 20[28]"Take heed to yourselves and to all the flock, in which the Holy Spirit has made you guardians, to feed the church of the Lord which he obtained with his own blood. [29]I know that after my departure fierce wolves will come in among you, not sparing the flock; [30]and from among your own selves will arise people speaking perverse things, to draw away the disciples after them."

(4) The radical attitude toward and use of possessions required of Christian disciples, seen throughout the Gospel and Acts, seems to take a slightly different twist in this speech. Using himself as an example Paul says: "I coveted no one's silver or gold or apparel. You yourselves know that these

hands ministered to my necessities, and to those who were with me. In all things I have shown you that by so toiling one must help the weak" (Acts 20:33-35a). He then cites the words of Jesus, "It is more blessed to give than to receive" (20:35b) to support his position. This picture of the leaders of the community working to support the community, especially the weak, appears unlike the situation described in Acts 2 and 4 where donations are placed at the feet of the apostles and all things are held in common (2:37-47; 4:32ff.). These differences will be addressed below, when we examine more closely Luke's teaching on possessions.

Conclusion

The most important aspects of Christian discipleship according to the call and commissioning stories in the Gospel are also found in the call stories in Acts. Thus, Luke presents the reader of his two-volume work with a consistent picture of what it means to be a Chrisian disciple. Jesus and his way of life are presented as examples for Christian disciples to emulate.[70]

One should believe Jesus because he is uniquely and intimately related to God and is the long awaited Messiah whose coming was promised by God throughout the Old Testament period. Those who become intimately associated with Jesus as they follow him on his way will gradually come to an understanding of his identity.

Potential followers of Jesus, from Luke's day to our own, are usually drawn to Christianity by the witness, in word and deed, of Christian disciples. According to the stories in Acts the first step to becoming a Christian is to hear the preaching of the word of God.[71] After hearing about Jesus and his message of forgiveness and reconciliation, would-be disciples respond by repenting, converting, being baptized into Jesus' new community, receiving the Holy Spirit and joyfully praising God. They soon learn that their life of faith is an intimate, eucharist-centered, prayer-filled journey with Jesus in which, following Jesus' example, they must do the will of God and place themselves at the service of others. This service ethic includes adopting a lifestyle which, in many respects, is radically opposed to the standards of the world. The greatest disciple is not the one with the most economic or political power, authority, and prestige, but rather: (1) the one who is the best servant, (2) the one who is not selfish, but uses wealth and possessions for the benefit of those in need, and (3) the one who suffers injustice rather than inflicting it on others. The person who follows Jesus on his way will come to know him as the Messiah who is the Son of God and the Servant of God. Such an individual will, then, fulfill the role of missionary and joyfully proclaim the saving message of and about Jesus to others.

4

Christology and Discipleship

The person and activity of Jesus Christ are at the center of Lukan theology because "there is salvation in no one else" (Acts 4:12). As we will see below, Luke believes that God has a plan for the salvation of all humanity. This plan includes the proclamation of salvation by Jesus during his earthly ministry and the proclamation about Jesus, the resurrected and exalted one, by the early church. Those who accept the message of and about Jesus are led to repent, believe, be baptized into Jesus' new community, and conduct their lives in accordance with his teaching and example. Because Jesus serves as a model for the disciple to follow, the question, "What does it mean to follow Jesus?" cannot be separated from the question of Jesus' identity, "Who is Jesus?"[1]

Jesus raises the question of his identity when he asks his disciples, "Who do the people say that I am?" (Lk. 9:18) and, following their answer queries, "But who do you say that I am?" (9:20). Luke's editorial activity also points to an interest in Jesus' identity. Because Luke has not included Mark 6:45-8:26 in his Gospel, Peter's identification of Jesus as the "Christ of God" (Lk. 9:20) follows closely after and answers Herod's question, "who is this about whom I hear such things?" (9:9; cf. Mk. 6:14-16). Herod's wish to "see" Jesus (9:9) is fulfilled eventually (23:6-12), but for him physical sight does not become the insight which leads to salvation.

There is an intrinsic connection between one's understanding of Jesus and one's understanding of what Christian discipleship entails. To discover Jesus' identity is to learn what true discipleship is, and vice versa. An incorrect understanding of Jesus will obviously result in an inadequate or misdirected following of Jesus. On the other hand, it seems clear that only by following Jesus does one come to understand who Jesus is.[2] Those who conclude, for example, that Jesus is a magician, not unlike other ancient Near Eastern miracle workers, do not become his disciples. Instead of seeing "the finger of God" in Jesus' powerful miracles, they conclude that he casts out demons by Beelzebul, the prince of demons (Lk. 11:14-26). Members of the crowd (11:16) and Herod (23:8) seek a sign from Jesus, some objective proof that his power comes from God. However, the one who wishes to know if God is at work in Jesus first must hear and heed his call to repentance. Only those who respond positively to the message of God's salvation are able to recognize the presence of God in the words and works of Jesus.

An immense body of literature has grown up around the question of Jesus' identity (Christology), making a comprehensive survey beyond the scope of this book. But because this is an important issue for Luke, it must concern us. In this chapter we will concentrate on the titles Luke uses for Jesus. While we recognize that "Luke does not just build his Christology on Jesus' titles,"[3] the fact is that he does use these titles throughout the Gospel and Acts to identify Jesus. One must not concentrate on these titles in the abstract, of course, but rather pay close attention to how they are used in Luke-Acts and how they affect Luke's understanding of discipleship.

In the first two chapters of Luke's Gospel, several important Christological titles are used by heavenly beings to identify Jesus. When the angel Gabriel appears to Mary he tells her that the child she will soon bear will be called holy, "the Son of God" (Lk. 1:35). Different titles are mentioned when the angel says to the shepherds who were out in the field, keeping watch over their flock,

> 2[10]"Be not afraid; for behold, I bring you good news of a great joy which will come to all the people; [11]for to you is born this day in the city of David a Savior, who is Christ the Lord."

In addition to these four important titles (Son of God, Savior, Messiah/Christ, Lord), attributed to Jesus by heavenly beings, we will discuss three titles which Jesus explicitly or implicitly uses for himself: "Son of Man," "Servant," and "Prophet." Luke frequently places the title "Son of Man" on the lips of Jesus and has Jesus speak of himself as the suffering Son of Man (Lk. 9:22). Since no Old Testament passage speaks of a suffering Son of Man one is led to see in these texts an allusion to the Isaian Suffering Servant. This conclusion is supported when Jesus quotes part of Isaiah 53:12 at the Last Supper and says that it finds its fulfillment in him (Lk. 22:37). Jesus refers to himself as a prophet when he says "it cannot be that a prophet should perish away from Jerusalem" (13:33), and implies the same when he notes, "no prophet is acceptable in his own country" (4:24).[4]

Luke presents Jesus of Nazareth as a human being (Lk. 2:6-7; Acts 2:22) who acts as God's agent in bringing the gift of salvation to humanity. Jesus shows mercy and compassion in his active concern for "the poor, the maimed, the lame, the blind" (Lk. 14:13; cf. 4:18), sinners (5:30; 7:34; 15:1), and other outcasts (5:12-16; 10:25-37; 17:11-19). There are things about this special emissary of God, however, that serve to set him apart from other human beings. Jesus is conceived through the power of the Holy Spirit (1:34-35), resurrected from the dead (e.g., 24:6; Acts 2:24, 32), and has ascended to God's right hand (Acts 2:33; 5:31; cf. 1:9). He has a special relationship to his heavenly Father (Lk. 2:49; 3:22; 9:35; 10:21-22; 23:46) and his ministry is guided by the Holy Spirit (3:22; 4:1,14,18; 10:21). Thus Luke presents Jesus as the risen Lord who rules from heaven and as a human being whose story is normative for Christian discipleship.

Son of God

The most significant title for Jesus in Mark's Gospel[5] is also found in Luke-Acts. In addition to the absolute term "Son of God," the third evangelist refers to Jesus as "Son of the Most High (God)" and "the/my Son." This title, and its variations, would appear to be an important designation for Jesus since heavenly beings use it to refer to him. It is the angel Gabriel who tells Mary initially that her son Jesus "will be called the Son of the Most High"(Lk. 1:32). He soon adds that the child "will be called holy, the Son of God" (1:35). Both times the voice from heaven speaks it uses this title to refer to Jesus. At the baptism the voice says, "Thou art my beloved Son; with thee I am well pleased" (3:22). And at the transfiguration the voice states, "This is my Son, my Chosen; listen to him!" (9:35). Luke found many references to Jesus as the Son of God in his sources. While the angel's words cited above are Lukan, the identification of Jesus as God's Son at the baptism and the transfiguration has Markan parallels (cf. Mk. 1:11; 9:7). Luke also includes Markan verses which show that the demons recognize Jesus as the "Son of God" (Lk. 4:41; Mk. 3:11) and the "Son of the Most High God" (Lk. 8:28; Mk. 5:7). Jesus seems to identify himself as the Son of God: (1) in the Parable of the Wicked Tenants when he speaks about the "beloved son" who will be killed (Lk. 20:13ff.; Mk. 12:6ff.), and (2) when he responds to the question of the Sanhedrin, "Are you the Son of God, then?" by stating, "You say that I am"(Lk. 22:70; cf. Mk. 14:61 where the high priest asks if Jesus is "the Son of the Blessed").

In two instances Luke has eliminated Markan references to Jesus as the Son of God (Mk. 13:32; 15:39).[6] When speaking about the time of the parousia, Jesus says "But of that day or that hour no one knows, not even the angels in heaven, nor the Son, but only the Father"(Mk. 13:32). This verse, in which Jesus seems to speak of his own ignorance with regard to the time of the parousia, is not included in Luke's Gospel. However, Luke makes a similar point in Acts 1:7. Jesus points out that God's timetable is not open to human knowledge or speculation when he says, "It is not for you to know the times or seasons which the Father has fixed by his own authority" (Acts 1:7).

According to Mark 15:39, the Roman centurion at the foot of the cross says of Jesus, "Truly this man was the Son of God!" In Luke's Gospel, however, the centurion says, "Certainly this man was innocent!" (Lk. 23:47). The Roman soldier thus joins a long list of individuals in Luke-Acts who declare that Jesus is innocent or righteous (δίκαιος): Pilate (Lk. 23:4,14, 22), Herod (23:14), the good thief (23:41), Peter (Acts 3:14), Stephen (7:52), Paul (13:28), and Ananias (22:14). The centurion "praised God" (a Lukan addition; cf. Mk. 15:39) because he recognized the meaning of this innocent death in God's plan. There is probably an allusion here to Isaiah 53:11 where God speaks of "the righteous one, my servant."

From his Q source Luke includes (a) the temptation scene in which "the devil" knows that Jesus is the Son of God (Lk. 4:3,9; Mt. 4:3), and (b) Jesus' identification of himself as the Son (Lk. 10:22; Mt. 11:27):

> 10²²"All things have been delivered to me by my Father; and no one knows who the Son is except the Father, or who the Father is except the Son and any one to whom the Son chooses to reveal him."

Before we conclude our comments on Luke's use of the title Son of God for Jesus we must look at two other Gospel pericopes and the use of this title in Acts. Jesus' comment during his Sermon on the Plain (6:35-36; cf. Mt. 5:43-48, the Sermon on the Mount) indicates that his disciples can become "sons of the Most High," a title ascribed to Jesus himself (Lk. 1:33; 8:28):

> 6³⁵"But love your enemies, and do good, and lend, expecting nothing in return; and your reward will be great, and you will be sons of the Most High; for he is kind to the ungrateful and the selfish. ³⁶Be merciful, even as your Father is merciful."

As a result of Lukan editing (Mk. 12:25), Jesus says something quite similar when he states that those who are resurrected "are equal to angels and are sons of God, being sons of the resurrection" (Lk. 20:36).

In Acts Jesus is identified as the Son of God only twice.[7] While he was preaching in the Damascus synagogues, Paul proclaimed Jesus, saying, "He is the Son of God" (Acts 9:20). And in a sermon to the Jews at Pisidian Antioch (13:33) Paul identifies Jesus as the Son spoken of in Psalm 2:7.

Elsewhere[8] we have argued that the title Son of God should be seen against its Old Testament background and understood primarily as denoting a moral or functional relationship. The title "Son of God" means "being chosen or elected to a task, thus participating in the work of God; it implies obedience, the obedience of a son to a father."[9] In Luke's Gospel, however, there is a uniqueness about Jesus' sonship that transcends the strictly functional, particularly in 10:22:

> 10[22]"All things have been delivered to me by my Father; and no one knows who the Son is except the Father, or who the Father is except the Son and any one to whom the Son chooses to reveal him."

Jesus demonstrates both obedience and faithfulness to God, even to death on a cross. This is seen clearly in the passion narrative and in Jesus' prayer while on the cross. After the Last Supper, Jesus and his disciples go to the Mount of Olives. Once there, Jesus prays, "Father, if thou art willing, remove this cup from me; nevertheless not my will, but thine, be done" (Lk. 22:42). The Father/Son relationship is also highlighted in the final words of the earthly Jesus while on the cross, "Father, into thy hands I commit my spirit!" (23:46).

Recognizing that Jesus is the Son of God has definite implications for discipleship. As Jesus was obedient to the will of God, so too must his followers be obedient to the will of God. Luke indicates that one discovers the will of God by listening to the words of Jesus when he reports that the heavenly voice said "This is my Son, my Chosen; listen to him!" (9:35). Jesus identifies as his relatives "those who hear the word of God and do it" (Lk. 8:21). These are the same individuals who are encouraged to follow Jesus' example (2:49) and address God as "Father" (11:2). God is the Father of Jesus (10:21-22; 22:29; 24:49) and of his disciples (6:36; 12:30,32). While Jesus is the unique Son of God,[10] his faithful disciples can become children of the Most High (cf. 20:36). In revealing God's Fatherhood (10:22), Jesus reveals the disciple's "sonship." The Christian stands in the same relationship to the Father as Jesus does, because Jesus' Sonship mediates the disciple's "sonship." Disciples, following the example of Jesus, are expected to be merciful as God is merciful, kind to the ungrateful and the selfish, love their enemies, do good, and lend, expecting nothing in return (6:35-36). In Luke 4:41 we learn that the demons recognize Jesus and cry out "You are the Son of God!" Luke immediately adds that Jesus "rebuked them, and would not allow them to speak, because they knew that he was the Christ" (4:41). The context here suggests that Luke equates the titles "Son of God" and "Messiah" (cf. 22:70 and 23:2). Because of this we will examine next Luke's use of the title "Messiah" or "Christ" for Jesus.

Messiah / Christ

A title Luke uses frequently for this remarkable individual, Jesus of Nazareth, is χριστός ("Messiah" or "Christ"). It is a comprehensive term which identifies Jesus as God's final, supreme agent in the history of salvation (Lk. 2:26; 9:20). Seen by many as the most important title for Jesus in Luke-Acts, χριστός would have suggested both royalty ("King") and Davidic descent ("Son of David") to Luke's original readers.

Luke uses the noun χριστός as a title for Jesus numerous times in his two-volume work.[11] Often in Acts it appears as almost a second name.[12] The term has a rich Old Testament background[13] and at the time of Jesus would probably have been understood to refer to a political king and military leader who would drive out the Romans. Luke, following Mark, has Jesus correct this title, thereby countering the political overtones. Peter identifies Jesus as "the Christ of God" (9:20; Mk. 8:29), but Jesus immediately commands his disciples to tell this to no one and states, "The Son of Man must suffer many things, and be rejected by the elders and chief priests and scribes and be killed, and on the third day be raised" (9:22; Mk. 8:30-31). When the Sanhedrin say to Jesus, "If you are the Christ, tell us" (22:67), he responds, "If I tell you you will not believe" (22:67). Jesus' evasive answer (cf. Mk. 14:62 where Jesus replies frankly, "I am.") shows that Luke is reluctant to have Jesus identify himself as the Christ.

In the Gospel, this title forms part of the accusations against Jesus (Lk. 23:2) and is used by both the rulers of the people

(23:35) and one of the criminals (23:39) to mock Jesus. Most distinctive, however, is Luke's idea that Jesus was a suffering Messiah. "The idea of a suffering messiah is found nowhere in the OT or in any Jewish literature prior to or contemporaneous with the NT."[14] The risen Jesus first asks his two companions on the road to Emmaus, "Was it not necessary that the Christ should suffer these things and enter into this glory?" (24:26). Later, when he opens the minds of his disciples to understand the scriptures, Jesus says, "Thus it is written, that the Christ should suffer and on the third day rise from the dead" (24:46). In Acts, Luke frequently reminds the reader that Jesus is the Christ who had to suffer (e.g., Acts 2:36; 3:18; 4:10; 17:3; 26:23). We will discuss below why the Christ who has to suffer should be understood according to the Suffering Servant motif.[15]

Luke's reluctance to identify Jesus as the Messiah/Christ in the Gospel is probably due to the political overtones this designation would have conveyed. Once Luke corrects this misunderstanding, however, and defines Jesus as the suffering, dying, rising Messiah, the title is frequently used to identify Jesus (e.g., Acts 2:36; 4:10; 9:22; 15:26; 17:3; 18:5,28).

Recognizing that Jesus is the suffering Messiah/Christ has specific implications for discipleship. The importance of acknowledging that Jesus is the Christ can be seen in the name by which his followers are called, "Christians" (cf. Acts 11:26). The one who believes that God's final, supreme agent in the history of salvation has come will look to that person for guidance. In the first century an announcement that the Messiah has come could easily have been greeted with a violent outburst directed at the Roman authorities. The popular expectation was that the Messiah would be a political king and military leader who would spearhead a violent revolution and drive out the Romans. Simply recognizing that Jesus is the Messiah, therefore, is not enough. Luke's presentation of Jesus as the suffering Messiah, rather than as a political/military figure, suggests that Christian discipleship involves the renunciation of violence. The one who wishes to travel with Jesus on his journey to God must realize that the road is often difficult and demanding. The suggestion that the Isaian Suffering Servant serves as a model for both Jesus and his disciples will be examined below.

Savior

The angel who announces to the shepherds that Jesus is the Christ also identifies him as a "Savior" (Lk. 2:11). Although the name "Jesus" means "God is salvation," Luke is the only Synoptic evangelist to use the title "Savior" (σωτήρ) for Jesus (Lk. 2:11). In using this title, used for God in the Hebrew Scriptures (1 Sam. 10:19; Isa. 45:15,21), Luke is suggesting that Jesus acts with divine authority.[16] God has determined to make available in Jesus the salvation that otherwise only he can accomplish. The third evangelist is obviously aware of the Hebrew tradition since Mary refers to God as "my Savior" in her Magnificat (Lk. 1:47).

Although the title "Savior" occurs only once in Luke's Gospel (2:11; cf. 1:69; 2:30), its prominent position in the words of the angel to the shepherds causes us to examine Luke's use of this title in his second volume. In Acts, both Peter (Acts 5:31) and Paul (13:23) use the title "Savior" to refer to Jesus. As part of their response to the high priest's charge, that they not teach in Jesus' name, Peter and the apostles state:

> 5:31"God exalted Jesus at his right hand as Leader and Savior, to give repentance to Israel and forgiveness of sins. 32And we are witnesses to these things, and so is the Holy Spirit whom God has given to those who obey him."

In this passage Luke suggests that repentance is the proper response of one who recognizes that Jesus is the "Savior." As we have already seen, repentance involves a radical conversion from all that is evil and a total commitment to God. It is closely connected with faith, thus suggesting obedience, trust and hope, and with baptism, thus suggesting that this process of conversion is accomplished within the Christian community. Mention of the Holy Spirit as a gift of God to those who are obedient points unmistakenly to an active discipleship. This includes both prayer (cf. Lk. 11:13) and hearing and doing the will of God.

In his synagogue address in Pisidian Antioch, Paul states that "God has brought to Israel a Savior, Jesus, as he promised" (Acts 13:23). The promises he has in mind are those made to David that he would have descendents who would rule after him forever (2 Sam. 7:12-16; 22:51; Pss. 89:29,36f.; 132:11f.). Luke suggests indirectly here what he has stated more clearly in Acts 5:31, that repentance is the appropriate response of the one who accepts Jesus as Savior. In the very next verse, Luke has Paul refer to John's preaching "a baptism of repentance to all the people of Israel" (13:24).

In applying the same title to God and Jesus, Luke is emphasizing that God has made salvation available in Jesus (Acts 4:12). Through his words and deeds, Jesus teaches us that God's salvation involves more than just deliverance from sickness, infirmity, and sin. During his ministry "to seek and to save the lost" (Lk. 19:10), Jesus teaches his disciples that the marginalized should participate fully in the ongoing life of the community. God's salvation is universal and all-encompassing; it has a present, as well as a future, dimension. This means that the message of salvation has economic, political and social consequences. The disciple who understands this will be led to proclaim the message of God's salvation and to work for social justice.

Lord

The last of the three titles used by the angel in Luke 2:11, "Lord" (κύριος), is the most frequently used title for Jesus in Luke-Acts.[17] As he did with "Savior," Luke uses the title "Lord" both for God and for Jesus. It is used for God in the Gospel (e.g. Lk. 1:6ff.,76; 19:38; 20:42) as well as in Acts (e.g., Acts 3:19; 4:26; 7:31ff.) and for Jesus in both the Gospel (e.g., Lk. 1:43; 2:11; 24:34) and Acts (e.g., Acts 1:6, 21; 2:36). The dominion, power, and authority that God and Jesus are said to exercise over human beings is emphasized by Luke's use of "Lord" (κύριος). Jesus is Lord because he is the one through whom God has chosen to exercise his rule.

One of the first things one notices about Luke's use of "Lord" for Jesus is that the Lord has a "way." John the Baptist, in fulfillment of the prophecies of Malachi and Isaiah, is identified as one who "will go before the Lord to prepare his ways"

(Lk. 1:76; cf. Mal. 3:1) and as "the voice crying in the wilderness: Prepare the way of the Lord" (Lk. 3:4; cf. Isa. 40:3). The way of the Lord is also the "way of peace" (Lk. 1:79). The way of the Lord is the way of Jesus (cf. Acts 18:25). The last strophe of Zechariah's prayer focuses on the rising light from on high in whom God has visited us and shown his mercy, namely, Jesus who will "guide our feet into the way of peace" (Lk. 1:79).[18] This should remind us of the journey motif associated with Christian discipleship.[19] Both the communal dimension of discipleship and the journey motif are found in Luke's use of the expression "the Way" to refer to the followers of Jesus.

The reader of Luke-Acts discovers that Luke has associated the title "Lord" with the chief components of discipleship. Many individuals are pictured listening to the word of the Lord (e.g., Lk. 10:39-41) and observing his powerful deeds (e.g., Lk. 5:12; 7:6-10,19ff.; 18:41-43). Of course, more is required for discipleship than merely hearing his words and seeing his deeds. In the Sermon on the Plain Jesus says, "Why do you call me 'Lord, Lord,' and not do what I tell you?" (Lk. 6:46). One of the things Jesus has taught his disciples is to be merciful, even as God is merciful (6:36). It should come as no surprise, therefore, when the Lord Jesus has compassion on the widow of Nain and brings her only son back to life (7:13ff.).

In a passage in which Jesus is identified as Lord, one learns that he preaches the good news of God's salvation to the poor (Lk. 7:19-23). The fact that the Lord is especially concerned with the marginalized comes as a surprise both to Peter and to the Roman centurion. In the initial call story in the Gospel Peter says, "Depart from me, for I am a sinful man, O Lord" (Lk. 5:8). The centurion, whose servant was at the point of death, does not deem himself worthy of approaching Jesus. Instead, he sends the following message with his friends: "Lord, do not trouble yourself, for I am not worthy to have you come under my roof; therefore I did not presume to come to you. But say the word, and let my servant be healed" (7:6). These individuals are mistaken, of course, because the Lord has come to seek and to save the lost" (19:8-10).[20] According to Luke, individuals are saved through believing in the Lord Jesus (Acts

15:11; 16:31) who is able to forgive sins (cf. Acts 7:60). This faith in the Lord Jesus (Lk. 17:5ff.; Acts 9:35,42; 11:17,21; 16:31; 18:8) leads to baptism in his name (Acts 18:8; 19:5; cf. 8:16). Apparently some think that the Lord favors a violent response to those who refuse to accept him. At the beginning of his journey to Jerusalem, Jesus is not received by some Samaritan villagers. When they see this, James and John say, "Lord, do you want us to bid fire come down from heaven and consume them?" (Lk. 9:54). Jesus responds by rebuking his disciples (9:55). Similarly, when one of his disciples cuts off the ear of the high priest's slave Jesus says, "No more of this!" and he touched his ear and healed him (22:49-51; cf. 22:38). The disciples who think that they are doing what the Lord wants when they respond violently against their opponents are mistaken. Paul provides a good example of what it means to follow the Lord Jesus when he says, "I am ready not only to be imprisoned but even to die at Jerusalem for the name of the Lord Jesus" (Acts 21:13; cf. Lk. 22:33). While Christians, like Paul, should be ready to suffer violence "for the name of the Lord Jesus," disciples of Jesus must not act violently themselves.

The Lord warns that salvation is not for workers of iniquity (Lk. 13:22-30); one must actually strive to be a good person and not merely give the appearance of being a good person (11:39ff.; 13:15). Among other things, a disciple of the Lord must be a person of prayer, generous, and mission-oriented. The Lord prays (11:1), teaches his disciples a prayer (11:2-4), and instructs them to pray always and not lose heart (18:1-8). The one who wishes to follow the Lord must not let anything interfere with this commitment (9:57ff.). And disciples of the Lord must not be selfish in their use of possessions. The rich tax collector Zacchaeus says to the Lord, "Behold, Lord, the half of my goods I give to the poor; and if I have defrauded any one of anything, I restore it fourfold" (19:8). Jesus is referred to as "Lord" when Luke describes the Jerusalem community and its sharing of possessions (Acts 4:33-37). And Paul reminds the Ephesian elders that it was "the Lord Jesus" who said, "It is more blessed to give than to receive" (Acts 20:35).

The missionary responsibility of the Christian disciple is seen when the Lord appoints the Seventy (Lk. 10:1) and Peter (Acts 10:36ff.) to preach the good news and commissions Paul (Acts 9:10ff., 28-29; 22:8ff.; 26:15ff.) to act as his witness (23:11) to the Gentiles. The one who recognizes that Jesus is the Lord must understand that Jesus joins with God in exercising dominion, power, and authority over human beings. However, he does not do this in a harsh or cruel way. The Lord acts with mercy and compassion and expects his disciples to follow his example. Those who listen to the Lord and see his powerful deeds are led to lead their lives according to his teachings. They must be concerned with the marginalized. They must repent, believe, and be baptized into the "church of the Lord." They must not react violently against their opponents and must be ready to suffer and die, if necessary, for his name. Disciples of the Lord must seek to be good people and not merely to appear to be good. Their lives must be characterized by prayer, generosity, and a commitment to spreading the word of the Lord. Because this title touches on so many aspects of discipleship it is perhaps fitting that in the final verse of Luke's two-volume work he refers to Jesus as "the Lord Jesus Christ" (Acts 28:31).

Son of Man

Luke also uses the traditional title "Son of Man" to refer to Jesus, the Son of God, the Messiah who is Lord and Savior. The titles "Son of God," "Lord," and "Savior," serve to highlight the power and authority now exercised by the risen Christ. Those who focus exclusively on power and glory, however, miss an extremely important aspect of Lukan Christology, suffering messiahship. Luke clearly believes that anyone who wishes to know Jesus must understand him as the suffering, dying Messiah. The risen Jesus reminds his disciples on two occasions that a correct understanding of messiahship must include suffering and death, as well as resurrection (Lk. 24:25-27, 44-46; cf. Acts 3:18; 17:3; 26:23). In order to emphasize this motif, Luke has included in the Gospel sayings about the suffering Son of Man and has deliberately portrayed Jesus as the Suffering Servant of Isaiah 40-55.

While some suggest that the book of Ezekiel forms the background for the title "Son of Man,"[21] most scholars identify Daniel 7 as the source for this title.[22] In Daniel 7:13-14 the prophet has a night vision in which "one like a son of man" (i.e. a human figure) rises on the clouds of heaven to the throne of God where he receives an eternal kingdom. Daniel's vision is then interpreted to mean that "saints of the Most High," the righteous Jews who will soon be liberated from their oppressors, "shall receive the kingdom, and possess the kingdom forever, forever and ever" (Dan. 7:18; cf. 7:22,27). Although the "son of man" is interpreted in Daniel as a collective symbol (i.e., "saints of the Most High"), later Jewish apocalyptic literature interprets the Danielic "son of man" as an individual heavenly figure.

In 1 Enoch 62:5, one reads that the kings and the mighty are terrified "when they see that son of man sitting on the throne of his glory." The author of 1 Enoch interprets Daniel 7:13-14 to mean that God has given his throne to the son of man, who assumes the role of apocalyptic judge. In IV Ezra 13:1-3, a work written at the end of the first century, one reads about a messianic redeemer who arises from the midst of a storm-tossed sea and flies "with the clouds of heaven." With Daniel 7 as its source, and in light of its use in Jewish apocalyptic literature, the title "Son of Man" refers to a heavenly figure who sits on the divine throne, executes judgement against sinners, and establishes the eternal kingdom of the righteous.

Luke uses the title "Son of Man" both to refer to Jesus' earthly ministry (Lk. 5:24; 6:5, 22; 7:34; 9:58; 12:10; 19:10; 22:48) and to his future coming in glory or judgment (9:26; 11:30; 12:8, 40; 17:22-30; 18:8; 21:27, 36; 22:69). This supports our earlier claim that Luke is interested in presenting Jesus as both a mortal and a heavenly figure. Our primary interest, however, lies in those "Son of Man" sayings which refer to the passion.[23] Relying for the most part on Mark[24] and Q, Luke identifies Jesus as the Son of Man who will be delivered into the hands of "men" and Gentiles (9:44; 18:32; 22:22; 24:7), to be killed, and be raised (9:22; 18:33; 24:7). These sayings highlight an important aspect of Lukan Christology and have profound implications for Christian discipleship. Jesus, the Messiah, Lord and Savior, is also the suffering Son of Man.

As such, he becomes a model for the suffering and persecution that his disciples endure. In the Sermon on the Plain Jesus says, "Blessed are you when people hate you, and when they exclude you and revile you, and cast out your name as evil, on account of the Son of Man!" (Lk. 6:22). The only time this title appears in Acts is on the lips of Stephen, the first Christian martyr:

> 7⁵⁵But Stephen, full of the Holy Spirit, gazed into heaven and saw the glory of God, and Jesus standing at the right hand of God; ⁵⁶and he said, "Behold, I see the heavens opened, and the Son of Man standing at the right hand of God."

Stephen sees Jesus in his role as the Son of Man who suffered and was vindicated by God (Lk. 9:22). As the suffering Son of Man, Jesus becomes a model for Christians.[25] The kind of suffering that the world inflicted on him it will also inflict on his disciples. This theme is amplified by Luke's portrayal of Jesus as the Isaian Suffering Servant.

Servant

In two passages Luke unambiguously applies quotations from the Isaian Servant Songs to Jesus' mission. At the Last Supper Jesus indicates that he is the fulfillment of Isaiah 53:12 when he says, "For I tell you that this scripture must be fulfilled in me, 'And he was reckoned with trangressors'; for what is written about me has its fulfillment" (Lk. 22:37). In Acts, one finds the story of Philip's encounter with an Ethiopian who is reading Isaiah 53:7f. In response to the Ethiopian's question, "About whom, pray, does the prophet say this, about himself or about someone else?" (Acts 8:34), Philip begins to tell him about the good news of Jesus. Luke's obvious dependence on the Isaian Servant Songs suggests that he identifies Jesus as the "Servant" of God in Acts 3:13, 26; 4:27, 30. While the term παῖς can mean either child or servant, in these verses it is best translated as referring to Jesus as the Servant of God.[26]

Luke may well have the Servant in mind also when, in the

programmatic passage at the beginning of his public ministry
(Lk. 4:16ff.), Jesus identifies himself as the fulfillment of Isaiah
61:1-2. Jesus went up to the synagogue at Nazareth on the
sabbath day, stood up and read from the book of the prophet
Isaiah:

> 4[18]"The Spirit of the Lord is upon me, because he has
> anointed me to preach good news to the poor. He has sent
> me to proclaim release to the captives and recovering of
> sight to the blind, to set at liberty those who are oppressed,
> [19]to proclaim the acceptable year of the Lord." [20]And he
> closed the book, and gave it back to the attendant, and sat
> down; and the eyes of all in the synagogue were fixed on
> him. [21]And he began to say to them, "Today this scripture
> has been fulfilled in your hearing."

"Since the [Isaiah 61] passage uses a language and style reminiscent of the earlier Servant passages it may have been interpreted in terms of the Servant of Yahweh."[27]

Luke's identification of Jesus as the Suffering Servant of
Isaiah 40-55 agrees with his presentation of Jesus as the suffering Messiah (Lk. 24:26, 46) and the suffering Son of Man.
There are numerous verses in the Gospel and Acts which
indicate that the way of discipleship also includes the possibility
of suffering. But in his use of the Servant theme, Luke does
not dwell exclusively on suffering.

When he refers to Jesus as proclaiming "the light to the
Gentiles" (Lk. 2:32; Acts 26:23) Luke is applying another aspect
of the servant theme to Jesus (cf. Isa. 42:6; 49:6).[28] The third
evangelist has the missionary dimension of discipleship in mind
here. When one reads Acts 26:23 an obvious question arises:
How can the resurrected Christ "proclaim light both to the
people and to the Gentiles"? The risen Lord proclaims this
light through his earthly representatives, the Christian missionaries. Both mission and suffering are seen when Luke
portrays Paul and Barnabas in the role of the servant. In Acts
13:46-47 (cf. Acts 26:15-18; 28:26-27) Paul and Barnabas boldly
declare their intention to take the gospel to the Gentiles. They
cite Isaiah 49:6 as scriptural support for this missionary enterprise. Jesus is God's Servant and light to the Gentiles (Lk.

2:32), but the mission of the Servant is also the task of Jesus' disciples who proclaim the light to the Gentiles (Acts 13:46-47). Luke intends to present Jesus as a model for his followers. Paul and Barnabas, therefore, serve as examples for all Christians who carry on the task of the Servant. While Luke admits that suffering and death might be the lot of the faithful disciple, he is much more interested in presenting the disciple as one who serves. In Luke-Acts Jesus is seen as the Servant who lives a life of service and teaches his disciples to do the same (e.g., Lk. 22:24-30). Three times in Acts verses from Isaiah are quoted to describe a missionary task:

> 13[47]"I have set you to be a light for the Gentiles, that you may bring salvation to the uttermost parts of the earth." (Isa. 49:6).

> 26[17]"I shall deliver you from this people and from the Gentiles to whom I send you, [18]to open their eyes, that they may turn from darkness to light..." (Isa. 35:5; 42:6-7).

> 28[26]"Go to this people, and say..." (Isa. 6:9-10).

Luke's presentation of Jesus as the Servant of God has obvious implications for Christian discipleship. Because the Servant suffered as part of his ministry, and because Jesus suffered and died as part of his ministry, the Christian may discover that the way of discipleship includes suffering and death. More important, however, is the service aspect of this title. The Christian must follow the example of Jesus, the one who serves. With mercy and compassion the disciple must take care of the weaker members of society. Working for social justice means providing food for respectable widows (cf. Acts 6:1-6), ministering to the poor who are hungry and covered with sores (cf. Lk. 16:19-31), and providing medical care for those in need, even if they are outside one's religious community (cf. 10:25-37).

Prophet

Early in the Gospel, Luke uses a passage from Isaiah, cited

above, as a programmatic statement on the nature of Jesus' entire ministry. Jesus enters the synagogue at Nazareth one sabbath day and reads from the Isaiah scroll, "The Spirit of the Lord is upon me, because he has anointed me to preach good news to the poor" (Lk. 4:18-19; cf. Isa. 58:6; 61:1-2). Shortly after this incident, Jesus encounters a man with an unclean demon and says to the demon, "Be silent, and come out of him!" (4:35). This agrees with what we have already said about Luke's portrait of Jesus. The third evangelist presents Jesus as one who speaks authoritatively and who performs numerous mighty acts. As the risen Lord went along the road to Emmaus with his two disciples they told him about "Jesus of Nazareth, who was a prophet mighty in deed and word before God and all the people" (Lk. 24:19). Of what significance is it for discipleship that Luke ascribes to Jesus the title "Prophet"?

In Luke-Acts a large number of passages speak of Jesus as a "Prophet." While in the Nazareth synagogue, Jesus implies that he is a prophet when he says, "Truly, I say to you, no prophet is acceptable in his own country" (Lk. 4:24; cf. Mk. 6:4). During his journey to Jerusalem, Jesus seems to identify himself as a prophet when he says, "I must go on my way today and tomorrow and the day following; for it cannot be that a prophet should perish away from Jerusalem"(Lk. 13:33). Jesus' disciples respond to his question, "Who do the people say that I am?" (Lk. 9:18) by noting that some say he is Elijah and others that one of the old prophets has risen (9:19; cf. Mk. 6:15). Their answer is supported: (1) by the Nain episode, where the people recognize Jesus as "a great prophet" after he has raised the dead boy (Lk. 7:16), (2) by the Herod episode, in which Luke notes that some identified Jesus as Elijah and others said that "one of the old prophets had risen" (9:8), and (3) by the Emmaus episode, in which Jesus is identified as "a prophet mighty in deed and word" (24:19).

These texts highlight several discipleship themes to which we have already referred. The difficulties involved in following Jesus, the Lord and Son of Man who has nowhere to lay his head (Lk. 9:57-62) are suggested when Jesus says that "no prophet is acceptable in his own country" (4:24) and indicates that a prophet cannot perish away from Jerusalem (13:33).

The necessity of acting with compassion is indicated when one reads that the great prophet Jesus, the Lord, has compassion on the widow of Nain (7:13-17). The importance of seeing and hearing to discipleship are suggested in both the Herod passage, when the king says "who is this about whom I hear such things?" (9:9) and Luke notes "And he sought to see him" (9:9), and the Emmaus episode, where Jesus is described as "a prophet mighty in deed and word" (24:19).

Jesus, the prophet, associates with sinners and forgives those who have great love and faith (7:39-50). And Jesus, who resembles the prophets in his suffering and death, serves as a model for his disciples (Lk. 6:22-23; cf. 13:33-34; Acts 7:52).

> 6²²"Blessed are you when people hate you, and when they exclude you and revile you, and cast out your name as evil, on account of the Son of Man! ²³Rejoice in that day, and leap for joy, for behold, your reward is great in heaven; for so their ancestors did to the prophets."

In certain texts (Acts 3:22-23; 7:37), Luke specifically presents Jesus as the "Prophet like Moses" promised in Deuteronomy 18:15-18:

> 3²²Moses said, "The Lord God will raise up for you a prophet from your brethren as he raised me up. You shall listen to him in whatever he tells you. ²³And it shall be that every soul that does not listen to that prophet shall be destroyed from the people."

The emphasis here on listening to Jesus, the prophet like Moses, should remind the reader of the words spoken by the voice from heaven at the transfiguration, "This is my Son, my Chosen; listen to him!" (Lk. 9:35). The disciple must hear and do the words of the Lord (6:46ff.), who is the Son of God and the prophet like Moses. In addition, the context of Acts 3:22-23 allows us to conclude that Luke understands Jesus to be the Servant of God (3:13, 26) and the suffering Messiah (3:18, 20).

It is widely accepted that Luke associates Jesus, rather than the Baptist (except in the infancy narrative), with the figure of Elijah.²⁹ In the Nazareth synagogue episode, for example, Luke presents Jesus as another Elijah (Lk. 4:24-25). A contrast between Jesus and Elijah is seen at the beginning of the Travel Narrative, however, when James and John want to call down fire from heaven to consume those who would not receive Jesus (9:51-56). By rebuking James and John, who want him to act like Elijah (cf. 2 Kgs. 1:9ff.), Jesus teaches his followers that Christian discipleship does not consist in the zealous punishment of those who reject Jesus and his mission.

The disciple who recognizes that Jesus is a prophet will understand that, as with the prophets of old, God has spoken through Jesus. This means that one must listen to his words and conduct one's life in accordance with his teachings. Jesus, the prophet, is ready to suffer persecution and death as he conducts his ministry of compassion and preaches the good news to sinners. His disciples must follow Jesus' example of generous service to those in need, even if suffering and death result.

Conclusion

Once Luke has established that God exercises active control over everything in heaven and on earth, he must explain to the reader exactly how this Sovereign Lord has made salvation available to human beings. To this end Luke presents his belief that God had a plan for the salvation of human beings which was worked out in the history of Israel, Jesus, and the early church. As the central figure in God's plan, Jesus of Nazareth unifies past, present and future. He is the one who was promised in the Jewish Scriptures, is God's primary agent in bringing salvation to humanity, and continues to perform this task after his resurrection and ascension through his selected representatives in the early church.

Jesus is the Son of God promised in the Hebrew Scriptures (Acts 13:33; cf. Ps. 2:7). This means that he has been chosen for a specific task and participates in the work of God. The title also implies obedience, the obedience of a son to a father (cf. Lk. 22:42; 23:46). As Jesus was obedient to the will of God, so too must his followers be obedient to the will of God. Luke indicates that one discovers the will of God by listening to the words of Jesus when he reports that the heavenly voice said "This is my Son, my Chosen; listen to him!" (9:35). Jesus identifies as his relatives "those who hear the word of God and do it" (Lk. 8:21). These are the same individuals who are encouraged to follow Jesus' example (2:49) and address God as "Father"(11:2). God is the Father of Jesus (10:21-22; 22:29; 24:49) and of his disciples (6:36; 12:30,32). While Jesus is the unique Son of God,[30] his faithful disciples can become children of the Most High (cf. 20:36) if they are merciful as God is merciful, kind to the ungrateful and the selfish, if they love their enemies, do good, and lend, expecting nothing in return (6:35-36).

Jesus is the Messiah/Christ promised in the Hebrew Scriptures. This title, a comprehensive term which identifies Jesus as God's final, supreme agent in the history of salvation (Lk. 2:26; 9:20), would have suggested both royalty ("King") and Davidic descent ("Son of David") to Luke's original readers. At the time of Jesus, it would have been understood to refer to a political king and military leader who would drive out the Romans. Luke reinterprets this title, thereby countering the political overtones, by presenting Jesus as the suffering Messiah (24:26,46). Once Luke corrects this misunderstanding, and defines Jesus as the suffering, dying, rising Messiah, he uses the title frequently to identify Jesus (e.g., Acts 2:36; 4:10; 9:22; 15:26; 17:3; 18:5,28). Luke's presentation of Jesus as the suffering Messiah suggests that suffering is not alien to Christian discipleship. The one who wishes to travel with Jesus on his journey to God must realize that the road is often difficult and demanding. The suffering Messiah, not the royal military leader, is the model Luke presents for his Christian readers to follow.

In the Hebrew Scriptures God is both Lord and Savior. In Luke-Acts these two titles are used to refer to Jesus, the one through whom God has chosen to exercise his rule. As Lord, Jesus joins with God in exercising dominion, power, and authority over human beings. In Luke-Acts, Jesus is the Lord who acts with mercy and compassion and expects his disciples to follow his example. Those who listen to the Lord and see his powerful deeds must be concerned with the marginalized. They must repent, believe, and be baptized into the "church of the Lord." They must not react violently against their opponents and must be ready to suffer and die, if necessary, for his name. Disciples of the Lord must seek to be good people and not merely to appear to be good. Their lives must be characterized by prayer, generosity, and a commitment to spreading the word of the Lord.

By applying the title "Savior" both to God and to Jesus, Luke is emphasizing that God has made salvation, which otherwise only he can accomplish, available in Jesus (Acts 4:12). Through his words and deeds, Jesus teaches us that God's salvation involves more than just deliverance from sickness, infirmity, and sin. During his ministry "to seek and to save the lost" (Lk. 19:10), Jesus teaches his disciples that the marginalized should participate fully in the ongoing life of the community. God's salvation is universal and all-encompassing; it has a present, as well as a future, dimension. This means that the message of salvation has economic, political and social consequences. The disciple who understands this will be led to proclaim the message of God's salvation and to work for social justice.

Jesus is also a prophet, specifically a "Prophet like Moses" who was promised in Deuteronomy 18. The disciple who recognizes that Jesus is a prophet will understand that, as with the prophets of old, God has spoken through Jesus. This means that one must listen to his words and conduct one's life in accordance with his teachings. Jesus, the prophet, is ready to suffer persecution and death as he conducts his ministry of compassion and preaches the good news to sinners. His disciples must follow Jesus' example of generous service to those in need, even if suffering and death result.

When Luke presents Jesus as the Danielic Son of Man and the Isaian Servant, he is once again emphasizing that Jesus is one who suffered. Jesus, the prophet who cannot die away from Jerusalem (Lk. 13:33) and the suffering Messiah (24:26,46), is also the suffering Son of Man and the Suffering Servant.

The titles "Son of God," "Lord," and "Savior," serve to highlight the power and authority now exercised by the risen Christ. Those who focus exclusively on power and glory, however, miss an extremely important aspect of Lukan Christology, suffering messiahship. Luke clearly believes that anyone who wishes to know Jesus must understand him as the suffering dying Messiah (9:44; 18:32; 22:22; 24:7). As such, he becomes a model for the suffering and persecution that his disciples endure. The kind of suffering that the world inflicted on him it will also inflict on his disciples. In his use of the Servant theme, however, Luke does not dwell exclusively on suffering. While Luke admits that suffering and death might be the lot of the faithful disciple, he is much more interested in presenting the disciple as one who serves. In Luke-Acts Jesus is seen as the Servant who lives a life of service and teaches his disciples to do the same (e.g., Lk. 22:24-30). The Christian must follow the example of Jesus, the one who serves. With mercy and compassion the disciple must take care of the weaker members of society. This includes providing food for widows (cf. Acts 6:1-6), ministering to the poor who are hungry and covered with sores (cf. Lk. 16:19-31), and providing medical care for those in need, even if they are outside one's religious community (cf. 10:25-37).

Only a correct understanding of Jesus leads to the adequate practice of Christian discipleship. The parallels between Jesus and his disciples in Luke-Acts point unmistakeably to the fact that Luke sees Jesus as a model for his followers. And the example he gives them is one of service. Doing the will of God means loving God and loving our neighbor. The Christian who prays and celebrates the Eucharist in community must also act with mercy and compassion toward those in need.

5

The Way to Discipleship

Thus far our study has been guided by the belief that:
(1) Luke is using a journey motif, a growth and development
model, to describe Christian discipleship and (2) that his
understanding of discipleship can best be found in the call and
commissioning stories in the Gospel and Acts. In this chapter
we will begin to focus on what could be referred to as the
circular dimension of Christian discipleship as we expand our
discussion beyond these call and commissioning accounts and
take a closer look at some of the themes already discussed.
This will help us arrive at a clearer understanding of what is
involved in responding positively to the call of Jesus.

The first arc in the circle is the invitation to Christian discipleship, extended to human beings by Jesus during his earthly
ministry and by the risen Lord through his agents, the Christian
missionaries, in the post-resurrection period. One becomes a
Christian by accepting the message of these missionary witnesses, that Jesus is the Messiah and Lord, and by adhering to
the risen Lord in personal faith. Acceptance of Christ and his
message, however, is only the beginning. This act necessarily
leads to the second arc, where the believer is baptized into the
Christian community, and to the third arc, where the believer
shares a life of fellowship together with other believers. The
fourth arc, the missionary dimension of Christian discipleship,
completes the circle. The church cannot focus exclusively on
itself, because it must bear witness to the risen Lord as it
preaches the good news in his name to all nations (Lk. 24:47-

48; Acts 1:8). The believer, who has accepted the word of God through the missionary preaching of the church, now takes the message of salvation to others as a member of the church.

In this chapter we will examine more closely the first half of the circle, the initial steps along the path to Christian discipleship as they are presented in Luke-Acts. (1) Hearing the words of and about Jesus, the message of (2) forgiveness and reconciliation, leads the disciple (3) to repent, believe in Jesus, and be baptized into Jesus' new community. In later chapters, we will examine the second half of the circle, the life of the disciple within the community itself and the missionary dimension of discipleship.

Listening/Hearing

In his sermon in the temple area (Acts 3:12ff.) Peter identifies Jesus as the eschatological prophet of whom it was said, "You shall listen (ἀκούειν) to him in whatever he tells you" (3:22; cf. Deut. 18:18ff.). This agrees with what the voice from heaven says at the transfiguration, "This is my Son, my Chosen; listen (ἀκούειν) to him!" (Lk. 9:35). Luke tells the reader that early in Jesus' public ministry a great many individuals hear/listen to his words (e.g., 5:1,15; 6:17).

Hearing/listening to Jesus is a necessary first step toward discipleship, but it is not enough for one who would be Jesus' follower. Those in the synagogue at Nazareth who *heard* Jesus read from the prophet Isaiah "were filled with wrath" and wanted to throw him headlong off the brow of the hill (Lk. 4:28-29). When he explains the parable of the Sower to his disciples Jesus notes that those in the story who fall away, those who are not saved, have all *heard* the word of God (8:11-18). The rich ruler becomes very sad when he *hears* Jesus tell him to ;ell all that he has and distribute it to the poor (18:23). Merely listening to the word of God does not guarantee one salvation.

In the Sermon on the Plain (Lk. 6:20-49), Jesus says that those who hear his words must also incorporate them into their lives (6:46-49):[1]

6⁴⁶"Why do you call me 'Lord, Lord,' and not do what I
tell you? ⁴⁷Every one who comes to me and hears my words
and does them, I will show you what that individual is like:
⁴⁸Such a one is like a person building a house, who dug
deep, and laid the foundation upon rock; and when a flood
arose, the stream broke against that house, and could not
shake it, because it had been well built. ⁴⁹But, the one who
hears and does not do them is like a person who built a
house on the ground without a foundation; against which
the stream broke and immediately it fell, and the ruin of
that house was great."

This same theme appears later in the gospel when Jesus
identifies his true family as "those who hear the word of God
and do it" (Lk. 8:21),[2] and when Jesus responds to the woman
who praises his mother by pronouncing as blessed "those who
hear the word of God and keep it" (11:28). The ones who will
be saved, according to Jesus' interpretation of the parable of
the Sower, "are those who, hearing the word, hold it fast in an
honest and good heart, and bring forth fruit with patience"
(8:15). The themes of hearing and doing are also emphasized
in the closely connected stories of Martha and Mary (10:38-
42), where it is reported that Mary listened (ἀκούειν) to Jesus
(10:39), and the good Samaritan (10:25-37), with its stress on
"doing" (10:25, 28, 37).[3] From these two pericopes one learns
that discipleship involves listening to the Lord's teaching as
well as actively showing mercy to those in need.

Because it is claimed by many that Mary, the mother of
Jesus, is portrayed by Luke as the ideal disciple,[4] we will
briefly consider Luke's presentation of her as one who hears
and does the word of God. Mary is an excellent example of
someone who has accepted God's word as the norm for her
life. (1) In the infancy narrative, she is seen as the faithful
Jewish virgin who hears the word of God and believes (Lk.
1:26-38). While the verb "to hear" (ἀκούειν) does not appear in
these verses, it is clear that Mary is listening to the word of the
Lord. She says to the angel Gabriel, "Behold, I am the hand-
maid of the Lord; let it be to me according to your word
(ῥῆμα)" (1:38). Elizabeth identifies the ultimate source of the
word which the angel spoke when she says, "And blessed is she

who believed that there would be a fulfilment of what was spoken to her from the Lord" (1:45).

(2) During the ministry of Jesus, Mary is portrayed as one who hears the word of God and bears good fruit (Lk. 8:19-21; cf. 8:11,15). When Jesus is informed that his mother and brothers have come to see him, he responds, "My mother and my brothers are those who hear (ἀκούειν) the word (λόγος) of God and do it" (8:21). Luke agrees with Mark,[5] that the relatives of Jesus have no priority in the Kingdom of God simply because of their physical relationship to him, "but here in Luke Jesus makes those of physical descent models for those who hear the word of God and keep it."[6]

(3) In the first chapter of Acts, Mary is presented as a member of the new community, faithfully gathered in prayer to await the outpouring of the Holy Spirit (Acts 1:12-13, cf. 1:8; Lk. 24:49). After all the members of this group of 120 Christians, including Mary,[7] were filled with the Holy Spirit, they proceeded to speak in other tongues (2:3-4). Luke uses the verb "to hear" (ἀκούειν) several times in this pericope (2:6,8,11) implying that there is a connection between hearing the word of Jesus and hearing the word of his Spirit-filled disciples.

The unity between Jesus and his disciples is made explicit in the Gospel when Jesus says to the Seventy, "The one who hears you hears me" (Lk. 10:16). Luke has taken a traditional saying found in Mark 9:37 (cf. Mt. 10:40; 18:5; Lk. 9:48) and editorially expanded it. To the traditional saying, "Whoever receives one such child in my name receives me; and whoever receives me, receives not me but the one who sent me," Luke adds that those who "hear" the Christian missionary "hear" Jesus (Lk. 10:16; cf. 9:48).

The listening/hearing motif is even more prominent in Acts than it is in the Gospel. Luke has included in his second volume some twenty-eight speeches which account for about thirty percent of the text.[8] As in the Gospel, those who hear the word are usually moved to action. In Acts 2, for example, one learns that after hearing (ἀκούειν) the words of Peter and the disciples at Pentecost (cf. Acts 2:6, 8, 11, 22, 33, 37) many respond positively and ask, "What shall we do?" (2:37). Peter's answer, "Repent, and be baptized, every one of you in

the name of Jesus Christ for the forgiveness of your sins"
(2:38), will be examined below. Similarly, the Samaritans "gave
heed to what was said by Philip, when they heard (ἀκούειν)
him and saw the signs which he did" (8:6). This includes
believing Philip "as he preached the good news about the
Kingdom of God and the name of Jesus Christ" and being
baptized (8:12-13). Examples from the preaching of Paul also
show the importance of hearing the word of God and responding positively to it. Luke mentions that the proconsul, Sergius
Paulus, a man of intelligence, "summoned Barnabas and Saul
and sought to *hear* the word of God" (13:7). In response to
their Spirit-filled preaching, the proconsul believed (13:12). On
the next sabbath almost the whole city of Antioch in Pisidia
"gathered together to *hear* the word of God" (13:44). Many
Gentiles who *heard* the word of God, as preached by Paul and
Barnabas, believed (13:48). Several chapters later, Luke reports
that "many of the Corinthians *hearing* Paul believed and were
baptized" (18:8). Elsewhere in Acts, on numerous occasions
one sees the disciples functioning as witnesses to what they
have seen and heard[9] and large numbers of people coming to
believe because they hear the word of God.[10]

Seeing/ Understanding

In our discussion of the call and commissioning stories,
"seeing" and "hearing" were frequently found together. In the
Gospel, individuals are presented as following Jesus only after
they have heard his words and observed his powerful deeds. In
Acts, it is more often the words of the Christian missionary
about Jesus and the missionary's own powerful deeds which
lead to repentance, belief, and baptism. A closer look at this
theme will reveal that Christian discipleship requires "seeing"
(δοκεῖν, ὁρᾶν) as well as hearing and doing.

Luke is neither the first nor the last New Testament author
to use physical seeing as a metaphor for spiritual insight. Mark,
for example, brackets the central section of his Gospel with
two stories in which Jesus heals the blind—the blind man at
Bethsaida (Mk. 8:22-26) and blind Bartimaeus (Mk. 10:46-52).
Between these stories of how Jesus cured physical blindness

one finds him attempting to cure the spiritual blindness of the disciples.[11] In John's Gospel, when Jesus heals the man born blind it is a sign that Jesus is the light of the world (Jn. 9:1ff.). Luke is also aware of the symbolic dimensions of physical seeing. At the outset and the conclusion of his two-volume work Luke places pericopes which implicitly equate one's response to Jesus with seeing the salvation of God. In the Gospel, one reads about the righteous and devout Simeon who was promised by the Holy Spirit that he would not die before he had "seen" the Lord's Christ, God's salvation (Lk. 2:26-32). At the conclusion of Acts Paul charges that although the Jews have heard and seen the salvation of God, they never understood or perceived (Acts 28:26-28).

In verses already identified as programmatic (Lk. 4:18-19), Jesus announces that he has come to proclaim recovery of sight to the blind. The fact that Jesus heals the blind is mentioned in response to the question John the Baptist's followers ask Jesus, "Are you the one who is to come, or shall we look for another?'" (7:18ff.). The reader of Luke's Gospel is led to conclude that Jesus' activity of healing the blind is a sign that he is the One Who is to Come.[12]

As it was not enough merely to "hear" Jesus' words, so it is not enough just to "see" his miraculous healings. The one who sees must perceive that these are the work of God's eschatological agent. When Simon Peter sees the miraculous catch of fish, he falls down at Jesus' knees, and says "Depart from me, for I am a sinful man, O Lord" (Lk. 5:8). The crowd that witnessed the healing of the paralytic "glorified God and were filled with awe, saying, 'We have *seen* strange things today.'" (5:26). Although Jesus healed ten lepers on his way to Jerusalem, only one returned and gave praise to God. What sets this individual apart from the others is his faith (17:19). Luke explains that after "he *saw* that he was healed," the Samaritan praised God with a loud voice and "fell on his face at Jesus' feet, giving him thanks" (17:16). The healing of the blind man near Jericho follows the same pattern. After he received his sight, the man followed Jesus, "glorifying God; and all the people, when they saw it, gave praise to God" (18:43). In this pericope, both the blind man and the crowd pass from blindness to sight (cf. Lk. 18:39). As Jesus and his disciples draw near to the Mount of Olives,

> 19³⁷ᵇ the whole multitude of the disciples began to rejoice and praise God with a loud voice for all the mighty works that they had *seen,* ³⁸saying "Blessed in the King who comes in the name of the Lord! Peace in heaven and glory in the highest."

In each of these cases "sight" means "insight." Those who "see" the miracles of Jesus understand that he does these mighty acts "by the finger of God" (Lk. 11:20) and they respond by giving glory and praise to God.

In Luke's Gospel Jesus himself, not only his miracles, is presented as the object of "seeing." After the angel appears to the shepherds, they decide to go to Bethlehem in order to *"see* this thing that has happened" (Lk. 2:15). After they *saw* (2:17), "the shepherds returned, glorifying and praising God for all they had heard and *seen,* as it had been told them" (2:20). What they had been told was that the baby, born in the city of David, is "a Savior, who is Christ the Lord" (2:11). This mention of both the visual and the auditory should come as no surprise, since seeing and hearing appear together frequently in Luke's Gospel (e.g., 7:22; 9:7-9; 10:21-24; 11:29-36).

Shortly after Simeon "sees" Jesus and understands him to be the salvation of God (Lk. 2:25ff.), Luke introduces John the Baptist's preaching by citing Isaiah 40:3-5. Only Luke, among the Synoptists, includes the prophecy that "all flesh shall *see* the salvation of God" (Lk. 3:6).[13] The resurrection appearances also fit into this theme of "seeing." As the risen Lord broke bread with the two disciples at Emmaus, "their eyes were opened and they recognized him" (24:31). They soon informed the other disciples how Jesus "was known to them in the breaking of the bread" (24:35). The Christian disciple must "see" Jesus, the risen Lord, in the Eucharist. After Luke informs the reader that "the Lord has risen indeed, and has appeared to Simon!" (24:34), he recounts the words of the risen Lord to his disciples,

24³⁸"Why are you troubled, and why do questionings rise in your hearts? ³⁹See my hands and my feet, that it is I myself; handle me, and see; for a spirit has no flesh and bones as you see that I have."

Those to whom the risen Lord appears "see" him and as a result they function as his witnesses (Lk. 24:36-49) from Jerusalem to the end of the earth.[14] Peter tells Cornelius that:

10⁴⁰God raised Jesus on the third day and *made* him *manifest*, ⁴¹not to all the people but to us who were chosen by God as witnesses, who ate and drank with him after he rose from the dead. ⁴²And he commanded us to preach to the people, and to testify that he is the one ordained by God to be judge of the living and the dead.

Paul agrees (a) when he informs the Israelites that for many days Jesus "*appeared* to those who came up with him from Galilee to Jerusalem, who are now his witnesses to the people" (Acts 13:31), and (b) when he recalls that he "saw" the risen Lord saying to him, "Depart; for I will send you far away to the Gentiles" (22:12-21; cf. 26:16). In the first account of Paul's conversion experience Ananias says, "Brother Saul, the Lord Jesus who appeared to you on the road by which you came, has sent me that you may regain your sight and be filled with the Holy Spirit" (9:17).

We have already discussed how, in the post-resurrection period, would-be disciples "hear" Jesus when they listen to the word of God preached by the Christian missionaries. In a similar fashion, individuals continue to "see" Jesus when they recognize the manifestation of the Holy Spirit in the works of Jesus' disciples. During his Pentecost sermon Peter says, "This Jesus God raised up, and of that we all are witnesses. Being therefore exalted at the right hand of God, and having received from the Father the promise of the Holy Spirit, he has poured out this which you *see* and hear" (Acts 2:32-33). Individuals also respond positively when they "see" the works performed by Philip and Paul. "The multitudes with one accord gave heed to what was said by Philip, when they heard him and *saw* the signs which he did" (8:6; cf. 4:13-14). Likewise, the proconsul Sergius Paulus responds positively to what he has seen. Paul, "filled with the Holy Spirit" (13:9), announces that the hand of the Lord will come upon Elymas the unbelieving magician and he will become blind (13:11). When this comes to pass, "Then the proconsul believed, when he *saw* what had occurred, for he was astonished at the teaching of the Lord" (13:12).

Christian discipleship thus involves "seeing." The follower of Jesus must see the finger of God in Jesus' miracles and those of his disciples, and come to understand who Jesus really is. This insight into the identity of Jesus and God's saving activity in him will lead the individual to give praise and glory to God and witness on his behalf to others.

Forgiveness/Reconciliation

Early in his ministry, Jesus "came to Nazareth, where he had been brought up; and he went to the synagogue, as his custom was, on the sabbath day" (Lk. 4:16). While in the synagogue he stood up and read from the book of the prophet Isaiah. These words of Jesus in the synagogue at Nazareth (4:18ff.) are programmatic as they foreshadow Luke's account of Jesus' entire ministry.

> 4[18]"The Spirit of the Lord is upon me, because he has anointed me to preach good news to the poor. He has sent me to proclaim release to the captives and recovering of sight to the blind, to set at liberty those who are oppressed, [19]to proclaim the acceptable year of the Lord."

Jesus announces that Scripture has been fulfilled in him (Lk. 4:21) and that he has been anointed to preach the good news of salvation (4:18-19). A short time later, Jesus will say that the very purpose for which he was sent was to "preach the good news of the Kingdom of God" (4:43). The message of Jesus' synagogue speech is that the good news has political ("release to the captives"), economic ("to set at liberty those who are oppressed"), and physical ("recovering of sight to the blind") consequences. This is obviously the meaning of these verses in their original context (Isa. 61 and 58) and the way they are understood by Luke.[15] What could be missed by some readers is that the good news also includes the message of forgiveness of sins. Elsewhere in his two-volume work, Luke uses ἄφεσις (translated here as "release" and "liberty") to mean forgiveness of sins (Lk. 1:77; 3:3; 24:47; Acts 2:38; 5:31; 10:43; 13:38; 26:18). Luke tells the reader that, through and in Jesus, individuals are being restored to physical, moral and economic wholeness; debts are being cancelled and a life of harmony, order, and peace begun (cf. Isa. 61:2).

Jesus tells those who listen to him that he has come to seek and to save the lost (Lk. 19:10; cf. 15:1-32). He accomplishes this by preaching the good news of salvation which includes the release of human beings from their debts (i.e., sins) in the sight of God. Early in his public ministry Jesus says to a paralytic, "your sins are forgiven" (5:20) and announces to the onlookers that "the Son of Man has authority on earth to forgive sins" (5:24). In the Sermon on the Plain he describes God as merciful (6:36) and tells his audience to forgive, and they will be forgiven (6:37). He also forgives the sins of the woman who anoints his feet (7:48). While on the journey to Jerusalem, Jesus teaches his disciples to pray, "Father . . . forgive us our sins" (11:2-4), announces that those who speak "a word against the Son of Man will be forgiven" (12:10), and urges his disciples to forgive those who, after having sinned against them, repent (17:3-4). As he hangs on the cross Jesus says, "Father, forgive them; for they know not what they do" (23:34). And as risen Lord he tells the eleven and those with them, "that repentance and forgiveness of sins should be preached in his name to all nations" (24:47).

Luke's interest in "the forgiveness of sins" is also evident in Acts. Peter does what the risen Lord has commanded when he advises his audience at Pentecost to repent and be baptized "in the name of Jesus Christ for the forgiveness of your sins" (Acts 2:38) and when he tells Cornelius that all the prophets bear witness to Jesus Christ so that "everyone who believes in him receives forgiveness of sins through his name" (10:43). Together with the apostles, Peter informs the Jewish council that God exalted Jesus "at his right hand as Leader and Savior, to give repentance to Israel and forgiveness of sins" (5:31). Paul, who is sent to the Gentiles by the risen Lord so that "they may receive forgiveness of sins" (26:18), also proclaims forgiveness of sins in Jesus' name (13:38-39).

When Luke looks back at the Christ-event, one way in which he sums up its effect is by the phrase "the forgiveness of sins."[16] The good news of the Kingdom, that Jesus has inaugurated the long awaited era of salvation (cf. Lk. 19:9; Acts 4:10-12), includes the message of the forgiveness of sins which is to be preached to all nations (Lk. 24:47; Acts 26:15-18).

Repentance, Belief, and Baptism
Repentance

Peter faithfully carries out the command of the risen Jesus, that "repentance" ($\mu\epsilon\tau\acute{a}\nu o\iota\alpha$)[17] as well as forgiveness of sins be preached in his name to all nations (Lk. 24:47), when he says to the crowd that has listened to his Pentecost speech, "Repent, and be baptized every one of you in the name of Jesus Christ for the forgiveness of your sins" (Acts 2:38; cf. 3:19; 8:22). The importance of preaching repentance, however, is not a post-resurrection insight. According to Luke, it appears first in the preaching of John the Baptist (Lk. 3:3, 8; cf. Acts 13:24) and is rooted in the ministry of the earthly Jesus.[18] After initially reporting that John "went into all the region about the Jordan, preaching a baptism of repentance for the forgiveness of sins" (Lk. 3:3) Luke then has John himself demand that those who came out to be baptized by him "bear fruits that befit repentance" (3:8). In the call of Levi pericope, Luke adds "to repentance" to his source (Mk. 2:17): thus, according to Luke, Jesus announces not simply that he has come to call sinners (Mk. 2:17), but that he has come to call sinners "to repentance" (Lk. 5:32). While Jesus warns that the one who does not repent will perish (13:3, 5; cf. 16:30), he also comforts his audience by speaking of the joy in heaven over one sinner who does repent (15:7, 10; cf. 15:22-24, 32). On his journey to Jerusalem Jesus reminds the crowds that the people of Nineveh "repented at the preaching of Jonah, and behold, something greater than Jonah is here" (11:32). He also tells the Seventy that Tyre and Sidon "would have repented long ago" if they had witnessed his mighty works (10:13). This agrees with what we have seen thus far, that both the authoritative words and the powerful works of Jesus should lead sinners to repentance.

In Acts, Peter urges his audience at Pentecost, "Repent, and be baptized every one of you in the name of Jesus Christ for the forgiveness of your sins; and you shall receive the gift of the Holy Spirit" (Acts 2:38). To those who hear him later in the temple area he proclaims, "Repent therefore, and turn again, that your sins may be blotted out, that times of refreshing may come from the presence of the Lord" (3:19). And to Simon the sorcerer he says, "Repent therefore of this wickedness of yours, and pray to the Lord that, if possible, the intent of your heart may be forgiven you" (8:22). Together with the other apostles Peter announces that God has exalted Jesus "at his right hand as Leader and Savior, to give repentance to Israel" (5:31). Later in Acts, the reader learns that God has "granted repentance unto life" to the Gentiles (11:18) as well as to Israel. Luke also portrays Paul as a missionary who preaches to all the message of repentance (Acts 17:30; 20:21; 26:20) which leads to baptism (19:4-5; cf. 13:24).

Belief

The positive side of repentance ($\mu\epsilon\tau\acute{a}\nu o\iota\alpha$) is faith ($\pi\acute{\iota}\sigma\tau\iota\varsigma$). In a general sense $\pi\acute{\iota}\sigma\tau\iota\varsigma$ implies obedience, trust, and hope as well as the acceptance of the "good news."[19] Luke understands this to include hearing the word of God, holding it fast in an honest and good heart, and bringing forth fruit with patience (Lk. 8:15). Faith begins with listening but does not end there. The Christian disciple must both hear and obey the word of God. The commitment to God, which $\pi\acute{\iota}\sigma\tau\iota\varsigma$ suggests, is seen as complementary to repentance.

Jesus implies that faith leads to salvation when he says that the devil will come and take away the word from some, "that they may not believe and be saved" (Lk. 8:12; cf. 8:50). The connection between faith and salvation is more explicit when Jesus says to the woman who anointed his feet, "your faith has saved you" (7:50) and when Paul says to his jailer, "believe in the Lord Jesus and you will be saved" (Acts 16:31).

Through his disciples (Acts 8:26-38; 10:44-48; 13:46-48; 14:8-10), the risen Jesus offers repentance, forgiveness of sins, and sanctification to those who have faith in him (26:17-18). Many who hear (ἀκούειν) the word of God (4:4; 8:12f.; 11:21; 14:1; 15:7; 18:8) or see the signs and wonders of the apostles (5:14; 9:42) come to believe. In fact, the one who hears the word of God is expected to believe (15:7; cf. 4:4; Lk. 1:20). In his sermon to Cornelius, Peter says that everyone who believes (πιστεύειν) in Jesus "receives forgiveness of sins through his name"(Acts 10:43; cf. 13:39, 48; 16:31). Paul agrees that God's salvation is universal when he says that both Jews (21:20; cf. 11:17) and Gentiles (21:25) have come to believe in the Lord Jesus Christ (20:21). In several places Luke notes that the early Christian community is composed of those "who believed" (2:44; 4:32; cf. 15:5).

Belief in Jesus includes knowing who Jesus is and faithfully following the example he has set. This is essential because only a proper understanding of Jesus can lead to true discipleship; an incorrect perception of Jesus will result in an inadequate or misdirected following of Jesus. As we saw in the previous chapter, Luke presents Jesus as God's Messiah (Lk. 9:20), God's primary agent in the history of salvation. Jesus is the one promised in the Hebrew Scriptures, God's prophet and Son, the bringer of God's salvation who, after his exaltation, continues this task through his disciples.

In their speeches in Acts, Peter and Paul identify Jesus as both "Savior"(Acts 5:31; 13:23; cf. Lk. 2:11) and "Lord"(e.g., Acts 2:36; 16:31; 20:21; cf. Lk. 2:11). Knowledge that Jesus is the Savior should lead the Christian disciple to repentance, forgiveness of sins (Acts 5:31; cf. 13:23ff.) and great joy (Lk. 2:10). And those who have faith in the "Lord Jesus" will be saved (Acts 16:31) as they listen to the words of the Lord and act upon them (Lk. 6:46; cf. 13:22-30; 19:8). The disciple is urged to help the weak because the Lord Jesus said, "It is more blessed to give than to receive" (Acts 20:35). Disciples are reminded of the difficulties of following Jesus when Paul states that he is willing to suffer martyrdom for the name of the Lord Jesus (Acts 21:13).

Paul also refers to Jesus as the "Son" of Psalm 2 (Acts 13:33). Jesus is the "Son of God" because, conceived by the power of the Holy Spirit (Lk. 1:35), he knows God intimately (10:22), and obeys God perfectly (4:3, 9). As Jesus was obedient to the will of God, so the one who wishes to join Jesus on the way must follow his example and be obedient to the will of God (which can be found now in the teaching of Jesus).

The title "Son of God," like "Lord" and Savior," serves to highlight the power and authority now exercised by the risen Christ. While the joy and confidence that this engenders in the disciple is good, if one concentrates only on these titles for Jesus then a distorted understanding of discipleship may result. Those who focus exclusively on power and glory miss an extremely important aspect of Lukan theology, suffering messiahship.

Luke, in agreement with Mark,[20] believes that anyone who wishes to know Jesus must understand him as the suffering and dying Messiah. The risen Jesus reminds his disciples on two occasions that a correct understanding of messiahship must include suffering and death, as well as resurrection (Lk. 24:25-27, 44-46; cf. Acts 3:18; 17:3; 26:23). In order to emphasize this motif, Luke has included in the Gospel sayings about the suffering "Son of Man"[21] and deliberately portrayed Jesus as the Suffering Servant of Isaiah 40-55 (cf. Lk. 22:37).[22] Jesus, as the Suffering Servant, becomes a model for his followers. His disciples may have to endure suffering and persecution themselves (cf. Lk. 6:22; Acts 7:56) as they follow the example of the one who serves (Lk. 22:26-27; cf. 9:48; Acts 23:46-47; 26:16-18).[23]

In Luke-Acts, "faith" ($\pi\iota\sigma\tau\iota\varsigma$) involves a personal commitment to Jesus (cf. Lk. 17:5; 18:8; 22:32; Acts 6:5; 11:24). This includes understanding Jesus' identity and conducting one's life in accordance with his example and teachings. The one who accepts Jesus and his message must bring forth the fruit that befits repentance.

Baptism

In addition to repenting and believing, Luke implies that the Christian disciple must be baptized in Jesus' name. Luke refers to the baptism ($\beta\acute{\alpha}\pi\tau\iota\sigma\mu\alpha$) of John numerous times in his two-volume work (cf. Lk. 3:3; 7:29; 20:4; Acts 1:22; 10:37; 13:24; 18:25; 19:3-4) and informs the reader that Jesus himself was baptized (Lk. 3:21; cf. Acts 1:22). John tells the multitudes that someone mightier than he is coming who "will baptize you with the Holy Spirit and with fire" (Lk. 3:16). This accounts for the absence of a baptizing ministry by Jesus or his disciples in Luke-Acts prior to Pentecost. The risen Jesus looks forward to the Pentecost event when he promises his disciples that they will "be baptized with the Holy Spirit" in the near future (Acts 1:5).

After the Holy Spirit comes upon the assembled group of disciples at Pentecost, these followers of Jesus begin their task of bearing witness to the resurrection of Jesus and his role in the divine plan of salvation. From Peter's Pentecost speech onward, the importance of baptism is constantly stressed. The necessity of baptism is implied (a) when Peter says "Repent, and be baptized every one of you in the name of Jesus Christ for the forgiveness of your sins; and you shall receive the gift of the Holy Spirit" (Acts 2:38), (b) when the Ethiopian eunuch, after hearing the good news of Jesus, asks Philip, "What is to prevent my being baptized?" and is promptly baptized by him (8:37-38), (c) when Paul hears the words of the risen Lord and is baptized (9:18), (d) when Peter baptizes those who heard the word of God at Caesarea (10:44-48), and (e) when those who believed the preaching of Philip were baptized (8:12).

Nowhere, however, does Luke state that baptism is absolutely necessary for salvation. The three thousand Pentecost-day converts were baptized (Acts 2:41), but no mention is made that any of the original disciples, including the mother of Jesus, was baptized (1:12-15). Although he states that Apollos, who had been instructed in the way of the Lord and spoke and taught accurately the things concerning Jesus, only knew the baptism of John (18:25), Luke does not report that Apollos ever received Christian baptism. As the narrative continues, Luke refers to some people in Ephesus as "disciples" even though they had received only the baptism of John (19:1-7).[24]

Peter's comment at Pentecost (cited above) suggests that there is a close connection between baptism and the Holy Spirit. This is supported elsewhere in Acts (1:5; 11:16). The exact relationship between baptism and the gift of the Holy Spirit, however, is much debated. One is tempted to answer that baptism is the occasion and/or means of the bestowal of the Holy Spirit (cf. 2:38). But several texts call this conclusion into question. While Luke narrates the coming of the Spirit upon the disciples at Pentecost, nowhere does he report that they received a baptism of water in the name of the Lord Jesus.[25] The Samaritans are evangelized by Philip and baptized by him, without receiving the Holy Spirit (8:12). The Jerusalem church sends to Samaria Peter and John who "laid their hands on them and they received the Holy Spirit" (8:14-17). The reverse order is seen in the Cornelius episode. While the centurion, his relatives, and friends listen to Peter proclaim the word of God, the Holy Spirit falls upon them (10:44). Peter concludes that this is a divine sign and he commands they be baptized (10:45-48).

Various solutions have been suggested concerning the relationship between baptism and Christian discipleship. An important insight is that Luke gives priority to the reception of the Holy Spirit.[26] This helps to explain the emphasis on the Spirit at Pentecost and the note that Apollos was "fervent in spirit" (Acts 18:25), although he only knew the baptism of John. It also suggests that Luke might not view John's disciples at Ephesus as full members of the Christian community. The importance of the Holy Spirit for Luke leads him to suggest that it is possible to receive the Holy Spirit apart from baptism with water. This is supported by the Cornelius story, the report of Paul's conversion (9:17-18), and the Samaritan episode (8:12, 15-17).

A careful reading of the evidence suggests that the reception of the Holy Spirit is not always tied to the moment of water baptism. Baptism can be the occasion and/or means of the bestowal of the Holy Spirit,[27] but individuals can receive the Holy Spirit apart from Christian baptism with water. One must remember, however, that while the necessity of baptism is not stated by Luke, it is clearly implied in several places (cf. Acts 2:38; 8:12, 37-38; 9:18; 10:48).

Because baptism is an important component of discipleship in Luke-Acts, one should not be surprised that references to other themes associated with discipleship are frequently included in the baptismal passages in Acts: faith,[28] repentance,[29] prayer,[30] forgiveness of sins,[31] and rejoicing.[32]

Conclusion

In this chapter we have examined more closely the call to Christian discipleship and its immediate consequences. The use of the term "call" suggests that there is both a caller and a recipient of the call. During the ministry of Jesus it is primarily Jesus himself who issues the invitation to discipleship. In the post-resurrection period it is the risen Jesus who issues the call through his agents, the Christian missionaries. The first step along the path of discipleship, therefore, is hearing/listening to the words of and about Jesus. Hearing is not enough, of course, since many who hear do not become disciples. One must not only hear the word, but also hold it fast in an honest and good heart and bring forth fruit with patience (Lk. 8:15).

The Christian disciple must also "see." Spiritual insight into the identity of Jesus is crucial for a proper understanding of discipleship. The would-be follower of Jesus must believe that Jesus is God's eschatological agent of salvation and must accept the fact that the words and works of Jesus and his disciples are accomplished by the power of the Holy Spirit. This sight or insight leads to the incorporation of Jesus' teachings into one's life. The person who hears, accepts, and does the will of God will also give praise and glory to God and witness on Jesus' behalf to others.

The good news of God's salvation includes the message of the forgiveness of sins and the restoration to wholeness or completeness. It is now possible to be reconciled with and to establish a correct relationship with both God and our neighbor. Those who understand and accept God's saving action in Jesus Christ cannot continue behaving in the same sinful way. Jesus announces that he has come to call "sinners to repentance" (Lk. 5:32). Would-be followers of Jesus, therefore, must cease to do evil and strive to conduct their lives according to the will of God. Those called to Christian discipleship must develop a personal faith in Jesus. This involves trust, hope, and obedience to his teaching. Jesus serves as a model for

Christian behavior; therefore, one must have a correct understanding of who Jesus is in order to have a correct understanding of Christian discipleship.

Luke, who teaches that Jesus received the Holy Spirit and
was baptized, highlights the importance of each disciple's
reception of the Holy Spirit and strongly suggests that baptism
in Jesus' name is a necessary element of discipleship. Baptism
incorporates the believer into Jesus' new community where
each follower of Jesus shares a life of fellowship together with
other believers. In the next chapter, we will begin to examine
further the life of the disciple within the Christian community
itself.

6

The Community and God's Plan

Thus far we have glanced at several texts which indicate that there is a communal dimension to Christian discipleship. The next three chapters will focus more specifically on this aspect of discipleship. In the present chapter, as we take a look at the larger context for community, we will see that this community, is inclusive and not exclusive. Membership in the community that confesses Jesus as Lord and Savior is open to all, regardless of race, gender, or economic status. This is not accidental, but the result of God's plan for the salvation of all. Chapter 7 will examine more closely the specific context for community. After focusing on those texts which unambiguously show that there is a communal dimension to Christian discipleship, we will examine the organizational structure of the community as it existed in Jerusalem, Antioch and Ephesus. Chapter 8 will examine what Luke has to say about life within this new community, especially with respect to the Eucharist marriage, prayer, possessions, and nonviolent behavior.

God's Plan

Although we have already seen many thematic motifs which serve to unite the Gospel and Acts, ultimately it is the divine plan of salvation which provides the unity of Luke's thought in his two-volume work. Luke believes that God, who is ultimately in control of his creation, has a plan by which human beings can gain eternal salvation. This plan was revealed by God in the Hebrew Scriptures, especially in the writings of Israel's prophets. These promises, which God has made, have been fulfilled in the life and ministry of Jesus Christ, especially in his death and resurrection. The fact the these prophecies/ promises have been fulfilled is presented by Luke as having been attested to by the apostles and other early Christian missionaries, who then invite the members of their audience to repent and be baptized.

God is in Control

Luke assures his readers that salvation has been made available to human beings by presenting the one who offers this salvation as ultimately in control of events both in heaven and on earth. Luke seems to depend primarily on the portrait of God in the Hebrew Scriptures as he presents his readers with the picture of a God who exercises sovereign control over history.[1] He emphasizes the supremacy of God when he describes God as both the Savior (Lk. 1:47) and the "Sovereign Lord" (δεσπότης) who made "the heaven and the earth and the sea and everything in them" (Acts 4:24; cf. Lk. 2:29).[2]

In Luke's understanding, however, the "Lord of heaven and earth" (Lk. 10:21) also cares personally for humanity and takes an active part in the history of salvation. God, who has been at work (directing, leading, planning) throughout the history of Israel (Acts 7:2-53; 13:16-41), entered human history in order to show his mercy (Lk. 1:72, 78; 6:36) and to bring salvation to human beings. God's numerous visits during the history of Israel culminate in his visitation to Israel in the person of Jesus (Lk. 7:16; Acts 15:14), who proclaims God's mercy (cf. Lk. 10:37; 15:1-32) and offers salvation to all human beings in fulfillment of Isaiah 40:5: "and all flesh shall see the salvation of God" (Lk. 3:6; cf. 19:10).

God's Promises in the Hebrew Scriptures

The first stage in God's plan for the salvation of all occurs when God interacts with the Israelite people during a period of well over a thousand years. In the text just cited, for example, one can see that Luke believes the mission to the Gentiles was promised during the ministry of Isaiah. Luke's understanding of God's plan is outlined in Stephen's speech (Acts 7:2ff.), where the author presents the history of Israel as interpreted by a Christian.[3] Stephen summarizes the interaction of God with Israel from God's appearance and promises to Abraham until "the coming of the Righteous One" who was betrayed and murdered. God is present throughout that history as he speaks to certain individuals and directs them to carry out his commands (cf. Acts 7:3ff., 30ff.). The dynamic nature of salvation is seen in God's rescue of Joseph, after the jealous patriarchs had sold him into Egypt (7:9-10), and his continued interaction with the people of Israel even after they refused to obey his chosen emissary Moses. Because they failed to understand that "God was giving them deliverance by his hand" (7:25), the Israelites persecuted the prophets and murdered the Righteous One. Stephen is claiming, therefore, that the prophets should have been listened to when they "announced beforehand the coming of the Righteous One" (7:52). And Jesus, the "Righteous One," should not have been betrayed and murdered.

As a result of this speech, Stephen stands out as a true heir of the promises of God to Abraham, one who correctly understands God's plan (cf. Acts 7:25). He is the correct interpreter of the law, who realizes that the salvation of God cannot be limited to one place or nation (cf. 6:13-14). As Luke narrates elsewhere, the "salvation of God has been sent to the Gentiles" (28:28) because it is written that repentance and forgiveness of sins should be preached in Christ's name to all nations (Lk. 24:47).

The Promises Fulfilled in Jesus Christ

The person and activity of Jesus Christ are at the center of Lukan theology because "there is salvation in no one else" (Acts 4:12). Luke presents Jesus of Nazareth as a human being (Lk. 2:6-7; Acts 2:22) who acts as God's agent in bringing the gift of salvation to humanity. Jesus shows mercy and compassion in his active concern for "the poor, the maimed, the lame, the blind" (Lk. 14:13; cf. 4:18), sinners (5:30; 7:34; 15:1), and other outcasts (5:12-16; 10:25-37; 17:11-19). Salvation is available to the poor as well as the rich, the ill as well as the healthy, and the marginalized as well as the pillars of society. There are things about this special emissary of God, however, that serve to set him apart from others. Jesus is conceived through the power of the Holy Spirit (Lk. 1:34-35), resurrected from the dead (e.g. Lk. 24:6; Acts 2:24, 32), and has ascended to God's right hand (Acts 2:33; 5:31; cf. 1:9). Clearly Jesus is an extraordinary human being, as we saw above in the chapter on Lukan Christology.

The career of Jesus as a whole, as well as numerous specific parts of that ministry, is seen in Luke-Acts as the fulfilment of earlier prophecy. Both the story of the beginning of the ministry of Jesus at Nazareth and the final scene of the Gospel contain references to the fulfilment of Hebrew prophecy. Luke tells his readers that Jesus entered the synagogue at Nazareth, read from Isaiah (61:1-2; 58:6), and then said, "Today this scripture has been fulfilled in your hearing" (Lk. 4:21). At the end of the Gospel, Jesus tells his disciples "that everything written about me in the law of Moses and the prophets and the psalms must be fulfilled" (Lk. 24:44-46) and "beginning with Moses and all the prophets, he interpreted to them in all the scriptures the things concerning himself" (24:27).[4]

"We All Are Witnesses"

Because Luke believes that there is salvation in no one else except Jesus Christ of Nazareth (Acts 4:12) and because he believes that God wills this salvation be made available to all, a universal mission is required. In order to bring the good news of salvation to all peoples the church needs to conduct a mission. This universal mission is foreshadowed by the travels of Jesus himself as he fulfills his role of preaching the good news (Lk. 4:34), and by Jesus' sending out of the Twelve (Lk. 9:1-6) and the Seventy (Lk. 10:1ff.). The importance of the universal mission becomes obvious in Acts 1:8 when the risen Lord tells his disciples that they shall be his "witnesses in Jerusalem and in all Judea and Samaria and to the end of the earth." Acts agrees with the Gospel when it pictures the urgent activity of the Christian mission and its almost miraculous triumph over obstacles. According to Luke, once the mission begins it is the power of Jesus that enables these early Christian missionaries to be successful (e.g., Acts 3:12, 16; 4:7-12) as they preach the Kingdom of God (Acts 8:12; 19:8; 20:25; 28:23, 31) in accordance with God's plan.

Luke believes that the promises made by God in the Hebrew Scriptures have been fulfilled in the life, death, resurrection, and ascension of Jesus. In order to appreciate this fact, however, more is needed than merely to read the Jewish Scriptures. The one who wishes to understand the promises of God and how they have been fulfilled in Jesus must have a trustworthy guide for the journey. In the Gospel Jesus himself is pictured as leading his disciples to those texts which were fulfilled and were about to be fulfilled in his life, death, and resurrection. After chiding the two disciples whom he joined on the road to Emmaus, "O how foolish you are! How slow of heart to believe all that the prophets have spoken! Was it not necessary that the Christ should suffer these things and enter into his glory?" (Lk. 24:25-26), Jesus began with Moses and all the prophets and "he interpreted to them in all the scriptures the things concerning himself" (24:27). The same theme is found even more clearly in the story of the conversion of the Ethiopian (Acts 8:26-40). When he comes upon an Ethiopian who is reading a passage from Isaiah, Philip asks, "Do you understand what you are reading?" (8:30). The Ethiopian responds, "How can I, unless some one guides me?" (8:31; cf. 13:27). Just as Jesus had to explain the Jewish Scriptures to his initial followers, so the Christian missionary must guide future disciples to a correct understanding of how these earlier prophecies have been fulfilled.

The mission to the Gentiles, in which repentance and forgiveness of sins should be preached (Lk. 24:47), is in complete agreement with God's plan (cf. Acts 14:16) as announced in the Hebrew Scriptures. Simeon cites Isaiah 49:6 when he identifies Jesus as "a light for revelation to the Gentiles" (Lk. 2:32). One finds included in Luke's story about John the Baptist (Lk. 3:4-6) verses from Isaiah (40:4-5) which are not found in Luke's source (cf. Mk. 1:2-3). Luke is claiming that the Gentile mission was foreshadowed in Isaiah's prophecy that "all flesh shall see the salvation of God." In Acts 15:16ff. James argues that Amos 9:11f. has been fulfilled in God's visitation to the Gentiles.

The role that the missionaries of the early church will play in God's plan is seen clearly when Paul says that Christ, being the first to rise from the dead, "would proclaim light both to the people and to the Gentiles" (Acts 26:22-23). The way in which Jesus, as risen Lord, proclaims this light to Jews and Gentiles is through the preaching of his missionary community.

Salvation is Available Now

While there is no doubt that Luke presents Jesus as the one who proclaims the good news of God's salvation, there is disagreement among scholars concerning when salvation becomes available. Is salvation available now or only in the distant future?

The influence of Hans Conzelmann in Lukan studies during the past half century has been enormous. His conclusion that Luke understands history to be divided into three stages[5] led him to claim that just as the eschaton was an event relegated to the far distant future by Luke, so too was eternal life "removed into the distance."[6] He also claimed that there is no "soteriological significance drawn from Jesus' suffering or death."[7] Although both these positions found early supporters, they have been challenged by recent scholarship.

Many scholars today argue that Luke does, in fact, have a theology of the cross. Luke has not eliminated the soteriological significance of the cross but has included material from his sources to explain Jesus' death as part of God's design. God's plan for universal salvation included the death of Jesus, who was saved because of his faith and obedience (Lk. 22:42; 23:46)[8] and whose resurrection-ascension makes universal salvation possible.[9]

There is also a scholarly consensus that salvation is available "today" and not in the far distant future as Conzelmann suggested.[10] It is often pointed out that Luke, in the Gospel, has included many examples of the imminence of salvation. The shepherds in the field are told by the angels that a Savior is born to them "this day in the city of David" (Lk. 2:11). After reading the saving prophecies of Isaiah, Jesus announces that "today this scripture has been fulfilled in your hearing" (4:21). It is "today" that sins are forgiven (5:26) and "today" that demons are cast out (13:32). Jesus tells Zacchaeus that "today salvation has come to this house" (19:9; cf. 19:5; Acts 26:29). And he says to the repentant thief, "Today you will be with me in paradise" (Lk. 23:43). The scholarly consensus, therefore, has moved away from Conzelmann's position on Lukan soteriology. It is now recognized that Luke has a theology of the cross and believes that salvation is available in the present. Because of the cross, salvation is now available through the activity of the Spirit within the Christian community.

Luke and the Jews

In the Gospel Luke teaches us that the promises God made to the people of Israel are fulfilled in the ministry of Jesus of Nazareth, God's promised Messiah. There are also indications both in the Hebrew Scriptures and in Luke's Gospel that, as part of God's plan of salvation, there will be a mission to the Gentiles. Does this mean that salvation is no longer available to the Jews?

Both continuity and discontinuity mark the relationship between Christianity and Judaism. The promises of God for the salvation of humanity were made to and kept alive by the Jews during the many centuries before the coming of Jesus. Yet, Christians claim that when the Messiah arrived in fulfilment of God's promises both he and his gospel were rejected by the Jews. What role does Luke see the Jews playing in the divine plan of salvation?

Scholars have long been interested in trying to understand the attitude of Luke, the Christian evangelist, toward Judaism. The reason that this area remains of interest to Lukan scholars is that Luke presents both positive and negative statements about Judaism.[11] Luke displays a considerable knowledge of Judaism and has a very positive attitude toward both the Law and the temple.[12] He is well acquainted with the Septuagint.[13] And it has even been claimed that for Luke "Christianity is true Pharisaism."[14] In spite of these positive factors, however, Luke severely criticizes the Jews for their refusal to accept Jesus and his gospel.

The importance of Israel in Luke's view is seen in the story about the need to reconstitute the Twelve after the death of Judas. The Twelve are witnesses not only to the salvation which God has made available through Jesus, but also to the judgment which threatened a stubborn and unrepentant Israel (Lk. 22:30). The fact that the Twelve function on a symbolic level is clear when one notices that although Matthias is chosen to replace Judas, no need is felt to replace James when he is put to death by Herod Agrippa (Acts 12:1). The Twelve, therefore, represent the twelve tribes of Israel and the group "is reconstituted so that it can confront Israel on the day of Pentecost and show that despite the death of God's anointed one, he still addresses the message of salvation first to the children of Abraham."[15]

But does "Israel first" mean that God's plan includes the complete rejection of Israel after the mission to the Gentiles has begun?

13[46]And Paul and Barnabas spoke out boldly, saying, "It was necessary that the word of God should be spoken first to you. Since you thrust it from you, and judge yourselves unworthy of eternal life, behold, we turn to the Gentiles."

18[6]And when the Jews opposed and reviled him, Paul shook out his garments and said to them, "Your blood be upon your heads! I am innocent. From now on I will go to the Gentiles."

28[28]"Let it be known to you then that this salvation of God has been sent to the Gentiles; they will listen."

Using Acts 13:46; 18:6; and 28:28 in particular, many would argue that Luke has abandoned the hope of converting Israel and that he understands the Christian mission to be directed exclusively to the Gentiles.[16] They conclude that "Luke saw the reception of the Gentiles and the Gentile mission as being the result of the Jews' rejection of the gospel."[17] The promises which were fulfilled in Christ belong to Israel; but because

Israel has been completely rejected, Luke must see the church as the new Israel. J. Jervell[18] takes a somewhat different position when he argues that the *acceptance* of the good news by the Jews, rather than its rejection, forms the basis for the Gentile mission.[19] He has a number of followers when he claims that Luke does not talk about an old Israel which has rejected Jesus and a new Israel (i.e., the church) which has taken its place. When he speaks of "Israel" Luke is talking about a reconstituted Israel, one made up of faithful Jews (i.e., Jewish Christians) and stubborn Jews. According to Jervell, Luke is not referring to a church which is made up of Jews and Gentiles, but to the reconstituted Israel with whom Gentiles have associated in order to realize a share in the fulfilled promises of God.[20]

Both Jervell's thesis and the more widely accepted position, that the rejection of the Gospel by the Jews provides the impetus for the Gentile mission, have been questioned.[21] "Luke knows that the mission to the Jews was a mixed success and is at a stalemate; however, in his composition he is careful to note that the mission to Israel is open-ended."[22] Both the blindness of the Jews (cf. Isa. 6:9-10) and the listening of the Gentiles (cf. Ezek. 3:6) are part of God's plan as foretold in the Hebrew Scriptures (Acts 28:26-28). But this does not mean that God has permanently rejected the Jews. The ignorance or blindness of Israel leads not to unforgiving condemnation and abandonment, but to the call for repentance. After all, God exalted Jesus "at his right hand as Leader and Savior, to give repentance to Israel and forgiveness of sins" (Acts 5:31). According to God's plan, the gift of salvation continues to be offered to all, Jews as well as Gentiles (Lk. 24:46-47; Acts 2:32-39; 3:13-21; 5:31; 10:42-43; 11:18; 13:26-39).

Both the rejection and the acceptance of the gospel are seen by Luke as components of the divine plan of God revealed in the Jewish Scriptures. As early as the prophetic speech of Simeon (Lk. 2:29-35), the mission to the Gentiles, as well as the mission to Israel, is seen as part of the divine plan. Luke's familiarity with the Jewish Scriptures has caused him to see the salvation of the Gentiles as a necessary part of the eschatological action of God.[23] The risen Lord announces that "repentance and forgiveness of sins should be preached in his name to all nations" (Lk. 24:47), a theme which is found throughout Acts (e.g., 3:25; 13:47; 15:16ff.).

We can conclude, therefore, that God's salvation was made available, and continues to be made available to both Jews and Gentiles. The gift of salvation will be offered to the Gentiles, with whom God has had previous contact (cf. Acts 14:11, 17; 15:14; 17:27), when God visits them anew by means of the rebuilt Israel in fulfillment of the prophecy of Amos 9:11f. (Acts 15:16):[24]

> 15[16]"After this I will return, and I will rebuild the dwelling of David, which has fallen; I will rebuild its ruins, and I will set it up, [17]that the rest of humanity may seek the Lord, and all the Gentiles who are called by my name, [18]says the Lord, who has made these things known from of old."

Those who hear the preaching of the Christian missionaries of and about Jesus, whether they be Jews or Gentiles, are expected to repent, believe, and be baptized. The new community which confesses Jesus as Lord and Savior is thus composed of Gentiles as well as Jews. But does this mean that salvation is available to *all* Jews and *all* Gentiles, regardless of gender or economic status?

The Marginalized

No discussion of the universalism of salvation would be complete without mentioning Luke's attitude toward the marginalized. The third evangelist presents Jesus as especially concerned with tax collectors, sinners, the poor, and women. Although the job of tax collector was considered a despicable occupation by first century Judaism,[25] Jesus associates freely with them (Lk. 5:29-30; 7:29, 34; 15:1; cf. 18:9-14). Jesus and his disciples sit at table with tax collectors and eat and drink with them (5:29-30). Tax collectors are in Jesus' audience when the disciples of John question him (7:29) and when Jesus teaches the parables of the lost sheep, the lost coin and the prodigal son (15:1). Jesus admits that he is widely known as a friend of tax collectors (7:34) and uses a repentant tax collector as a positive example in the parable of the Pharisee and the publican (18:9-14). Even more striking is the fact that the famous tax collectors Levi (5:27-32) and Zacchaeus (19:1-10) are numbered among Jesus' disciples. Association with sinners was something to be avoided according to the Pharisees. They based their conclusion in this matter on Leviticus 10:10, "You are to distinguish between the holy and the common, and between the unclean and the clean." Because moral wickedness is not distinguished from impurity in the Hebrew priestly literature the sinner is considered to be unclean. Uncleanness was considered infectious, therefore, a human being might become unclean by contact with any sinner.[26] Salvation according to the Pharisees, then, was to be sought by separating oneself from one's unclean surroundings. Luke presents Jesus as operating on a different principle. Jesus does not ignore and avoid sinners, rather he associates with them (e.g., Lk. 7:36-50; cf. 6:32-34), seeking the lost (15:1-32) in an effort to bring them to repentance (5:32).

When Jesus stands up in the synagogue and reads from the Isaiah scroll (Lk. 4:16ff.), one of the things he announces is that he has been anointed to preach good news to the poor (4:18). Thus early in his ministry Jesus proclaims that the good news of God's salvation is intended for the poor. Those living in the ancient world might expect that salvation would be available to the rich.[27] After all, these people had political and economic power that guaranteed their prosperity. They were large landholders and wealthy merchants involved in export and import trade as well as those in political power who through inheritance or present land ownership were wealthy. The poor, on the other hand, had no economic security and no financial ability to improve their position in the economic system. They were the masses involved in subsistence living as small peasants, tenant farmers, craftspeople, small traders, day laborers, the destitute and beggars. Because the poor have the good news of salvation preached to them, they can repent, believe, and be baptized into Jesus' new community. Although they are excluded from full participation in their secular society, the poor can be included as full members of the Christian community. The Christian community that gathered together at Jerusalem pooled its resources and distributed goods to those in need (Acts 2:45). This approach to poverty appears to have been successful as Luke notes that as a result of the distribution "there was not a needy person among them" (4:34). Because Jesus teaches that salvation belongs to those who hear the word of God and do it (Lk. 8:21) the reader should not be surprised to learn that even a beggar can be saved (16:22).

Luke's belief that salvation is universal is also found in Jesus' association with women. In the Jewish society of Jesus' day a woman was seen as subordinate to her father or her husband.[28] The inferior status of women in late first-century Judaism, reflected in John 4:27 and the early rabbinical writings, is also well known. In the wider Greco-Roman world in which Luke writes, women do not enjoy the same privileges that men enjoy. Scholars have pointed out for some time that in Luke-Acts stories about a man are frequently paralleled by stories about a woman.[29] Women, at least one of whom is married, are pictured as providing for Jesus and the Twelve "out of their means" (Lk. 8:1-3). Women (4:39; 8:3; 10:40) as well as men (Acts 6:2; 19:22) follow the example of Jesus (Lk. 22:26f.; cf. 12:37) and serve (διακονεῖν). Women speak prophetically (Acts 21:8-9) and function as missionaries (Acts 18:8, 26). In suggesting that an equality exists between men and women, Luke the Christian is more progressive than his Jewish or Greco-Roman contemporaries.

Luke understands that God has made salvation available to all through Jesus Christ. His favorable portrayal of women supports this in two ways. First, the universalism of salvation is suggested by the fact that the Gospel is available to all without regard to gender. Luke shows his readers that women received the good news and helped to promote it in the church. Second, as we have seen above, Jesus came to seek and save the lost, the disadvantaged, and the marginalized. One cannot ignore the fact that in first-century Israel women, as well as tax collectors, sinners, and the poor, were among society's marginalized. By presenting Jesus' association with women in such a positive light, whether they symbolize half of society because of their gender or more than half of society because of their social status, Luke has clearly shown that he believes that the gift of salvation is universal.

Because salvation is available to Jews as well as Gentiles, women as well as men, the marginalized as well as the affluent,[30] individuals in all these categories can become members of the Christian community.[31] The new family of Jesus is composed of those who strive to do the will of God regardless of their race, gender, or economic status.

The Community and the Kingdom

Salvation is available to those who hear the word of and about Jesus and respond by repenting and believing in him. Because salvation is available in the present and repentance and belief lead to baptism, one is led to ask about the relationship between the church and the Kingdom of God. Does membership in the Christian community guarantee salvation?

The Kingdom of God, which is made present in Jesus, should be (but is not *de facto*) made present in the community of disciples. These individuals, having repented and been baptized, should be leading their lives in accordance with the will of God. However, this does not always happen. Although Judas Iscariot is one of the twelve whom Jesus named apostles (Lk. 6:12-16), he betrays Jesus into the hands of the Jewish authorities (22:47ff.). Luke's narration of the Lord's Supper also indicates that membership in the Christian community is no guarantee of salvation. Unlike Matthew (Mt. 26:21-25) and Mark (Mk. 14:18-21), Luke locates the prediction of the betrayal of Jesus after the meal (Lk. 22:21-22). The nature of Judas' offense is thus intensified as the reader learns that even presence at the Lord's table is no guarantee against apostasy. That members of the Christian community can still sin is evident also in Acts. In Acts 5:1-16 Luke presents Ananias and Sapphira as two members of the community who attempt to get credit for donating all the proceeds from the sale of a piece of property to the church when, in fact, they are giving only a portion of the proceeds. Their act of deception is considered a very serious sin and is characterized as lying to or tempting the Spirit of the Lord.

In spite of these shortcomings, Luke presents the Christian community as prefiguring, imitating, and spreading the reign of God. The church is seen as a "contrast-society" embodying, more or less faithfully, a whole different ethos from the world around it. This is the key to the meaning of salvation as a communal event. The Kingdom is not confined to the church, nevertheless, the church is defined, discovers its identity, in terms of the Kingdom.

Conclusion

Having taken a closer look at the Christian community, we can conclude that this community is inclusive and not exclusive. Membership in the community that confesses Jesus as Lord and Savior is open to all, regardless of race, gender, or economic status. In a society dominated by wealthy and powerful men, a society that views the marginalized as relatively unimportant, Jesus demonstrates a preferential option for the poor, the powerless, and women as he preaches the good news of salvation to all. Many of the marginalized, those individuals on the fringes of society, receive the good news of God's salvation and become members of the Christian community.

This inclusiveness is not accidental, but the result of God's plan for the salvation of all. The divine plan of salvation provides the unity of Luke's thought in his two-volume work. Luke believes that God, who is ultimately in control of his creation, has a plan by which human beings can gain eternal salvation. The promises contained in God's plan, revealed in the Hebrew Scriptures, especially in the writings of Israel's prophets, have been fulfilled in the life and ministry of Jesus Christ, especially in his death and resurrection. The fact that these prophecies/promises have been fulfilled is presented by Luke as having been attested to by the apostles and other early Christian missionaries, who then invited the members of their audience to repent and be baptized.

According to Luke-Acts, the divine plan calls for the good news of salvation to be preached first to the Jews and then to the Gentiles. This does not mean, however, that the Jews are to be ignored once the Gentile mission has begun; salvation is still available to the Jews. God desires the salvation of all and to this end the good news must be preached to the Jews as well as the Gentiles, even after the resurrection of Jesus. The salvation of God is available now, not only at some far distant time. This means that the reign of God can and should become manifest in the Christian community. As important as membership in the visible community of disciples is for one who is called to acknowledge the Lordship of Jesus, it does not by itself guarantee salvation. What is necessary for salvation is membership in the Kingdom of God which: (1) exists within the Christian community but is not identical with it and (2) should be made visible in the lives of the disciples.

7

The Community:
Its Existence and Structure

In the previous chapters we have seen that God's salvation is available to all who hear the message of Jesus and his disciples and respond positively to it. Personal repentance, a prerequisite to the reception of the Holy Spirit, must occur after one hears about the forgiveness of sins and the possibility of reconciliation with God and one's neighbor. This leads both to spiritual insight as the individual "sees" who Jesus really is and to baptism into Jesus' new community. In this chapter we will examine more closely the specific context for community. After focusing on those texts which unambiguously show that there is a communal dimension to Christian discipleship, we will examine the organizational structure of the community as it existed in Jerusalem, Antioch, and Ephesus.

The Community Exists

Luke found two texts in Mark's Gospel which point to the fact that the call to Christian discipleship includes a call to become a member of a new community (Mk. 3:20-35; 10:28ff.).[1] He has included both texts in his Gospel and added other pericopes which also suggest that discipleship has a communal dimension. In the Gospel, Luke alludes to an organized and communal way of life for Christians when he says that "those who hear the word of God and do it" are

Jesus' mother and brothers (Lk. 8:21; cf. 18:29-30), when he says that several women provided for Jesus and his disciples out of their means (8:1-3), and when he portrays the followers of Jesus as gathered together (24:33) and spending time together at the Jerusalem temple (24:52). While he follows Mark in using the image or model of "family" as a way of understanding the community of disciples, Luke's editorial activity (cf. 14:26; 18:29-30) suggests that one's "family" could present a possible challenge to the discipleship community.

Luke 8:21

> 8²¹"My mother and my brothers are those who hear the word of God and do it."

Luke retains Jesus' words about his eschatological family, but in a context and setting that betrays a much more positive attitude toward the natural family of Jesus. According to Mark 3:21 the natural family of Jesus went out to seize him because they thought that he was out of his mind. His family is joined in its negative assessment of Jesus by the scribes from Jerusalem who say, "He is possessed by Beelzebul, and by the prince of demons he casts out demons" (Mk. 3:22). A short while later, when Jesus is told that his mother and brothers are outside asking for him, Jesus looks around on those who are sitting about him and says, "Here are my mother and my brothers! Whoever does the will of God is my brother, and sister, and mother" (Mk. 3:35). This arrangement seems to distinguish between those who are outside, Jesus' natural family and the scribes, and those who are inside, his disciples. While it is still possible that members of Jesus' natural family might eventually participate in his new community composed of those who do the will of God, Mark is clearly not interested in presenting the members of Jesus' natural family as models of Christian discipleship.

Luke, however, presents a favorable view of both the community and Jesus' natural family. The third evangelist excludes Mark 3:20-21, where the family of Jesus tries to seize him because they believe he is crazy, distances this pericope from the Beelzebul controversy, and eliminates the contrast between those outside and those inside. The parable of the sower and its explanation (Lk. 8:4-18) now immediately precede the pericope about Jesus' true family; the Beelzebul controversy occurs three chapters later (11:14ff.). The result is that the mother and brothers of Jesus are presented in a very positive manner. Almost immediately after he praises "those who, hearing the word, hold it fast in an honest and good heart, and bring forth fruit with patience" (8:15), Jesus uses similar language to speak about his eschatological family, "My mother and my brothers are those who hear the word of God and do it" (8:21). By eliminating the contrast found in Mark between those inside and those outside the house, Luke is suggesting that the natural family of Jesus is an example of the seed that has fallen in good soil.[2]

Luke 18:29-30

For Luke, however, the image of "family" can also be one of potential conflict of loyalties between natural and spritual families. Mention of the fact that one of the women traveling with Jesus and his disciples was married (Lk. 8:1-3) highlights the radical nature of Christian discipleship. While Luke records that Joanna was the wife of Chuza, Herod's steward, he mentions neither that her husband is with the group nor that Chuza has died. The reader of Luke 8:1-3 is left with the impression that Joanna has left her husband in order to accompany Jesus and his disciples. This reading is reinforced when one realizes that on two other occasions Luke notes the possibility of leaving one's spouse for the sake of the Kingdom (14:26; 18:29-30).

When Peter reminds Jesus that he and the other disciples have left their homes and followed him, Jesus replies, "Truly, I say to you, there is no one who has left house or wife or brothers or parents or children, for the sake of the Kingdom of God, who will not receive manifold more in this time, and in the age to come eternal life" (Lk. 18:29-30). These verses, which are dependent on Mark 10:29-30, have been revised significantly by Luke.[3] In spite of the fact that Luke replaces Mark's specific list of what the faithful disciple will receive "in this time" with the unspecific phrase "manifold more," scholars generally conclude that Luke agrees with Mark and understands that the "more" which one will receive in this life means association with the new family of Jesus, i.e. the church.[4] Some who are members of this new community apparently have left their spouses in order to follow Jesus. Mark lists house, brothers, sisters, mother, father, children, and lands as who and what one might have to leave in order to accompany Jesus (Mk. 10:29). Although Luke shortens the list by not mentioning sisters or lands and by using the collective term "parents," he makes a significant addition to the list when he includes "wife" as someone who could be left behind "for the sake of the Kingdom" (Lk. 18:29). Is the thought here that the disciple might have to renounce merely the possibility of marriage or does this text refer to the breakup of an existing marriage?

Luke 14:26

Material from his Q source, which Luke includes in chapter 14, suggests that Luke is referring to the breakup of an existing marriage.

> 14[26]"If any one comes to me and does not hate his own father and mother and wife and children and brothers and sisters, yes, and even his own life, he cannot be my disciple."

Matthew tones down this passage and has Jesus say that the one who loves father, mother, son, or daughter, more than him is not worthy of him (Mt. 10:37). Luke, however, has included "wife" here as among the relatives one must hate in order to be Jesus' disciple. In the preceding pericope, the parable of the Great Supper (Lk. 14:15-24; cf. Mt. 22:1-10), Luke alone reports the third excuse for refusing the master's invitation, "I have married a wife, and therefore I cannot come" (Lk. 14:20). The radical nature of Christian discipleship demands that no thing or person, even one's spouse, be allowed to stand in the way of one's allegiance to Jesus. It is not inevitable that this will happen, as elsewhere the Lukan Jesus speaks about the permanency of marriage (Lk. 16:18), but should it happen one's relationship to Jesus must be preferred.

Luke 8:1-3

In the Gospel, Luke gives several indications that Jesus' new family should live in the world as a visible community. On the way to Jerusalem Jesus passes through cities and villages, preaching and bringing the good news of the Kingdom of God. The community which foreshadows the church discovers its identity in the context of the Kingdom preaching. With Jesus are the Twelve, Mary Magdalene, Joanna, the wife of Herod's steward, Susanna, and many other women "who were serving them out of their possessions" (Lk. 8:3). During the ministry of Jesus, therefore, a large company of individuals traveled with him as he journeyed toward Jerusalem.

> 8 ¹Soon afterward he [Jesus] went on through cities and villages, preaching and bringing the good news of the Kingdom of God. And the Twelve were with him, ²and also some women who had been healed of evil spirits and infirmities: Mary, called Magdalene, from whom seven demons had gone out, ³and Joanna, the wife of Chuza, Herod's steward, and Susanna, and many others, who were serving them out of their possessions.

As we saw in chapter 2, "to be with him" is a technical expression for discipleship in Luke's sources as well as in Luke-Acts. Luke omits this characteristic from Mark 3:14 in his version of the choosing of the Twelve (cf. Lk. 6:13), but includes it here. The presence of this theme in Luke 8:1-3 supports the conclusion that "being with Jesus" is the central fact of community in the Gospel.

The journey motif, discipleship as "following" Jesus, is also emphasized in this pericope. Jesus and his male and female disciples are pictured as traveling along through various cities and villages, preaching the good news of the Kingdom of God (Lk. 8:1). In Acts, Luke conveys a special corporate sense of following by designating the early Palestinian Christian community as "the Way." Luke's conception of the life of faith as a pilgrimage, always on the move, is seen both in his absolute use of this term (Acts 9:2; 19:9,23; 22:4; 24:14,22) and in his use of the expressions "a way of salvation" (16:17), "the way of the Lord" (18:25), and "the way of God" (18:26). While the origin of this expression ("the Way") is debated,[5] it does serve to recall the motif of discipleship as following Jesus along his way. Mention of the women here foreshadows the appearance of women at the crucifixion of Jesus (Lk. 23:49), at the empty tomb (24:10), and as members of the Jerusalem community in Acts. This serves as a corrective to an overly male-oriented understanding of Christian discipleship. After the death and resurrection of Jesus these women who provided the financial resources for Jesus and his disciples during the ministry are gathered together with the other disciples waiting prayerfully for the coming of the Holy Spirit (Acts 1:14). Like the seed that grows and develops into a plant, so the group that traveled with Jesus during his ministry grows and develops into the Christian community. In Acts, the Spirit creates the community, both bonding and expanding the group.

This pericope also touches on several other themes: (1) Women are among Jesus' most faithful followers and are qualified to function as his witnesses. They are with Jesus early in his ministry (Lk. 8:1-3), accompany him from Galilee to Jerusalem and are present at his crucifixion (23:55), discover the empty tomb (24:1-11,22-24), and are members of the early Christian community (Acts 1:14). They have been included in the company of Jesus' disciples from the baptism of John until the day when Jesus was taken up (Acts 1:22). The risen Lord appeared to these women and to the others "who came up with him from Galilee to Jerusalem, who are now his witnesses to the people" (Acts 13:31).[6]

(2) The use of "to serve" ($\delta\iota\alpha\kappa\circ\nu\epsilon\hat{\iota}\nu$) to describe what the women are doing emphasizes the service component of Christian discipleship. Luke reports that at the Lord's Supper a dispute arose among the disciples of Jesus concerning which one of them was to be regarded as the greatest. And Jesus said to them:

> 22²⁵"The kings of the Gentiles exercise lordship over them; and those in authority over them are called benefactors. ²⁶But not so with you; rather let the greatest among you become as the youngest, and the leader as one who serves. ²⁷For which is the greater, one who sits at table, or one who

> serves? Is it not the one who sits at table? But I am among
> you as one who serves."

These verses are important for understanding how Luke views the structure of the Christian community. They seem to take for granted that there are differences in rank within the community. The point being made is that those in authority behave appropriately only when they follow the example of humble service given them by Jesus. Earlier in the Gospel Jesus presents his disciples with the same image of himself as servant when he says, "Blessed are those servants whom the master finds awake when he comes; truly, I say to you, he will gird himself and have them sit at table, and he will come and serve them" (Lk. 12:37). In Luke's Gospel, as in Mark's,[7] it is women who follow the example of Jesus and serve. In addition to the women mentioned in Luke 8:3, Luke uses "to serve" ($\delta\iota\alpha\kappa\rho\nu\hat{\epsilon}\iota\nu$) to refer to the activity of both Peter's mother-in-law (4:39) and Martha (10:40). In Acts, Luke uses the noun "service" ($\delta\iota\alpha\kappa\rho\nu\acute{\iota}\alpha$) to refer to Christian preaching (Acts 6:4) and missionary work (12:25; 20:24; 21:19), the office of apostle (1:17,25) and support for other members of the community (6:1; cf. 11:29). "Every office in the congregation, from the service at table to the teaching mission of the Apostles, can be called $\delta\iota\alpha\kappa\rho\nu\acute{\iota}\alpha$, because it means serving God in the community."[8]

(3) The editorial use of "possessions" ($\tau\grave{\alpha}$ $\dot{\upsilon}\pi\acute{\alpha}\rho\chi\rho\nu\tau\alpha$) looks forward to other passages dealing with the disciple's proper use of wealth (Lk. 12:15,33; 14:33; 16:1; 19:8; Acts 4:32).[9] Jesus first warns the multitudes that one's life does not consist in the abundance of one's possessions (Lk. 12:15) and then says, "whoever does not renounce all their possessions cannot be my disciple" (14:33). Jesus provides an example of what he means when he says to his disciples, "Sell your possessions, and give alms; provide yourselves with purses that do not grow old, with a treasure in the heavens that does not fail, where no thief approaches and no moth destroys" (12:33). He urges the rich not to waste their possessions (16:1) but to use them as a means of making friends for themselves. Jesus explains what he means a few verses later when he tells his audience the story of the rich man and Lazarus (16:19-31).

Individuals should listen to Moses, the prophets, and Jesus and use their wealth to "make friends" with the poor, treat those in need with mercy and compassion. The consequences of failing to heed this recommendation are serious: the rich man who ignored the needs of poor Lazarus is tormented in Hades after his death. Luke gives his readers further examples of the correct use of possessions in the Zacchaeus story and in the story of the early church in Acts. The wealthy tax collector named Zacchaeus provides evidence of his conversion by giving half his goods (τὰ ὑπάρχοντα) to the poor and paying back fourfold anyone he has defrauded (19:8). Luke informs the reader that "the company of those who believed," i.e. the early Christian community gathered together in Jerusalem in the post-resurrection era, "were of one heart and soul, and no one said that any of the things which he possessed was his own, but they had everything in common" (Acts 4:32).

Luke 24:33

According to Luke, the group of disciples that gather around Jesus in Galilee at the outset of his ministry and travel with him to Jerusalem remain together during the Passion account and are found together after the resurrection of Jesus. Mark reports that all the male disciples fled after Jesus was taken captive (Mk. 14:50). In the remainder of the Mark's Gospel, the only disciples who appear are Peter and the women who followed Jesus from Galilee (15:40, 47; 16:1-8). Luke, however, gives the reader the impression that the followers of Jesus remained together throughout Jesus' ordeal. Luke excludes Mark 14:50, so no mention is made of fleeing disciples. And according to Luke, not only the women (cf. Mk. 15:40) but "all his acquaintances" who had followed Jesus from Galilee stood at a distance and witnessed his crucifixion (Lk. 23:49).

After his resurrection Jesus appears to two of his disciples who are going along toward a village named Emmaus. Because it is late in the day the three travelers stop to have a bite to eat. While at table, Jesus acts the part of the host as he takes the bread, blesses it, breaks it, and gives it to his companions. When they recognize Jesus in the breaking of the bread he vanishes out of their sight (Lk. 24:31,35). The two disciples immediately set out for Jerusalem to tell the other disciples what had happened. The communal dimension of discipleship is seen when Luke reports that "they found the eleven gathered together and those who were with them" (24:33). This is undoubtedly the same group that is referred to at the end of the Gospel: after Jesus blessed them and parted from them, they "returned to Jerusalem with great joy, and were continually in the temple blessing God" (24:50-53); at the beginning of Acts, "all these with one accord devoted themselves to prayer, together with the women and Mary the mother of Jesus, and with his brothers" (Acts 1:14).

While the Gospel passages just examined clearly indicate Luke's interest in the communal dimension of discipleship, the most obvious examples of this theme appear in his second volume. In Acts, the disciples of Jesus are said to be of "one accord" as they pray together (Acts 1:14) and to be of "one heart and soul" as they live in common, their generosity insuring that there will be no needy among them (4:32; 2:44-45). The word Luke chooses to designate this group which gathered together for apostolic instruction, fellowship, prayer, and the breaking of bread (2:42ff.) is κοινωνία (association or fellowship).

The Structure of the Community

Luke understands the community to be organized, although he is somewhat vague about its exact structure. In the Gospel there is little horizontal distinction among the followers of Jesus as the Twelve and the Seventy are assigned the same tasks.[10] Jesus called together the Twelve and "gave them power and authority over all demons and to cure diseases, and he sent them out to preach the Kingdom of God and to heal" (Lk. 9:1-2). Likewise, he sends the Seventy on ahead of him (10:1), giving them authority (10:19) to "heal the sick" (10:9), to proclaim that "the Kingdom of God has come near" (10:9), and to cast out demons (10:17). In Acts, however, one finds a proliferation of roles and functions as the early church solidifies and struggles with troublesome issues. A distinction is made, for example, between those who help with the daily food distribution to the widows and those who "devote themselves to prayer and to the ministry of the word" (Acts 6:1-4). The same can be said concerning vertical distinctions. While Jesus is presented on two occasions as virtually forbidding vertical differentiation (Lk. 9:46-48; 22:24-30), the fact that it does exist is seen in Luke's account of the Lord's Supper[11] and in the prominent role of Peter in the Gospel (cf. 22:31-32). Jesus responds to the first argument among his disciples as to which of them was the greatest by saying that "the one who is least among you all is the one who is great" (9:48). After the second argument about the same topic, Jesus draws the disciples' attention to the way the Gentile kings exercise their power and authority over their subjects. He then tells his disciples that it is not to be that way with them (22:25-26). The remainder of the Last Supper pericope, however, takes for granted that there are differences in rank within the community (22:26-27). Jesus presents himself as a servant and indicates that this model of service must be followed by those in positions of authority within the community. In Acts it is clear that some individuals and groups (e.g., Peter, James, the elders) function in leadership roles. The exact nature of their roles, however, is not always clear.

The Twelve, Apostles, and Disciples

We have already seen that many people answered the call to discipleship issued by Jesus and the early Christian missionaries. While the most popular designation for these individuals is "disciples," Luke also refers to some of them as "the apostles" and "the Twelve." What must concern us at this point is the relationship between the Twelve, the apostles, and the disciples. Are these terms interchangeable? If they are distinct groups then how are they related to one another? What role does each group play in the governance of the Christian community?

In general, the term "disciple" presupposes a relationship to "the master." A disciple, from the verb "to learn," is a student who accepts and follows a given teacher. The term "apostle" has a more centrifugal connotation as it designates one who is sent out. "The Twelve," of course, has a connection with the Jewish tradition and is symbolic of the twelve tribes of Israel.

One could conclude, therefore, that any distinctions are first of all in connotation and only secondarily, if at all, functional or structural. They are indicative of relationships before they are of offices. Throughout his two-volume work, Luke uses "disciple" as a general term to refer to believers in Christ, i.e. Christians (cf. Acts 11:26).[12] Because only some of these believers are referred to as "the Twelve" or "the apostles," it will be more profitable if we confine our study specifically to these terms. In the Gospel Luke uses the term "the Twelve" six times (Mt. four, Mk. ten),[13] "the eleven" twice,[14] and "the apostles" six times (Mt. once, Mk. twice).[15] Unlike Matthew, neither Luke nor Acts uses the phrase "twelve apostles" (cf. Mt. 10:2) or "twelve disciples" (cf. Mt. 10:1; 11:1; 20:17). In Acts "eleven apostles" occurs once (Acts 1:26), "the eleven" once (Acts 2:14), and "the Twelve" once (Acts 6:2).

The existence of a communal dimension of discipleship has already been suggested. The little band which literally followed the historical Jesus grew into the church of thousands and settled down in many different places after his death and resurrection. Our attempt to understand the role and function of the Twelve, the apostles, and the disciples in Luke-Acts, thus has implications for what will be said about Luke's picture of the Christian community and leadership within that community.

(1) The Twelve in the Gospel

Many people would begin and end their response to the questions just raised by quoting Luke 6:13: "And when it was day, he called his disciples, and chose from them twelve, whom he named apostles." It is obvious, they say, that: (1) the "disciples" are a larger group than the Twelve, (2) the Twelve are disciples, and (3) the Twelve and "the apostles" are interchangeable terms. While the first two conclusions are universally accepted, scholars urge caution in equating "the apostles" and "the Twelve."

At the outset one must admit that Luke 6:13 is probably not the best place to begin an investigation into Luke's use of "the

Twelve." While it is true that the number twelve appears in this verse, it is also true that the title "the Twelve" does not occur here. The Twelve are referred to by this title only six times in the Gospel (Lk. 8:1; 9:1,12; 18:31; 22:3,47) and once in Acts (6:2). Luke does not seem to be especially interested in this title since four of the six instances in which Luke refers to the Twelve in the Gospel are found in his Markan source. He follows Mark when he mentions that twelve are chosen from among a wider group of disciples (Lk. 6:13; Mk. 3:14), and that "the Twelve" are sent out on a missionary journey (Lk. 9:1; Mk. 6:7), and compose the audience for Jesus' third passion-resurrection prediction (Lk. 18:31; Mk. 10:32). Luke also follows Mark in noting that Judas is numbered among the Twelve (Lk. 22:14,47; Mk. 14:10,43).

More interesting are those references to the Twelve which Luke has added, altered, or omitted. The two remaining references to the Twelve in Luke's Gospel are found in 8:1 and 9:12. In the story about Jesus and his followers (Lk. 8:1-3), which has no parallel in Mark's Gospel, the Twelve are singled out as a group that is with Jesus on his journey. Luke's mention of the Twelve here may account for the change he makes a few verses later. Mark reports that "those who were about him with the Twelve" asked Jesus about the parables (Mk. 4:10). Luke tells the reader that Jesus' "disciples asked him what this parable meant" (Lk. 8:9). It is difficult to determine exactly why Luke changed "the Twelve" to "his disciples" here. Perhaps Luke made this change because: (1) he inserted a pericope only a few verses earlier (Lk. 8:1) in which the Twelve were mentioned or (2) he wanted to point out that the teaching of Jesus is addressed to all disciples. The suggestion that Luke feels comfortable referring to the Twelve as disciples is supported by Luke 9:12, the final instance in the Gospel in which Luke refers to the Twelve. Unlike the previous example (Lk. 8:1), this verse does have a Markan parallel. The third evangelist replaces Mark's reference to Jesus' disciples (Mk. 6:35) with a comment that it was the Twelve who came to Jesus and tried to get him to send away the crowd before the Feeding of the Five Thousand (Lk. 9:12).

In addition to substituting "his disciples" for the Twelve in 8:9, Luke has replaced Mark's reference to the Twelve at the

Last Supper. Luke has identified the "apostles" as the group that was with Jesus at table (Lk. 22:14) whereas Mark has the Twelve as Jesus' dinner companions (Mk. 14:17). Elsewhere the third evangelist also appears to equate the Twelve and the apostles. In Luke 6:13 twelve disciples are chosen and named apostles. And although Luke tells the reader that it was the Twelve whom Jesus sent out on a missionary journey (Lk. 9:1) he reports that it was "the apostles" who told Jesus what they had done upon their return (9:10).

On four occasions Luke has simply eliminated references to the Twelve which he found in his Markan source. (1) Luke may have eliminated Mark's comment that Jesus "appointed the Twelve" (Mk. 3:16) because he has just (Lk. 6:13; cf. Mk. 3:14) referred to the fact that Jesus chose twelve from among his disciples.[16] (2) Jesus' words after the dispute about greatness (Lk. 9:46ff.) are not addressed to the Twelve as in Mark 9:35 but to a group previously identified as "his disciples" (Lk. 9:43). (3) Mark's reference to Jesus and the Twelve going together to Bethany (Mk.11:11) is eliminated by Luke because of a change in chronology. According to Luke Jesus does not enter the temple, look around and leave, only to return the next day. (4) Luke's elimination of Mark's comment (Mk. 14:20) that one of the Twelve will betray Jesus seems insignificant since, as mentioned above, he follows Mark on two other occasions in identifying Judas as one of the Twelve.

Although the Twelve are chosen from among the other disciples to form a special group, Luke does not appear to be very interested in referring to them as the Twelve. He has adopted only four of Mark's ten references to the Twelve and replaces this term twice, once with "the apostles" (Lk. 22:14) and once with "his disciples" (8:9). In order to determine if this preliminary conclusion is correct we must ask if there anything unique about the Twelve in Luke's Gospel. What do we learn about "the Twelve" in passages which explicitly refer to them by this term?

Luke's use of "to choose" ($\dot{\epsilon}\kappa\lambda\dot{\epsilon}\gamma\epsilon\sigma\theta\alpha\iota$) in 6:13 might be significant since only this group and Jesus are said to have been chosen: The voice from the cloud at the Transfiguration says, "This is my Son, my Chosen; listen to him!" (Lk. 9:35). In considering this possibility one must ask if it is important that the twelve disciples who were chosen are not identified as "the Twelve." Further comment on this will have to wait until we examine Acts.

In the Feeding of the 5,000 Luke has included a reference to the Twelve (Lk. 9:12) where Mark has "his disciples" (Mk. 6:35). Is this a significant change or merely a stylistic alteration? Luke refers to "the apostles" in 9:10 and the disciples in 9:14. Is he referring to the same group of people in 9:10, 12, and 14?

Other references to the Twelve seem less significant. Luke specifically mentions that the Twelve were with Jesus on his journey through the cities and villages of Galilee (Lk. 8:1-3), but so were Mary, Joanna, Susanna, and many others. The Twelve are given authority to exorcise and heal and are sent to preach the Kingdom of God (Lk. 9:1-6). As was mentioned above, however, the Seventy are able to do the same things. The third passion-resurrection prediction is the only one clearly addressed to the Twelve. The first two predictions appear to be addressed to a wider audience. Even if Luke intends to refer to the Twelve when he says "the disciples" in 9:18 and 9:43 he has not referred to them as the Twelve. The information given to this group in the third prediction is much more detailed than in the other predictions but there is no indication that Luke intended the reader to understand the Twelve as possessing some kind of special knowledge. Reference to Judas as a member of the Twelve seems to suggest that even a member of this chosen group could fail. Peter's denial, of course, teaches the same thing.

Luke may intend to refer to the Twelve in some instances when he uses the term disciples. It is clear, however, that the disciples are normally seen as a group larger than the Twelve. Luke may intend the Twelve and the apostles to be interchangeable terms. Our preliminary conclusion, however, is that Luke is not especially interested in the title "the Twelve."

(2) The Twelve in Acts

The only specific reference to the Twelve in Luke's second volume occurs in the story of the appointment of the seven (Acts 6:1-6; cf. 1:26; 2:14):

6¹Now in these days when the disciples were increasing in number, the Hellenists murmured against the Hebrews because their widows were neglected in the daily distribution. ²And the Twelve summoned the body of the disciples and said, "It is not right that we should give up preaching the word of God to serve tables. ³Therefore, brethren, pick out from among you seven individuals of good repute, full of the spirit and of wisdom, whom we may appoint to this duty. ⁴But we will devote ourselves to prayer and to the ministry of the word." ⁵And what they said pleased the whole multitude, and they chose Stephen, a man full of faith and of the Holy Spirit, and Philip, and Prochorus, and Nicanor, and Timon, and Parmenas, and Nicolaus, a proselyte of Antioch. ⁶These they set before the apostles, and they prayed and laid their hands upon them.

Since this is the only specific mention of the Twelve in Acts one must conclude that this designation is not extremely important for Luke. Our earlier conclusion suggested that the Twelve were singled out because they were "chosen" (ἐκλέγεσθαι). In Acts 1 the reader is reminded that Jesus chose "the apostles" (Acts 1:1) and is told that it was the Lord who chose Matthias to replace the traitor Judas (1:21-26) thereby restoring the number of this little group to twelve. In Acts 6:1ff., however, we encounter something unexpected. Thus far in Luke-Acts it has been either Jesus or God who has chosen (ἐκλέγεσθαι) individuals. But in Acts 6:1ff. the choice is not made directly by Jesus or God, but indirectly through the use of human agents. It might surprise some to learn that the Twelve did not choose these seven individuals. While the Twelve do appear as leaders, summoning the body of disciples (6:2), and the apostles do lay their hands upon the seven who have been set before them (6:6), it is the whole multitude of disciples who choose (ἐκλέγεσθαι) Stephen, Philip, Prochorus, Nicanor, Timon, Parmenas, and Nicolaus (6:3, 5).

Elsewhere in Acts we find that: (1) as in the Gospel, God chooses (Acts 13:17; 15:7) and (2) the council (the apostles, the elders, and perhaps others) chooses individuals to accompany Paul and Barnabas to Antioch (15:22, 25). The fact that some are chosen serves to set them apart from the rest of the disciples and to indicate that they have some special function to perform. The importance that we placed on the choosing of the Twelve in our preliminary conclusion must be tempered, however, by what we find in Acts. Many who are not members of the Twelve are chosen (ἐκλέγεσθαι). Nowhere in Acts does it say that the Twelve are the ones who choose others. Matthias is chosen by the Lord (1:24) and elsewhere it is either the multitude of disciples (6:3, 5) or the apostles together with the elders (15:22,23) who choose individuals for specific purposes. Judas Barsabbas and Silas are chosen and sent as missionaries (15:22ff.) while the seven disciples chosen in Acts 6 are appointed to serve tables (6:2).

Earlier it was suggested that Luke's understanding of the role of the Twelve might be found in the Feeding of the 5,000 where he replaces Mark's reference to "his disciples" (Mk. 6:35) with "the Twelve" (Lk. 9:12). In Acts 6:1ff., however, the Twelve specifically indicate that they intend to devote themselves to prayer and to the ministry of the word (Acts 6:4) and not to waiting on tables (6:2). Eucharistic allusions, often associated with the Feeding of the 5,000, are not associated with the Twelve as "the Twelve" either in the Gospel or in Acts. At the Lord's Supper Luke reports that Jesus sat at table with the apostles (Lk. 22:14) not with the Twelve (Mk. 14:17). In the Emmaus story (Lk. 24:13-35), with its obvious eucharistic theme, mention is made of Cleopas and an unnamed disciple, but not the Twelve.

One is left to conclude that Luke's interest in this group called the Twelve is limited. After Judas is replaced (Acts 1:15-26), the Twelve virtually disappear as a group. Elsewhere in Acts they are mentioned only in the Pentecost account (2:14) and in the story about the selection of the seven table servers (6:1ff.). Luke reports that James is killed by Herod Agrippa (12:2), but he does not tell the reader that anyone is chosen to replace James as one of the Twelve. The fact that Luke reports at such length the selection of Matthias to replace Judas indicates, however, that the Twelve are important for him in some way. It is usually suggested that in their role as witnesses they serve as a vital link between Jesus and the early church. Many suggest that the Twelve constitute the "twelve-tribe" framework upon which the new Israel is to be formed.[17]

After they serve this function, they become unimportant for Luke, at least until the final judgement. Although not stated as clearly as in Matthew 19:28, perhaps Luke intends the reader to understand that the Twelve will be seated upon twelve thrones "judging the twelve tribes of Israel" (Lk. 22:30).[18]

(3) The Apostles in the Gospel

While Luke refers to the apostles only six times in the Gospel (Lk. 6:13; 9:10; 11:49; 17:5; 22:14; 24:10), he uses this term some 28 times in Acts. The third evangelist includes in his Gospel the only reference to the apostles found in Mark (Mk. 6:30; Lk. 9:10) and seems to portray the apostles and the Twelve as identical. It is the Twelve that Jesus calls together and to whom he gives power and authority (Lk. 9:1), but when this group returns Luke refers to them as the apostles (Lk. 9:10). Further indication that Luke understands the Twelve and the apostles to be identical is found in 6:13 where one reads that "he called his disciples, and chose from them twelve, whom he named apostles." Also supporting this conclusion is Luke's reference to the apostles (Lk. 22:14) as Jesus' dinner companions where the Markan parallel has "the Twelve"(Mk. 14:17). Although Jesus says he will eat the passover with his disciples (Lk. 22:11) the reader soon learns that it is the apostles who sat at table with him. The identification of the apostles and the Twelve is also suggested in this pericope when Jesus speaks to the apostles about the twelve tribes of Israel:

> 22[28]"You are those who have continued with me in my trials; [29]as my Father appointed a Kingdom for me, so do I appoint for you [30]that you may eat and drink at my table in my Kingdom, and sit on thrones judging the twelve tribes of Israel."

Reference to the fact that apostles, like the prophets before them, will be persecuted and killed (Lk. 11:49) seems to look forward to Acts. Also foreshadowing the situation in Acts are Jesus' words about service. The reader learns that the apostles are on the journey with Jesus to Jerusalem when in 17:5 they say, "Increase our faith!" This gives Jesus the opportunity to comment on service as well as faith. Perhaps this pericope looks forward to Acts when the apostles will be leaders in the community. They need faith and must behave as servants, a fact we learn elsewhere in Luke-Acts. The last reference to the apostles in the Gospel (Lk. 24:10) occurs when Mary Magdalene and Joanna and Mary the mother of James and the other women with them told the apostles what they had experienced at the empty tomb, only to have their words be appraised as an idle tale, and not be believed. There is some question about who is meant by "the apostles" however.

> 24^{9b} they told all this to the eleven and to all the rest. ^{10}Now it was Mary Magdalene and Joanna and Mary the mother of James and the other women with them who told this to the apostles; ^{11}but these words seemed to them an idle tale, and they did not believe them. ^{12}But Peter rose and ran to the tomb; stooping and looking in, he saw the linen cloths by themselves; and he went home wondering at what had happened.
> ^{13}That very day two of them were going to a village named Emmaus, about seven miles from Jerusalem . . . .
> ^{18}Then one of them, named Cleopas . . . .

The most common conclusion is that "two of them" in verse 13 refers to "all the rest" in verse 9.[19] The basic assumption is that Luke has equated "the apostles" and "the Twelve" intentionally in his two-volume work. It follows from this that Cleopas, who is "one of them" (Lk. 24:18; cf. 24:13) but not one of the Twelve (cf. 6:14-16), cannot be an apostle (i.e., one of the eleven mentioned in 24:9).

The approach we are taking here, however, does not allow us to assume at the outset that "the apostles" and "the Twelve" are interchangeable terms. This is what must be proved or disproved; it cannot be the starting point for our investigation of Luke 24:9ff. This is especially true in light of Acts 14:4,14 where Barnabas and Paul are clearly referred to as apostles (see below).

It is entirely possible that Luke did not intend to equate "the apostles" and "the eleven" in the present passage (Lk. 24:9ff.).

One could easily interpret these verses to mean that Cleopas was an apostle. "Of them" in verse 13 could refer to its closest antecedent, "the apostles" mentioned in verse 10. The term "the apostles" would then be inclusive of "the eleven and all the rest" who are referred to in verse 9.[20] If this interpretation is correct then Luke is not being inconsistent, as is often claimed, when he refers to Paul and Barnabas as apostles in Acts 14. This would lead to the conclusion that the term "apostle" is not meant to be interchangeable with and exclusively reserved for the Twelve. This will be examined in more detail below.

In texts which refer clearly and unambiguously to the apostles how does this group function in Luke's Gospel? (1) In 6:13 we learn that the apostles were chosen and named. The importance of being chosen will be examined below. In the Gospel only the apostles (Lk. 6:13) and Peter (Lk. 6:14) are "named." This serves to set them apart from the wider circle of disciples. (2) While it was the Twelve whom Jesus sent out on a missionary journey, it was the apostles who "told him what they had done" when they returned (Lk. 9:10). Although this text seems to identify the apostles and the Twelve, as mentioned above, what was said of the Twelve was said of the Seventy. Therefore, there is nothing unique here which sets the apostles apart from the Seventy. Their name "apostles" ($\dot{\alpha}\pi\acute{o}\sigma\tau o\lambda o\iota$ = people sent out) seems to suggest their function.

The final three references to the apostles in the Gospel (Lk. 17:5; 22:14; 24:10) imply a leadership role for them. While the individuals who accompany Jesus on his journey from Galilee to Jerusalem are referred to most often as Jesus' "disciples,"[21] the Twelve are singled out in 18:31 and the apostles are mentioned in 17:5. Luke identifies those who said to Jesus, "Increase our faith!" (17:5) as the apostles. After responding to their request in terms of faith, Jesus launches into a story about service. Luke may have intended the reader to see this story as directed only to the apostles and not to the disciples mentioned a few verses earlier (17:1). According to this scenario the apostles would be seen by the reader as those who expect to be served their supper by a servant who has just completed a hard day's work in the field. The meaning of the story appears in 17:10 when Jesus identifies the apostles as unworthy servants. They must not sit back and expect to be waited on by their "servants." They too have a duty to perform; they must do what has been commanded. As will be seen below, although Luke portrays the Christian community as hierarchical in structure he insists that its leaders must follow the example of Jesus, the Suffering Servant, and place themselves at the service of the Lord and the members of Christian community.

Leadership and service are also connected in Luke's account of the Lord's Supper. Unlike Mark, who has Jesus eating with the Twelve (Mk. 14:17), Luke tells the reader that it was the apostles who were at table with Jesus (Lk. 22:14). Although a similar story is found in Mark 10:42-45, it is generally accepted that Luke's tradition provided the story of the dispute about greatness in the Kingdom which he included in his account of the Lord's Supper.[22] Jesus responds to the argument among his followers by saying:

> 22[25]"The kings of the Gentiles exercise lordship over them; and those in authority over them are called benefactors. [26]But not so with you; rather let the greatest among you become as the youngest, and the leader as one who serves. [27]For which is the greater, one who sits at table, or one who serves? Is it not the one who sits at table? But I am among you as one who serves.
>
> [28]You are those who have continued with me in my trials; [29]as my Father appointed a Kingdom for me, so do I appoint for you [30]that you may eat and drink at my table in my Kingdom, and sit on thrones judging the twelve tribes of Israel."

Luke's introduction to the conversation is more general and timeless than the similar story found in Mark 10:35ff. According to Mark the dispute arises because James and John request the places of honor in the Kingdom. Jesus responds that his disciples should not be interested in precedence. The Lukan story, on the other hand, takes for granted that there are differences in rank within the community. Jesus' concern in the Third Gospel is the appropriate behavior of those in authority.

In verse 25 Luke informs his readers that those in power normally lord it over their people. Jesus then says that it cannot be that way for Christian leaders. In 2 Corinthians 1:24 Paul uses the same verb, "to be lord or master" *(κυριεύοσιν)*, in speaking about attitudes to be avoided by those in leadership positions in the church. Jesus addresses those who "are great" (Lk. 22:26) in contrast to Mark 10:43 where he speaks of those who wish to be great. Luke seems to be referring to leaders in the early church when he contrasts greater/junior and leader/servant. The term "ruler" or "leader" (*ἡγούμενος*) is used for leaders of the community in Hebrews 13:7, 17, 24 and Judas Barsabbas and Silas are called "leaders (*ἡγούμενος*) among the brethren" in Acts 15:22. By including servant (*διάκονος*) in his contrast, Luke has clearly indicated that church leaders must behave as servants. When Jesus says "I am among you as one who serves" (Lk. 22:27) he is identifying himself with the lowly position of the house servant and calling for humility among church leaders as he defines their role in terms of service.

The future leadership role of the apostles is also suggested in Luke 22:19 when Jesus commands the apostles to "Do this in remembrance of me" and in 22:28-30 when Jesus appears to be referring to future Eucharistic celebrations in the church.[23]

The apostles are also singled out in Luke 24:10 as a group to whom the women should tell their story about the empty tomb. A hierarchical structure within the community is suggested whether or not "the apostles" is a term which includes "all the rest." Luke distinguishes "the eleven" from "all the rest" (Lk. 24:9; cf. 24:33) even if all of these disciples can be called apostles.

(4) The Apostles in Acts

Luke mentions the "apostles" more times in Acts than his combined references to the disciples and the Twelve. The reader is reminded in Acts 1 that Jesus chose (*ἐκλέγεσθαι*) the apostles (cf. Lk. 6:13). As indicated above, however, others who are not specifically called apostles are also chosen. The fact that those chosen (e.g., Jesus, the Twelve, some of the seven, Judas

Barsabbas, Silas) function as missionaries has led some to speculate that there is a connection between being chosen and missionary work. The problem with this conclusion is that many who function as missionaries are not specifically mentioned as having been chosen (e.g., the Seventy, Paul). When Luke informs the reader that Matthias "was enrolled with the eleven apostles" (Acts 1:26) he seems to be indicating that the apostles and the Twelve/Eleven are interchangeable terms. A serious challenge to this conclusion arises, however, when one realizes that Barnabas and Paul, not members of the Twelve, are called apostles (14:4,14). Putting this aside for the moment, let us ask how the group known as "the apostles" functions in Acts.

After Peter's Pentecost sermon he "and the rest of the apostles" (Acts 2:37) are addressed by the crowd. Although Peter is the only one who responds, we learn that those who were baptized that day (about 3,000) "devoted themselves to the apostles' teaching" (2:42). The apostles witness to the resurrection of Jesus by giving public testimony (4:33), and have the proceeds of what was sold by the members of the Jerusalem community laid at their feet for distribution to those in need (4:35, 37; cf. 5:2). They give Joseph the name Barnabas (4:36). Many wonders and signs were also done through the apostles (2:43; 5:12). They were arrested, thrown in prison (5:18) and beaten (5:40). Peter and the apostles also gave public testimony before the Jewish council (5:29ff.). They prayed and laid hands upon the seven chosen by the community to be table servers (6:6) and Peter and John laid hands upon the Samarian converts (8:18). When a great persecution arose against the church in Jerusalem all scattered except the apostles (8:1). When they heard that Samaria had received the word of God, the apostles sent Peter and John to them (8:1). Luke specifically mentions that it was the apostles and the brethren who were in Judea who heard that the Gentiles received the word of God (11:1). When Paul and Barnabas escape to Jerusalem it is Barnabas who introduces Paul to the apostles (9:27).

Prior to Acts 14, where Luke refers to Barnabas and Paul as apostles, the apostles appear to occupy leadership positions in the community. In the rest of Acts, however, they are never mentioned alone. It is "the apostles and the elders" who are mentioned in connection with Luke's report of the Jerusalem council (Acts 15:2, 4, 6, 22, 23; cf. 16:4). After the council, the apostles disappear from the structure of the Jerusalem church and, in fact, the term "apostle" is not found anywhere in the last twelve chapters of Luke's second volume (Acts 17-28). Much of what is associated with the "apostles" in the first half of Acts will be applied subsequently to Paul. The apostles teach in the temple (Acts 5:21, 25, 42) and in Jerusalem (5:28); Paul teaches at Antioch (11:26), Cyprus (13:12), Athens (17:19), Corinth (18:11), Ephesus (20:20), and Rome (28:31). The apostles perform signs and wonders (2:43, 5:12), but so does Paul (14:3, 15:12). The apostles witness to the resurrection of Jesus by giving public testimony (4:33). The risen Lord says to Paul, who preaches the resurrection (17:18; cf. 24:15, 21; 26:23), "Take courage, for as you have testified about me at Jerusalem, so you must bear witness also at Rome" (23:11). Like the apostles (5:18, 40), Paul is arrested (21:27), thrown in prison (16:23) and beaten (16:37). Paul, as well as the apostles (5:21-41), appears before the Sanhedrin (22:30-23:10). And prayer plays an important role in the life of both Paul (9:11; 14:23; 16:25; 20:36; 21:5; 22:17; 28:8) and the apostles (6:6). These parallels between Paul and the apostles should remind us of the similar parallels (referred to earlier) between Jesus and his followers in Luke-Acts.

Our examination of Luke-Acts thus far leads to the following conclusions: (1) The "disciples" of Jesus are those who hear the word of and about him, repent, obey the will of God, and accept Jesus as Lord and Savior. The group known as the "disciples" includes, but is not limited to, the Twelve and the apostles.

(2) Because Luke distinguishes "the eleven" from "all the rest" (Lk. 24:9; cf. 24:33), retains the title "the Twelve," and narrates the selection of Matthias to replace Judas (Acts 1:15-26) one can talk about a special apostolate of the Twelve.[24] Their most important function, however, rests in their symbolism. As the twelve tribes of Israel descended from the twelve sons of Jacob, so the Christian community (the new Israel) begins with the proclamation of the good news of and about Jesus by the Twelve. After the formation of the new com-

munity, the primary function of the Twelve is eschatological as Jesus has appointed them to "sit on thrones judging the twelve tribes of Israel" (Lk. 22:30).
(3) While the Twelve are apostles (Lk. 6:13), Luke did not intend to reserve the title "apostles" exclusively to the Twelve. Paul and Barnabas are unambiguously referred to as apostles (Acts 14:4, 14); the sending of the Twelve finds a parallel in the sending out (ἀποστέλλειν) of the Seventy (Lk. 10:1); and Luke may intend that the travelers to Emmaus be understood as apostles (Lk. 24:9-13).[25]

Luke's use of the journey theme and the growth and development model suggests that, in the parallels between "the apostles" and Paul, the third evangelist is primarily interested in emphasizing "the expansion that the Holy Spirit gives the church through the apostolic witness."[26] The parallels between Jesus and his disciples suggest that "what God began in Jesus he continues in Jesus' followers."[27]

Church Models in Acts

When the disciples of Jesus gathered together in Jerusalem after his resurrection what organizational structure did they adopt for their community? If after providing the vital link between the ministry of Jesus and the early church the Twelve then become insignificant until the final judgement, who exercises leadership in the Christian community? Is the structure of the Jerusalem church transported to other Christian communities as an essential part of discipleship? The first step in answering these questions is to realize that Luke actually presents the reader with several different models for the church in Acts: (1) the idealized Jerusalem community, (2) the community which is centered around Antioch and its missionary activity, and (3) the community which is reflected in Paul's speech to the Ephesian elders (20:18ff.).[28]

The Jerusalem Community

The community of believers who gathered together in Jerusalem are described by Luke as "devoted to the apostles' teaching and fellowship, to the breaking of bread and the prayers" (Acts 2:42; cf. 2:46-47). "All who believed were together and had all things in common; and they sold their possessions and goods and distributed them to all, as any had need" (2:44-45). Some members of this community (i.e., the Twelve), in their role as witnesses, serve as a vital link between Jesus and the early church. They appear to function in a leadership role, yet after Judas is replaced (1:15-26), the Twelve virtually disappear as a group.[29] Luke reports that James is killed by Herod Agrippa (12:2), but he does not say that anyone is chosen to replace James as one of the Twelve. Individuals referred to as "the apostles," who may or may not be identical with the Twelve (see above), initially perform leadership tasks, but they disappear from the scene after the council of Jerusalem (15:1ff.). The administrative structure that soon emerges for the Jerusalem church involves James and the elders (cf. 21:18). Although they may have existed simultaneously in the Jerusalem church, the exact relationship among "the Twelve," "the apostles," the seven table-servers (6:1-6),[30] and "James and the elders," is unclear.

It seems as though the community is directed by a council. The apostles function as preachers and teachers, perform miracles and oversee the distribution of goods to the needy in the community. The Twelve summon the body of disciples together to discuss the problem of the daily distribution to the widows (Acts 6:1ff.). During this meeting the Twelve announce that they will devote themselves to prayer and to the ministry of the word. The seven individuals who were chosen were then set before the apostles and "they" (the Twelve? the apostles?) prayed and laid their hands upon them (6:6). In Acts 15 it is "the apostles and the elders" who gather together to discuss accepting the Gentiles without imposing on them the Law of Moses, especially circumcision (15:1ff.). In these brief pictures of the Jerusalem community Luke shows us that "the Twelve" presided over the meeting called to resolve the problem of food distribution and "the apostles and the elders" were in charge of the meeting held to discuss the problem of Gentile converts.

The Community at Antioch

The situation becomes more complex when one considers the evolution and growth of the early church. After the death of Stephen, Christians left Jerusalem and carried on the missionary enterprise outside of Israel. Some traveled as far as Antioch and conducted a mission among the Jews who lived there. They were joined later by missionaries from Cyprus and Cyrene who preached the Lord Jesus to the Greeks as well (Acts 11:19-20). When news of the great number of converts in Antioch reached Jerusalem Barnabas was dispatched to Antioch by the Jerusalem church. He was very successful in his Antiochene mission, adding "a large company to the Lord" (11:24). Barnabas then went to find Paul and together they returned to Antioch. They met with the church at Antioch for an entire year (11:25ff.).

The reader soon learns that the Christian community which was established at Antioch is served by prophets and teachers (Acts 13:1). Five individuals are listed: Barnabas and Saul/ Paul, Symeon, who was called Niger, Lucius of Cyrene, and Manaen, a member of the court of Herod the tetrarch. Luke does not tell us which individuals were prophets and which were teachers. It appears as if they functioned together as a group but, since Paul and Barnabas are sent on a missionary journey, apparently the church can get along without them. When these two missionaries return to Antioch (14:24-28) Luke reports that "they gathered the church together and declared all that God had done with them, and how he had opened a door of faith to the Gentiles" (14:27). No mention is made of any other church leaders at this point in the text. The Christian community at Antioch has leaders called by titles not previously mentioned in Acts (cf. 1 Cor. 12:28), but the exact structure of the Antiochene church eludes us.

What we do learn from this text is that the church at Antioch is inspired by the Holy Spirit to appoint Paul and Barnabas as its own missionaries (Acts 13:2). This is the first foreign mission which is planned and carried out by representatives of a particular church. Previous missionary efforts were conducted by individuals, usually as the result of persecution. Sent out by the Holy Spirit and the deliberate decision of the Antiochene church (13:2-4), Paul and Barnabas conduct a missionary campaign on the island of Cyprus and in Asia Minor (Acts 13-14). At the end of their Spirit-led missionary journey, Paul and Barnabas return to Antioch where they report to the church about their work, i.e., "all that God had done with them, and how he had opened a door of faith to the Gentiles" (14:27). On the basis of this text the missionary requirement of discipleship appears to be fulfilled when a particular church sends out its representatives who, upon completion of their journey, report back to the community. This missionary effort of the church at Antioch is not subject to the Jerusalem church; after their successful journey is completed, Paul and Barnabas report to the church at Antioch, not Jerusalem.

As part of their missionary work of preaching the word of God, Paul and Barnabas appointed leaders in every church. These local church leaders are referred to by Luke as "elders" (Acts 14:23). This is the first reference to elders (πρεσβύτεροι) outside of the Jerusalem church, although they are also found in the church at Ephesus (20:17). How they function within these communities founded by Barnabas and Paul is neither stated nor demonstrated.

The Community at Ephesus

After completing his missionary campaign in Macedonia and Achaia (Acts 15:36-18:17), Paul returns once again to Antioch. He spends some time at Antioch and then begins his third missionary campaign (18:23ff.) which takes him to Ephesus. It is here that we discover a third structural model for the church. Because we learned earlier that Paul and Barnabas appointed elders (πρεσβύτεροι) in every church (14:23), it should come as no surprise to learn that the leaders of the church at Ephesus are called "elders" (20:17). What is different about the church at Ephesus, however, is that the elders are also described as "guardians" or "bishops" (ἐπίσκοποι), appointed by the Holy Spirit "to feed the church of the Lord" (20:28). As they care for the church, they are told to be especially alert to dangers both from without and within the community (20:29-30) and not to be greedy for material gain (20:33-35). No mention is made of the church at Ephesus sending out missionaries. Luke presents its leaders as more inward directed as they seek to shepherd the church of the Lord and protect it from danger.

Conclusion

While the various Christian communities appear to have a hierarchy of roles, titles, and authority, there is little evidence that any role or function, except membership in the Twelve, was limited by racial, economic, or gender factors. Gentiles as well as Jews can become members of this new community (Lk. 24:46-47; Acts 2:32-39; 3:13-21; 5:31; 10:42-43; 11:18; 13:26-39). Christian discipleship is possible for the rich (e.g., Lk. 19:1-10, Acts 16:11-15) as well as for the poor, and women as well as men. Women, for example, perform some of the more important functions in the early church. Women are' designated as witnesses by the risen Lord (Lk. 24:48; cf. 24:22, 33), "serve" (Lk. 4:39; 8:3; 10:40) as missionaries (Acts 18:18), engage in teaching converts (Acts 18:26), and speak prophetically (Acts 21:8-9).

It is difficult to decide which, if any, model of church leadership Luke prefers, because he presents each structure (Jerusalem, Antioch, and Ephesus) in a positive light. The exact organizational relationship within the Jerusalem church among James and the elders, the apostles, the Twelve, and the seven table servers is unclear. Equally puzzling is the Antiochene church with its prophets and teachers and its missionaries who establish other churches and appoint elders to lead them. How is their hierarchy structured? What is the relationship between the church at Antioch and the churches founded by its missionaries? Between the individual missionary and these new Christian communities? The church at Ephesus is the only one mentioned in Acts as being led by elders who are called "bishops." They are specifically told to feed the church of the Lord, protect the church from "fierce wolves" both without and within, and to be generous as they toil to help the weak. It is impossible to tell whether or not these elders/bishops perform the same function at Ephesus as the elders do in the other churches.

According to the author of Luke-Acts, as the early church begins and continues its journey, new roles and functions emerge. Luke presents the reader with a church that is in the process of growing and developing as it is guided through history by the Holy Spirit in accordance with the plan of God

(Acts 1:8; cf. 4:31; 6:4; Lk. 12:12). Luke takes for granted that a hierarchy exists within the Christian community. However, he does not appear to be interested in presenting the reader with an ideal structural model. What Luke is concerned with is the appropriate behavior of those in authority, whether they be bishops, elders, prophets, teachers, or apostles. This leads him to point out quite clearly that church leaders must pattern their behavior after Jesus, who gave himself as servant, and must conduct themselves humbly as servants of all (Lk. 22:25-27).

8

Life Within the Community

We began our discussion of the Christian community several chapters ago when we pointed out that those who accept Jesus Christ and his message of salvation are usually led to be baptized into the Christian community. The existence of this community, which confesses Jesus as Lord and Savior, was supported by our closer examination of several relevant texts. This led to the conclusion that without a doubt there is a communal dimension to Christian discipleship according to Luke-Acts. In spite of the fact that Luke presents the reader with several different models of community structure, we were able to conclude that he understands there to be a hierarchy of roles and functions within the community.

We also learned that God has a plan for the salvation of all. This insight is important for any discussion of the Christian community. The message of God's salvation includes the invitation to repent, believe in Jesus, and be baptized into the community that confesses him as Lord and Savior. Membership in the church, therefore, is open to all regardless of race, gender, or economic status.

While Luke believes that salvation is possible for those who are not members of the visible community of disciples, he does not dwell on this. The third evangelist is much more interested in strengthening the faith of his Christian readers and influencing those who are not yet Christians to become believers in Jesus Christ and members of the Christian community. Following Luke's lead, in this chapter we will focus on the life of the Christian within the community of believers.

At the beginning of his second volume, Luke reports that members of the early church gathered together with one accord and devoted themselves to prayer (Acts 1:14). Since this group of disciples is composed of both men and women, it is appropriate to ask: What does Luke-Acts teach about marriage and Christian discipleship? And what about the related issue, children? Does the community that counts among its members Jews and Gentiles, rich and poor, men and women, also include within it the very young?

After discussing what Luke has to say about (1) marriage and children, we will examine his teaching on (2) the Eucharist, (3) Prayer, and (4) Possessions, themes which are highlighted in the pericope about life within the Jerusalem community (Acts 2:42-46):

> 2⁴²And they devoted themselves to the apostles' teaching and fellowship, to the breaking of bread and the prayers. ⁴³And fear came upon every soul; and many wonders and signs were done through the apostles. ⁴⁴And all who believed were together and had all things in common; ⁴⁵and they sold their possessions and goods and distributed them to all, as any had need. ⁴⁶And day by day, attending the temple together and breaking bread in their homes, they partook of food with glad and generous hearts, praising God and having favor with all the people.

The radical social challenge contained in Luke's teaching on the use of possessions is also found in his presentation of (5) Jesus' attitude toward violence. Having already discussed Luke's portrayal of Jesus as the Isaian Suffering Servant and the parallel between the suffering of Jesus and that of his followers, we must now ask what Luke-Acts teaches about discipleship and the use of violence.

Marriage and Children

Marriage

As we examine Luke-Acts from our late twentieth century perspective, we know that most Christians marry and live out their Christian discipleship in a married vocation for the greater part of their lives. Throughout much of Christian history, however, the married state has been seen as inherently inferior to the celibate state. Does Luke present the vocation of marriage as an inferior form of Christian discipleship?

There is no campaign in Luke-Acts on behalf of sexual abstinence nor any clear indication that marriage is an inferior way of following Jesus. Jesus speaks of marriage as a state proper to this age (cf. Lk. 17:27) when he says:

> 20[34]"The children of this age marry and are given in marriage; [35]but those who are accounted worthy to attain to that age and to the resurrection from the dead neither marry nor are given in marriage, [36]for they cannot die any more, because they are equal to angels and are children of God, being children of the resurrection."

Scholars[1] agree that these verses present marriage and procreation as necessary for the continuation of the human race. Because of resurrection and immortality, in the age to come people will no longer die and procreation will no longer be necessary.

The key to Jesus' attitude toward marriage and the family in Luke-Acts is his concern for the dignity of women, which goes far beyond contemporary Jewish attitudes and customs. Jesus allowed himself to be touched by the woman with the hemorrhage, even though this made him ritually unclean (Lk. 8:43-44; cf. Mk. 5:25-27). He also violated the sabbath law in order to heal a "daughter of Abraham" (13:10-17). Jesus' insistence on the permanency of marriage primarily benefits women as it goes against the Jewish practice which allowed a husband the freedom to divorce his wife and remarry.

> 16[18]"Every one who divorces his wife and marries another commits adultery, and he who marries a woman divorced from her husband commits adultery."

The texts we have cited thus far present marriage as the normal state of life in the world and the marriage bond as permanent. In Acts, Luke even portrays a married pair, Priscilla and Aquila, as the ideal missionary couple (Acts 18:2,18,26). Elsewhere, however, Luke warns that the concerns of marriage must never stand in the way of one's relationship with Jesus and one's dedication to the Kingdom of God. While on the journey to Jerusalem, Jesus says to the multitudes:

> 14²⁶"If any one comes to me and does not hate his own father and mother and wife and children and brothers and sisters, yes, and even his own life, he cannot be my disciple."

Later, when Jesus is dining at the house of a ruler of the Pharisees, a person says to him, "Blessed is the one who shall eat bread in the Kingdom of God!" (Lk. 14:15). In his reply, Jesus indicates that an unacceptable response to this invitation to share in the eschatological banquet would be, "I have married a wife, and therefore I cannot come" (Lk. 14:20).

In two other pericopes, Jesus seems to de-emphasize blood ties. Jesus states that his presence on earth will cause division among members of a household (Lk. 12:49-53) as family members take sides for or against him. And in two exchanges with potential disciples Jesus places allegiance to the Kingdom of God above familial responsibilities:

> 9⁵⁹To another Jesus said, "Follow me." But he said, "Lord, let me first go and bury my father." ⁶⁰But he said to him, "Leave the dead to bury their own dead; but as for you, go and proclaim the Kingdom of God." ⁶¹Another said, "I will follow you, Lord; but let me first say farewell to those at my home." ⁶²Jesus said to him, "No one who puts a hand to the plow and looks back is fit for the Kingdom of God."

The obvious conclusion is that while marriage is the normal and acceptable state for a Christian, blood ties are less important than fidelity to the will of God. This is especially clear when Luke edits his source (Mk. 10:29-30) and includes "wife" as one whom a man might have to leave "for the sake of the Kingdom of God" (Lk. 18:29-30).

Children

Although one's children are among those an individual must "hate" in order to be Jesus' disciple (Lk. 14:26) and among those one might have to leave for the sake of the Kingdom of God (18:29-30), Luke-Acts as a whole presents the reader with a very positive picture of children. In fact, Luke implies that children are baptized members of the Christian community. The young, as well as the old, can be members of the church. Several times in Acts Luke narrates the conversion of a whole "house" to Christianity.[2] According to Peter, an angel appeared to Cornelius and commanded him, "Send to Joppa and bring Simon called Peter; he will declare to you a message by which you will be saved, you and all your household"(Acts 11:13-14). Later in Acts, Luke reports that during Paul's missionary campaign in Macedonia and Achaia he had occasion to stay at Philippi for a few days. While Paul was at Philippi, a seller of purple goods from Thyatira, whose name was Lydia, responded positively to his preaching and "was baptized, with her household" (16:15). Life in Philippi soon became more difficult for Paul and his fellow missionary Silas. After they cured a possessed slave girl, her owners saw to it that Paul and Silas were thrown into jail. All was not lost, however, because while they were confined they preached the good news of salvation to their jailer.

> 16[31]"Believe in the Lord Jesus, and you will be saved, you and your household." [32]And they spoke the word of the Lord to him and to all that were in his house. [33]And he took them the same hour of the night, and washed their wounds, and he was baptized at once, with all his family.

After they were freed from prison, Paul and Silas continued their missionary journey. Soon they parted, with Paul going to Athens and Silas and Timothy, another missionary, remaining at Beroea. From Athens Paul went to Corinth, where he met the married couple mentioned above, Aquila and Priscilla. When Silas and Timothy joined him, they found Paul engaged in preaching the word of God. In response to his message, Crispus, the ruler of the synagogue, "believed in the Lord, together with all his household; and many of the Corinthians hearing Paul believed and were baptized" (Acts 8:8).

Does this mean that very young children in a family were baptized when a "house" entered the Christian community? One can not be absolutely certain but, as G. R. Beasley-Murray[3] points out, it is likely that children were members of these households and, therefore, reasonably certain that they were baptized.

Although Luke 18:15-17 has nothing to do with the baptism of infants,[4] it does indicate that Jesus had a positive attitude toward children.

> 18[15]Now they were bringing even infants to him that he might touch them; and when the disciples saw it, they rebuked them. [16]But Jesus called them to him, saying, "Let the children come to me, and do not hinder them; for to such belongs the Kingdom of God. [17]Truly, I say to you, whoever does not receive the Kingdom of God like a child shall not enter it."

Jesus takes this opportunity to teach his audience that the Kingdom of God belongs to children and to adults who are like them. He also warns them that entry into the Kingdom will be denied to anyone who is not prepared to receive it like a child. In this pericope Luke presents children as an ideal model for adult disciples.

But what is it about the way a child receives that Jesus wants adults to emulate? In the eyes of the ancient world a child was considered of little importance and had no social status. Since children were powerless and no one in society owed them anything, everything they received was the result of the love and generosity of their parents and other adults. In this comparison Jesus appears to be focusing on the sheer receptivity of children, especially infants, who cannot do anything to merit entry into the Kingdom. Readers of Luke's Gospel should learn from these words that the Kingdom must be received as a gift from God.

The current location of this passage also sheds light on its meaning. Luke has placed this pericope in between other stories that describe what is involved in Christian discipleship. Scholars recognize that there is a close connection between this passage and the stories of the Pharisee and the publican (Lk. 18:9-14) and the rich young ruler (18:18-30). "The children, like the publican, are nearer the Kingdom than they could suppose themselves to be; the rich young man, like the Pharisee, is farther from it than he supposed himself to be."[5] The publican realizes that "one achieves uprightness before God not by one's own activity but by a contrite recognition of one's own sinfulness before him."[6] Like the children, then, he is an example of one who trusts in God and not in his own

achievements. Luke is using these stories to teach the reader
that the entry of anyone "into eternal life or into the Kingdom
is a miracle of God's grace, which cannot be earned but only
accepted with humility and faith."[7]
    According to Luke-Acts, therefore, children can become
members of the Christian community. Jesus welcomes them
himself (Lk. 18:16) and tells his disciples that they should do
likewise:

> 9[48]"Whoever receives this child in my name receives me,
> and whoever receives me receives him who sent me; for the
> one who is least among you all is the one who is great."

Jesus also presents them to his audience as a model for
discipleship (18:16-17). The community that includes Jew and
Gentile, male and female, rich and poor, also includes children
as well as adults.

The Eucharist

    Luke describes the daily activity of the Christian community
at Jerusalem by saying that "they devoted themselves to the
apostles' teaching and fellowship, to the breaking of bread and
the prayers" (Acts 2:42) and "attending the temple together
and breaking bread in their homes, they partook of food with
glad and generous hearts" (2:46). Mention of "breaking bread"
should remind the reader of the numerous table-fellowship
stories in Luke's Gospel, especially the Lord's Supper and
Jesus' command "Do this in remembrance of me" (Lk.
22:19b).[8] After the resurrection the disciples gathered together
frequently for these shared meals.
    The six banquet/dinner scenes reported earlier in Luke's
Gospel (Lk. 5:29-32; 7:36-50; 9:12-17; 10:38-42; 11:37-44; 14:1-
24) look forward to the Lord's Supper, the Eucharistic
celebrations of the early church, and the eschatological banquet. In the Near East, both ancient and modern, meals are
expressions of peace, trust, and community.[9] The fact that
Jesus shares these meals with tax collectors, sinners, and
women indicates that the Kingdom of God is open to all.

It is clear from the four New Testament reports of the Lord's Supper (Mt. 26:26-29; Mk. 14:22-25; Lk. 22:15-20; 1 Cor. 11:23-25) that its structure was taken over from the Jewish ritual meal.[10] The primary differences, however, are (1) that Jesus identifies himself with the bread and wine; it is his body that is broken and his blood which is poured out,[11] and (2) that Jesus invites his disciples to establish a new community (a new covenant)[12] in which his presence will be recognized in the bread. The inclusion of the command to repeat this rite makes it clear that Luke views the Lord's Supper as the foundation of the eucharistic celebrations in the early church.

The Christian community, as Luke presents it, is very much concerned with the celebration of the Eucharist.[13] This motif appears in the multiplication of the loaves (Lk. 9:10-17) and in the Emmaus story (24:30ff.) as well as in Luke's account of the Lord's Supper (22:14ff.). The same formula—take, bless, break, and give—appears in all three pericopes (9:16; 22:19; 24:30). Because the Emmaus meal takes place after the Lord's Supper, it is likely that Luke intends this meal to be understood as a eucharistic celebration. It is in this post-resurrection account that the disciples of Jesus recognize him in the breaking of the bread (24:30-31, 32). "The lesson in the story is that henceforth the risen Christ will be present to his assembled disciples, not visibly (after the ascension), but in the breaking of the bread. So they will know him and recognize him, because *so* he will be truly present among them."[14]

In Acts, Luke indicates that the religious life of the community is centered in the Eucharist when he mentions the breaking of the bread in his account of life in the Jerusalem community (Acts 2:42,46). The disciples of Jesus are pictured as following the command which he gave at the Lord's supper, "Do this in remembrance of me" (Lk. 22:19).[15] Later in Acts, Luke reports that "on the first day of the week," when the Christian community at Troas was "gathered together to break bread, Paul talked with them" (20:7; cf. 20:11). While he was talking a young man named Eutychus, overcome by sleep, fell down from the third story and appeared dead. Paul embraced him and said, "Do not be alarmed, for his life is in him" (20:10). In this story, Luke is suggesting that the Eucharist, which was celebrated by the converts at Troas,[16] should serve as a sign of encouragement for the reader of Acts. The same Lord who gave life to Eutychus through Paul is present in the breaking of the bread (Lk. 24:30-31,35). Luke may intend that Acts 27:35 also be understood eucharistically. When Paul is on board ship heading for Rome, Luke reports that "he took bread, and giving thanks to God in the presence of all he broke it and began to eat." This resembles the take-break-bless-give sequence found in Jesus' feeding of the multitudes (Lk. 9:16), at the Lord's Supper (22:19), and in the Emmaus story (24:30). It is possible that Paul was celebrating the Eucharist since Luke regularly refers to this as the breaking of bread. However, in this account Luke could simply be describing an ordinary meal.

Luke-Acts highlights the importance and centrality of the Eucharistic celebration. Instituted by Jesus himself at the Last Supper, this meal symbolizing peace, trust, and community is joyfully celebrated by Jesus' disciples in response to his command, "Do this in remembrance of me" (Lk. 22:19). After the ascension, the community is united through the Lord's supper to the risen one who is present in the Eucharist.[17]

Because the issue of leadership in the Christian community was raised earlier, it is not enough simply to conclude that the Christian disciple celebrates the Eucharist with other members of the church. We must ask if there is any evidence in Luke-Acts to suggest who presided at these Eucharistic celebrations.

In the Gospel Jesus issues the command, "Do this in remembrance of me" (Lk. 22:19), to "the apostles" (22:14) who were with him at table. It is difficult to decide whether or not Luke understands this to mean "the Twelve," because Luke has replaced "the Twelve," which he found in his source (Mk. 14:17), with "the apostles."[18] Even if Luke understands that "the Twelve" were Jesus' dinner companions at the Last Supper, nowhere in Luke-Acts does it say that any of the Twelve actually presided at the Eucharist. According to Acts, the Twelve devoted themselves "to prayer and to the ministry of the word" (Acts 6:4), while "the apostles" were teachers and miracle workers (2:42-43) who supervised the distribution of goods to those in need (4:34-35). If Acts 27:35 is meant to be read as a Eucharistic text, a doubtful conclusion, Paul can be seen as presiding at a Eucharistic celebration. It is also possible to conclude that Paul presided at the breaking of bread at Troas (20:7,11), but this is far from certain. "Thus there is simply no compelling evidence for the classic thesis that the members of the Twelve always presided when they were present, and that there was a chain of ordination passing the power of presiding at the Eucharist from the Twelve to missionary apostles to presbyter-bishops."[19]

Prayer

The community of Christian disciples that gathered together to celebrate the Eucharist is also identified as a community dedicated to prayer. Luke presents the followers of Jesus as devoting themselves to prayer as they await the descent of the Holy Spirit at Pentecost (Acts 1:14). And the Jerusalem community is identified as one which gathers to pray and to praise God (2:42, 47). Where did Luke find this prayer motif? Is it really that significant for discipleship? Why does the Christian pray?

The fundamentals of prayer are found early in the Biblical narrative.[20] Throughout the Pentateuch (the first five books of the Hebrew Bible) human beings are depicted as conversing with God. This personal contact with God was designed to affect the nature and course of the relationship. In the Hebrew Scriptures individuals sought to converse with God for a variety of reasons, e.g. to thank God for past favors, to ask God to intercede on their behalf in some present crisis, for personal guidance. Prayer could be public or private, meditative or vocal, but no matter what form it took it was an important component of every believing Jew's life. Therefore, one should not be surprised to learn that Jesus, following in the footsteps of his ancestors, was a person of prayer.

Luke's source for this portrait of Jesus as one who prays was Mark's Gospel. Although he does not emphasize prayer as much as Luke does, Mark does speak about prayer in several places.[21] Jesus is seen as one who prays before beginning various stages of his ministry (Mk. 1:35; 6:46) and after he separates from his disciples in Gethsemane (14:32-39). And Jesus urges his disciples to pray that they may be able to endure their own times of tribulation (13:18; 14:32). Prayer does not mean flight from the world, but action in the world in accordance with the will of God. Usually well aware of the harsh realities of human existence, the one who prays is listening for the voice of God in an effort to discern God's will for the present. Luke has significantly expanded the prayer motif which he found in Mark. In the Gospel Luke portrays Jesus as one who prays (Lk. 3:21; 5:16; 6:12; 9:18, 28, 29; 11:1; cf. 23:34, 46), who teaches his disciples a prayer (11:2-4) and who urges his disciples to pray always and not lose heart (11:5-8; 18:1-8; cf. 22:40). In Acts, the early church is pictured as following Jesus' teaching and example concerning faithfulness in prayer (e.g., 1:14-24; 2:42, 46, 47; 4:24-31; 12:5, 12; 20:36; 21:5).[22] This has led many to conclude that Luke considers prayer to be among the more important elements of discipleship.[23] Luke wants to show that prayer is the means by which God has guided his people throughout history,[24] but he also wants his readers to understand the importance of prayer in the life of the Christian disciple.[25]

A good place to begin a discussion of prayer in Luke-Acts is by looking at two pericopes which appear only in Luke's Gospel. The third evangelist introduces the parable of the widow and the judge (Lk. 18:1-8) by noting that Jesus told his disciples "a parable to the effect that they ought always to pray and not lose heart" (18:1). A similar call for constant prayer is found at the end of Jesus' apocalyptic discourse (21:5-36) when he says, "But watch at all times, praying..." (21:36). Luke then proceeds to present Jesus as, in effect, praying always and urging his disciples to do the same.

Luke's interest in prayer is evident as early as the infancy narrative. In the first two chapters of the Gospel the importance of prayer in Jewish piety is reflected. An angel informs Zechariah, a priest and the father of John the Baptist, that his prayer has been heard and his wife, Elizabeth, soon will bear a son (Lk. 1:13). After John is born, Zechariah praises the Lord God of Israel who has raised up salvation for his people (1:67-79). Mary, the Jewish virgin who becomes the mother of Jesus, echoes the song of Hannah, Samuel's mother, in her thanksgiving hymn (1:46-55; cf. 1 Sam. 2:1-10). Only Luke speaks of "the heavenly host praising God" (Lk. 2:14) and of Simeon who blesses God and issues his hymn of praise and thanksgiving (2:28-35). Luke has further emphasized the prayer motif by bracketing the entire Gospel with references to the Temple. The story of Jesus begins in the Temple with the Zechariah episode and ends with the note that after Jesus departed from his disciples "they returned to Jerusalem with great joy, and were continually in the temple blessing God" (24:53). Luke reports that Jesus "was praying" (Lk. 3:21; cf. Mk. 1:9) after he had been baptized "and the Holy Spirit descended upon him in bodily form, as a dove, and a voice came from heaven, 'Thou are my beloved Son; with thee I am well pleased'" (Lk. 3:22). This is the same Spirit that leads Jesus into the wilderness (4:1) and then into Galilee (4:14). Jesus goes next to the Nazareth synagogue where he reads from the Isaiah scroll:

> 4[18]"The Spirit of the Lord is upon me, because he has anointed me to preach good news to the poor. He has sent me to proclaim release to the captives and recovering of sight to the blind, to set at liberty those who are oppressed, [19]to proclaim the acceptable year of the Lord."

The Spirit that motivates Jesus and guides him in his ministry is the same Spirit that leads his disciples in the post-resurrection period.

One day his disciples saw Jesus praying and they asked him to teach them a prayer. After teaching them the Lord's Prayer (Lk. 11:2-4), Jesus notes that the heavenly Father will give the Holy Spirit to those who ask him (11:13). Luke appears to have altered his Q source here since the Matthean parallel promises that the Father will give "good things" to those who ask him (Mt. 7:11). This passage, therefore, provides us with one more instance of Luke's emphasis on the role of the Spirit throughout Luke-Acts. In Acts, the Holy Spirit comes upon the members of the early church and guides their worldwide missionary efforts. The risen Lord maintains a close personal relationship with his disciples when he pours out the Holy Spirit upon those who repent and are baptized (Acts 2:33, 38). It is the "Spirit of Jesus" (16:7) that serves as the bond of union between Jesus and his disciples[26] and empowers them to function as his representatives as they bring the message of the salvation of God to the end of the earth. To be a disciple, for Luke, is to be filled with and led by the Spirit; the community is bound together and impelled outward by the Spirit. During his ministry Jesus prays after the healing of the leper (Lk. 5:19), before choosing the Twelve (6:12), and before asking his disciples the important question concerning his identity, "Who do you say that I am?" (9:18-21). The transfiguration takes place as Jesus is praying (9:28-29). Jesus prays for his executioners (23:34) and his last words while on the cross take the form of a prayer, "Father, into thy hands I commit my spirit!" (23:46).

The disciples of Jesus learn the importance of prayer from his example and from his urging them to pray always and not lose heart (Lk. 11:5-8; 18:1-8; cf. 22:40). In Acts the followers of Jesus gather together in prayer to await the coming of the Holy Spirit (Acts 1:14-26). The life of the Jerusalem community is characterized by prayer (2:42-47; 4:24-31). Luke informs us that the church prayed for Peter when he was in prison (12:5) and pictures the disciples gathered together in prayer at the house of Mary, the mother of John Mark, when Peter arrives after having been freed (12:12). When Paul had completed his farewell address to the Ephesian elders "he knelt down and prayed with them all" (20:36). And before he departed from Tyre, Paul knelt down with the entire community and prayed (21:5).

While it is obvious that the life of Jesus and his disciples is permeated by prayer, three questions remain: (1) What are some of the common features of prayer in Luke-Acts? (2) Why should a follower of Jesus pray? (3) What should the disciple pray for?

Common Features of Prayer in Luke-Acts

(a) Communion with God is one feature of the prayers of Jesus. This is apparent when Jesus is transfigured "as he was praying" (Lk. 9:29) and suggested in the baptism scene, with the descent of the Holy Spirit (3:22), in Jesus' withdrawal to the wilderness (5:16), and in his night-long prayer before choosing the Twelve (6:12).

(b) Joyful praise and thanksgiving also characterize prayer in Luke-Acts.[27] Only in Luke is Jesus presented as rejoicing in the Holy Spirit (cf. Mt. 11:25) as he prays:

> 10[21]"I thank thee, Father, Lord of heaven and earth, that thou has hidden these things from the wise and understanding and revealed them to babes; yea, Father for such was thy gracious will." [22]All things have been delivered to me by my Father; and no one knows who the Son is except the Father, or who the Father is except the Son and any one to whom the Son chooses to reveal him."

The prayer of Zechariah predicts that there will be joy, gladness, and rejoicing at the birth of John the Baptist (Lk. 1:14). Mary, in her song of praise, says "my spirit rejoices in God my Savior"(1:47). The angel speaks of the "good news of great joy which will come to all people" (2:10) immediately before the multitude join with him in praising God (2:13-14).

After they had seen the infant Jesus, "the shepherds returned, glorifying and praising God for all they had heard and seen" (Lk. 2:20). Similarly, the paralytic who was healed went home "glorifying God" (5:25) and all the people who witnessed this miracle "glorified God and were filled with awe, saying, 'We have seen strange things today'" (5:26). Those who watch Jesus bring the widow's dead son back to life "glorified God, saying, 'A great prophet has arisen among us!'" (7:16). The bent woman whom Jesus healed "praised God"(13:13) while the onlookers "rejoiced at all the glorious things that were done by him"(13:17). The Samaritan leper returned to praise God (17:15). The blind man who is healed near Jericho "glorifies God" and all the people give "praise to God" (18:43). When Jesus descends the Mount of Olives, his disciples "began to rejoice and praise God for all the mighty works that they had seen" (19:37; cf. Acts 3:8-9).

In the post-resurrection period, the disciples are joyful at seeing the risen Jesus (Lk. 24:41) and after his departure they "returned to Jerusalem with great joy, and were continually in the temple blessing God" (24:52-53). In Acts, Jesus' followers continue to be joyful. The apostles left the Jewish council "rejoicing that they were counted worthy to suffer dishonor for the name" (Acts 5:41). After his baptism by Philip, the Ethiopian went home rejoicing (8:39). And after his baptism by Paul, the Philippian jailer "rejoiced with all his household that he had believed in God" (16:34). The connection between prayer and rejoicing is even closer in the story of Paul at Pisidian Antioch. When the Gentiles heard Paul's preaching "they were glad and glorified the word of God" (13:48).

(c) Prayer can also take the form of an intercession or petition. As we saw above, the angel informed Zechariah that his prayer had been heard and his wife would soon bear a son (Lk. 1:13). Similarly, in Luke's second volume Cornelius is told "your prayer has been heard" (Acts 10:31). Jesus himself issues a prayerful request when he says, "Father, if thou art willing, remove this cup from me; nevertheless not my will but thine, be done" (Lk. 22:42). And Jesus' advice to his disciples is relevant here, "Rise and pray that you may not enter into temptation" (22:46).

In addition to personal petitions, one can pray for other individuals or the church at large. In the Gospel, Jesus says to Peter, "I have prayed for you that your faith may not fail; and when you have turned again, strengthen your brethren" (Lk. 22:32). In Acts, Peter kneels down and prays before he raises Tabitha from the dead (Acts 9:40-41). And Paul, while on the island of Malta, heals the ailing father of Publius after praying and laying hands on him (28:8).

Why Should One Pray?

Christian discipleship in Luke-Acts involves following the example of Jesus and his disciples. Both by word and by deed, Jesus showed himself to be a person of prayer. His disciples ask Jesus to teach them a prayer and are seen obeying his command to pray always and not lose heart. One should pray with confidence because God loves his people more than a parent loves a child (Lk. 11:11-12). And God will show mercy and compassion to those in need, if they only ask in prayer (11:5-10).

One should also pray because God gives "the Holy Spirit to those who ask him!" (11:13).[28] This is the same Holy Spirit that comes upon Jesus at the beginning of his ministry and empowers him during his earthly career, the same Spirit that comes upon the church at Pentecost and guides both the disciples and the church. The Holy Spirit enables and assists the disciple of Jesus to follow his example and preach the good news to the poor, proclaim release to captives, recovery of sight to the blind and to set at liberty those who are oppressed. The Holy Spirit, given by the Father in response to prayer, helps the disciple to see that God desires the liberation of his people from all forms of injustice. Thus, prayer has profoundly "this-worldly" consequences. The disciple who comes to understand that God's will includes justice for all is led to work for liberation and justice in this world.

For What Should One Pray?

One day when Jesus was praying, his disciples said to him, "Lord, teach us to pray, as John taught his disciples." Jesus said to them, "When you pray, say:

11²"Father, hallowed be thy name. Thy Kingdom come. ³Give us each day our daily bread; ⁴and forgive us our sins, for we ourselves forgive every one who is indebted to us; and lead us not into temptation."

According to Jesus, therefore, one should pray for daily bread, forgiveness, protection from temptation, and the coming of the Kingdom.

(a) The petition for daily bread is usually understood to be a request that God will continue to supply the physical needs of the disciples. Although the Christian tradition later interprets this petition as a reference to the Eucharist, this does not seem to be Luke's primary intent here.[29]

(b) Even the Pharisees agree that God is the one who can forgive sins (Lk. 5:21). In Acts, Peter says to Simon Magus "Repent therefore of this wickedness of yours, and pray to the Lord that, if possible, the intent of your heart may be forgiven you" (Acts 8:22). This could remind one of the publican who prays, "God, be merciful to me a sinner!" (Lk. 18:13). With the coming of Jesus the time of the new covenant (22:20) is now here, a time when sins will be remembered no more (Jer.

31:31-34). In the Gospel Luke often pictures Jesus forgiving sins.

(c) In praying "lead us not into temptation," the disciple is asking God for help in facing the temptations of daily life.[30] Both Jesus (Lk. 4:13; 22:28) and his disciples (22:28; Acts 14:22; 20:19) undergo temptations but, empowered by the Holy Spirit, they are not tempted beyond the point of endurance.

(d) The petition "thy Kingdom come" is usually understood in an eschatological sense. The disciple prays that God's reign, his dominion over human life and existence, be brought to full realization.[31] There are ancient textual variants, however, which suggest that this petition could also be a plea for the gift of the Holy Spirit.[32] And, as we know from Jesus' words in Luke 11:13, God gives the gift of the Holy Spirit to those who ask in prayer.

Possessions

Mary's song of praise can be seen as a prayer for liberation and justice. The mother of Jesus recalls that God has

> 1[51b] "scattered the proud in the imagination of their hearts, [52]he has put down the mighty from their thrones, and exalted those of low degree; [53]he has filled the hungry with good things, and the rich he has sent empty away."

Part of the good news for the poor (Lk. 4:18), therefore, is that the rich and powerful people who tyrannize them will ultimately be dealt with harshly by God. What implications does this insight have for the relationship between the Christian and material possessions?

Luke's concern about the proper relationship between the Christian disciple and wealth is widely recognized.[33] In the Gospel, Luke includes all Markan pericopes devoted to wealth and possessions (except the anointing at Bethany with its controversial saying, "The poor you will always have with you" [Mark 14:7]), all appropriate Q texts, and many other relevant passages not found elsewhere in the New Testament. In Acts, Luke presents several positive examples of almsgiving and describes the early Jerusalem community as sharing wealth and possessions. As a result of this editorial activity, Luke's two-volume narrative compels the reader to consider the place of possessions in Christian life and Christian community. Luke includes in his Gospel the well-known saying of Jesus, "For it is easier for a camel to go through the eye of a needle than for a rich person to enter the Kingdom of God" (Lk. 18:25). This saying, found in the story of the rich ruler (18:18-30; cf. Mk. 10:17-31), imples that it is virtually impossible for the rich to enter the Kingdom of God.[34] In this pericope one also learns of Jesus' demand that this would-be follower leave "everything" and follow him (Lk. 18:22). This same radical attitude toward possessions is found in the call of the first disciples (5:11) and the call of Levi (5:28). In the Sermon on the Plain Jesus says, "Blessed are you poor, for yours is the Kingdom of God" (6:20), "but woe to you that are rich, for you have received your consolation" (6:24). This reminds one of Mary's comment that God "has put down the mighty from their thrones, and exalted those of low degree; he has filled the hungry with good things, and the rich he has sent empty away" (1:52-53). The story of the widow's mite (21:1-4; Mk. 12:41-44) also suggests that the rich face great difficulties in their attempt to enter the Kingdom of God.

In exclusively Lukan passages the reader learns that the wealthy are fools (Lk. 12:20), who have no treasure in heaven (12:21), and that they will be sent away empty (1:54). The good news for the poor (4:18) turns out to be bad news for the rich as one discovers that the rich will weep and mourn and hunger (6:25-26). Those who love money are said to be an abomination in the eyes of God (16:14); those who do not use their riches to provide for the poor are guilty of a serious injustice and are deserving of eternal punishment and torment (16:23).

This harsh attitude toward wealth and possessions is modified slightly in Acts when Luke presents the members of the early church as sharing wealth and possessions. There are hints of this position in the Gospel itself, especially in the story of the conversion of the rich tax collector Zacchaeus (19:1-10).[35] In this pericope one learns that the salvation of the rich is possible (cf. 18:27). In order to be saved, however, a rich person must receive Jesus joyfully and share Jesus' active concern for the poor and the cheated. It is hard for those who have wealth to divest themselves of their material possessions, and the power and security that seems to come with them, but it is possible. One who follows Jesus must realize that restitution is to be made for past wrongs and that wealth and possessions must be shared with the poor.

In his second volume, Luke does not suggest that would-be disciples are required to sell all their possessions. The model Luke presents in the early chapters of Acts is one in which possessions are shared with other members of the community. The members of the Jerusalem church "had all things in common; and they sold their possessions and goods and distributed them to all, as any had need" (Acts 2:44-45; cf. 4:32). There was not a needy person among them, because those who possessed land or houses, "sold them, and brought the proceeds of what was sold and laid it at the apostles' feet; and distribution was made to each as any had need" (4:34-35). Elsewhere, however, Luke presents almsgiving as the way of handling possessions. Tabitha and Cornelius are commended for their almsgiving (9:36; 10:2, 4, 31), while the Ephesian elders who are helping the weak are reminded of Jesus' words, "It is more blessed to give than to receive" (20:35).[36] When one examines Luke's description of the use of possessions by Christian missionaries the situation becomes even more complex. Jesus tells the Twelve and the Seventy to take nothing for their journey (Lk. 9:3; 10:3-4), yet he later revokes these instructions (22:35-36). The descriptions of the missionaries in Acts, especially Paul, present yet another picture.

Luke informs the reader that Paul is a tentmaker (Acts 18:3) who works to support himself. He also has his own money to spend when James and the elders ask him to pay the expenses of four men participating in a rite of purification (21:24). Paul serves as a model for the Ephesian elders to follow as he takes care of his own needs and the needs of his companions (20:34). The narrative suggests that leaders of a Christian community should work to support both themselves and the weaker members of their community (20:35). It is better to give help to others than to amass further wealth for oneself.

The Christian ideal, as Luke presents it, is a community in which there are no needy people (cf. Acts 4:34). But does Luke give any practical advice on how one reaches this goal? Should Christians create a community in which all goods are held in common? Or, is a community characterized by private stewardship and almsgiving a better model for Christian living? Is the Jerusalem community of goods an ideal which Luke is urging his readers to emulate? Or, is it simply the first of many stages on the journey of the church?

The reader of the Gospel encounters several verses that suggest the disciple must leave "everything" in order to follow Jesus (Lk. 5:11, 28; 14:33; 18:22). In the early chapters of Acts, however, one finds Christians sharing possessions with other Christians as the need arises (Acts 2:42-47; 4:32-37; cf. Lk. 8:1-3). It seems unlikely that Luke would have provided such a favorable description of the Jerusalem community in Acts if he wanted to urge his readers to return to an ideal past when disciples left everything in order to follow Jesus. Is the Jerusalem community then the norm?

Later in Acts, Luke presents in a positive light both almsgiving (Acts 9:36; 10:2, 4, 31; cf. Lk. 11:41; 12:33; 16:9; 18:22; 19:8-10) and the picture of community leaders working to support other members of the community as well as themselves (Acts 20:34-35). If Luke saw the attitude toward possessions in the Jerusalem church as normative, then these models found later in Acts should have been described as a deviant departure from the pure original form. Since these practices are not presented as departures from the original ideal, it is likely that Luke sees each as a transformation or outgrowth of an earlier stage. This could mean that the normative model is to be found in Paul's speech to the Ephesian elders. But Luke and his readers do not live in the time period described in Acts. As the church continues its journey with Jesus, the risen Lord, from the days of Paul to the time of Luke, perhaps a new model for the correct use of possessions has emerged which, though different, is in continuity with the past.

Regardless of the model adopted, one must remember that in Luke's eyes how one handles possessions is an indication, a symbol, of one's interior disposition, whether one is responding positively or negatively to the word of God.[37] Luke does not portray possessions as evil in themselves, nor do they necessarily prevent a positive response to the word of God (cf. Lk. 18:28). But Luke is convinced that one must choose between serving God and serving mammon (16:13). Wealth can be used for good, but in many cases it creates priorities which prohibit the rich from doing the will of God.

Violence

We have already seen that Luke presents the Christian community as a contrast society; the structure of life among Jesus' followers is radically different from life in the surrounding society. Christian discipleship is characterized by humility and service, not by domination and exploitation. This revolutionary approach to interpersonal relationships has profound social and political implications. Luke's portrait of Jesus and the early church shows that violence has no place within this new community guided by the Holy Spirit. Does this also mean that followers of Jesus should not resort to violence in their dealings with those outside the Christian community? How do Jesus and his disciples respond when they are the victims of violence?

Before we examine specific passages in Luke-Acts to determine the appropriate Christian response to violence, it is important to mention that there are at least three options available to any individual who is confronted by violence:[38] (a) nonresistance (where people refrain from actions that would involve them in doing physical violence to others and from directly confronting those responible for existing evils; they seek solidarity with those who are suffering from these evils; they offer no defense if they are subjected to violence by those who have power; their hope is that their own commitment and example will eventually inspire changes in the attitudes and actions of others); (b) nonviolent resistance (where people avoid violence to persons but challenge the existing evils in a nonviolent way; they believe that these challenges can serve as a creative means of initiating a dialogue that may eventually result in a favorable change of behavior); (c) violent resistance.

Each of these positions was represented among the Jewish people in the first century A.D. It should not be surprising to discover that there was a warlike spirit alive in Palestine at the time of Jesus. We have already pointed out that the general Jewish expectation was that the Messiah would be a military leader who would drive out the Romans. In the first century, with the rise of the Zealot movement,[39] this belief leads many to the conclusion that violence should be used to achieve social reform.

Nonviolence and nonresistance were also live options in the first century.[40] Josephus, a first century Jewish historian, gives us at least two examples of nonviolent resistance during this period. In *Antiquities* 18:3:1, he reports the incident of the military standards. Out of respect for Jewish scruples, previous procurators had forbidden troops to carry their banners with images on them into Jerusalem. Pilate sent the offensive standards into Jerusalem after nightfall and with these figures covered. When they discovered what had happened, the Jews engaged in a five-day nonviolent protest at the residence of the Roman governor. Threatened with death if they did not end their protest, the Jews bared their throats to the Roman sword, declaring that they would gladly welcome death rather than violate their law. Pilate, fearing a revolt, ordered the offensive images returned to Caesarea (§ 261-309; cf. *War* 2:9:3 § 184-203). A second example of Jewish nonviolent resistance is found in *Antiquities* 18:8. When the Romans attempted to place a statue of the Emperor Caligula in the Jerusalem Temple, the Jewish people engaged in an economic protest. A general strike, which left the fields untilled for a month, prevented the Romans from carrying out their plan.

During the first century, the Pharisees appear to have become apolitical and adopted an attitude of nonresistance to foreign powers. "It seems likely that the Pharisees cooperated with, or at least did not oppose, Roman rule in Judea."[41] As long as they had religious freedom, they were indifferent to rulers and the forms under which they ruled.

What stance does Luke attribute to Jesus? While it is possible that Jesus chose a Zealot as one of the Twelve (cf. Lk. 6:15; Acts 1:13),[42] Jesus is neither a Zealot nor a Zealot sympathizer. Although Brandon energetically searches for evidence of a violent Jesus in the Gospels, he reluctantly admits that Luke-Acts emphasizes the pacific character of Jesus. Luke portrays Jesus "as peaceable in disposition and action, and uninvolved in Jewish nationalist politics."[43] For example, Jesus shows no sign of hatred or vengeance when he is told about "the Galileans whose blood Pilate had mingled with their sacrifices"(Lk. 13:1ff.). At a time when religious fanatics were ready to punish sinners, speedily and without mercy, and take revenge on their sins, Jesus calls his followers to the way of repentance and forgiveness.[44]

Some sayings of Jesus do contain the imagery of violence, but a close examination shows that they do not contradict the ethic of non-violence. When Jesus talks about casting fire upon the earth and about divisions that will take place within families because of his person and message (Lk. 12:49-53), he is not acquiescing in whatever strife and conflict his ministry caused. Rather, his words should be seen to "constitute a recognition of the serious strife his teachings are engendering, without representing any endorsement for the use of harsh measures by his disciples."[45] One must remember that earlier in his ministry Jesus rebuked James and John when they proposed that he call down fire from heaven to destroy the Samaritan villagers (9:51-56). A similar misunderstanding of the spirit of Jesus' teaching takes place at the conclusion of the Last Supper after Jesus says,

> 22[36b] "Let the one who has no sword sell his mantle and buy one. [37]For I tell you that this scripture must be fulfilled in me, 'And he was reckoned with transgressors'; for what is written about me has its fulfilment."

Jesus' disciples interpret his words to mean that they should literally take up arms as they respond, "Look, Lord, here are two swords" (22:38). Jesus is frustrated with their lack of comprehension and breaks off the discussion by saying "Enough of this" (22:38).[46] It is reasonable to conclude, therefore, that according to Luke Jesus takes a stand against violence.

With regard to Jewish authorities and structures, Jesus' stance can best be described as nonviolent resistance. While Luke reports numerous confrontations between Jesus and the

Jewish leaders, only in the story about the cleansing of the temple is there any hint of possible violence (Lk. 19:45, "And he entered the temple and began to drive out those who sold"). A detailed comparison of Luke and Mark, however, clearly shows that in this pericope Luke abbreviates and tones down Mark's account; he leaves out the buyers, the overturning of tables and chairs, and the preventing of anyone carrying things through the temple (cf. Mk. 11:15-16). In Luke's account, this verse merely reports Jesus' entry into the temple which he will use for his subsequent teaching. Jesus' teaching, rather than the cleansing of the temple, is the motive for the hostile reaction of the Jewish leaders.[47] In the story of Jesus' arrest (Lk. 22:47-53), Jesus explicitly rejects the use of violence:

> 22[49]And when those who were about him saw what would follow, they said, "Lord, shall we strike with the sword?" [50]And one of them struck the slave of the high priest and cut off his right ear. [51]But Jesus said, "No more of this!" And he touched his ear and healed him.

Both Jesus' words ("No more of this!") and actions (he touched the slave's ear and healed him) are Lukan additions to his source (cf. Mk. 14:47-52). According to Luke, therefore, Jesus explicitly rejects violent resistance and acts with compassion toward an enemy. After he heals the high priest's servant, Jesus speaks to the chief priests and captains of the temple and elders (Lk. 22:52). This leads Charles Talbert to conclude that "nonviolent confrontation aimed at dialogue and hoping for a change of behavior seems the best description of the Lukan Jesus' stance toward the Jewish structures."[48]

What is Jesus' stance toward the state and its political leaders? According to Hans Conzelmann, Luke presents both the gospel and Jesus' kingship as non-political.[49] The Jews are seen as responsible for the death of Jesus and the persecution of the church, while the representatives of the Roman Empire declare both Jesus and his followers innocent. Because Luke realizes that the parousia will not occur imminently, he narrates the story of Jesus and the early church in such a way that Christians will be seen as loyal citizens of the Empire. Conzelmann believes that Luke wants to show that the Christian movement is politically nonsubversive and that Luke is attempting to enter into a conversation with the Empire "in order to achieve a permanent settlement."[50] Conzelmann's thesis concerning Luke's political apologetic has been challenged by several scholars. Richard Cassidy argues against Conzelmann's view that Luke does not place Jesus "in conflict with the existing social and political conditions and that Jesus was primarily concerned with a heavenly kingship."[51] Cassidy admits that "there is one passage (6:27-31) in which Jesus appears to adopt a position bordering on nonresistance, but most of Luke's descriptions show Jesus vigorously challenging those responsible for the existing social patterns."[52] His conclusion, therefore, is that Jesus' teachings and deeds were economically, socially, and politically revolutionary. Therefore, Jesus presented a serious threat to the Roman Empire.[53] Cassidy believes that:

> Although Jesus did not constitute the same type of threat to Roman rule as the Zealots and the Parthians, the threat that he posed was, ultimately, not less dangerous. Unlike the Zealots, the Jesus of Luke's gospel does not make the overthrow of Roman rule the central focus of his activity, nor does he support any of the other forms of government (including that probably advocated by the Zealots) that might have been considered as replacements for Roman rule. Nevertheless, by espousing radically new social patterns and by refusing to defer to the existing political authorities, Jesus pointed the way to a social order in which neither the Romans nor any other oppressing group would be able to hold sway.[54]

John Howard Yoder also believes that Jesus was an agent of radical social change.[55] In his inaugural speech in the synagogue at Nazareth (Lk. 4:16ff.), Jesus proclaims "the acceptable year of the Lord." Yoder understands this to refer to the jubilee year, the year of liberation appointed by God in which fields lay fallow, persons returned to their own homes, debts were canceled, and slaves set free (cf. Lev. 25). Thus he concludes that the ministry of Jesus begins "a visible sociopolitical, economic restructuring of relations among the people of God."[56] What needs to be seen, according to Yoder, is that "the primary social structure through which the gospel works to change other structures is that of the Christian community."[57] While the message of Jesus requires that his disciples be active participants in the creative transformation of the world, Jesus' example of nonviolence demands that Christians not use violence to achieve this end.

> Jesus (does not) reprimand his disciples for expecting him to establish some new social order, as he would have had to do if the thesis of the only-spiritual kingdom were to prevail. He rather reprimands them for having misunderstood the character of that new social order which he does intend to set up. The novelty of its character is not that it is not social, or not visible, but that it is marked by an alternative to accepted patterns of leadership. The alternative to how the kings of the earth rule is not "spirituality" but servanthood.[58]

The position of Cassidy and Yoder, rather than that of Conzelmann, has found support in recent scholarship. At the conclusion of his study of "peace" (eirēnē) in Luke's Gospel, Willard Swartley states that Luke's major attention to social themes shows "the eirēnē-gospel to be of revolutionary consequence, socially, economically, and politically—here and now."[59] Charles Talbert believes that Yoder is correct in emphasizing Luke's focus on the Christian community as the primary social structure through which the gospel works to change other structures. Talbert states that "by embodying structures of social relationships that reflected the new life in the Spirit under the Lordship of Jesus, the Christian community functioned in the larger society as an agent of social change."[60]

The person and message of Jesus Christ, therefore, have profoundly this-worldly consequences. According to Luke, Jesus calls individuals to a new way of life. As this visible socio-political, economic restructuring of relations begins to take place among the followers of Jesus, the Christian community will begin to function in the larger society as an agent of social change. While they are engaged in the task of creatively transforming the world, Christians must follow the example of Jesus and reject the use of violence. The way of Jesus is the way of love and forgiveness, not the way of violence.

Conclusion

One who accepts the call to become a disciple of Jesus is baptized into the community that confesses him as Lord and Savior. This community recognizes the dignity of women and the importance of marriage. Jesus speaks out against divorce and remarriage and generally presents a positive picture of the family. He welcomes children and teaches his audience that the Kingdom of God belongs to children and to adults who are like them. Jesus also warns that entry into the Kingdom will be denied to anyone who is not prepared to receive it like a child. In other places, however, one learns that allegiance to Jesus and the Kingdom take precedence over familial responsibilities. The obvious conclusion is that while marriage is the normal and acceptable state for a Christian, blood ties are less important than fidelity to the will of God.

The Christian community, young and old, rich and poor, Jew and Gentile, frequently breaks bread together. Luke-Acts highlights the importance and centrality of the Eucharistic celebration. Instituted by Jesus himself at the Last Supper, this meal symbolizing peace, trust, and community is joyfully celebrated by Jesus' disciples in response to his command, "Do this in remembrance of me" (Lk. 22:19). After the ascension, the community is united through the Lord's Supper to the risen one who is present in the Eucharist. While the community is hierarchial and logic suggests that someone presided at the Eucharistic celebrations, there is no clear indication in Luke-Acts who presided at these ritual meals.

Prayer also marked the religious life of those who gathered together in Jesus' name. Throughout history God has guided his people though prayer. Jesus, like his Jewish ancestors, is a person of prayer. He serves as a model for his disciples as he teaches them a prayer and urges them to pray always and not lose heart. Prayer can take the form of joyful praise and thanksgiving, intercession, or petition. While prayer can be described generally as communication with God, Jesus tells his disciples specifically what to pray for. The disciples are told to pray for daily sustenance, forgiveness, protection from temptation, the coming of the Kingdom, and the gift of the Holy Spirit. The Holy Spirit who guided Jesus in his life is given by God to those who ask. This same Spirit motivates the Christian to carry on the work of Jesus and work for liberation and justice for all.

One injustice that the Christian must address is economic injustice, both inside and outside the Christian community. The poor and the oppressed must be set at liberty. The willingness of Jesus and his disciples to help those in need set them at odds with the values and structures of the pagan world in which they lived. If one has material possessions, one must freely give to those who are in need. This can take many different forms, e.g., communal living in common, like the Jerusalem church, or private possessions and almsgiving. The point is that for the Christian, sharing material goods must replace possessing them as a value. Regardless of the model adopted, one must remember that in Luke's eyes how one handles possessions is an indication, a symbol, of one's interior disposition, whether one is responding positively or negatively to the word of God.

While the wealthy have a right to use their possessions for the necessities of life, what remains belongs to the poor. The story of the rich man and Lazarus (Lk. 16:19-31) teaches us that the rich are in possession of the goods of the poor even if they have aquired them honestly or inherited them legally. If they are to be saved, the wealthy must follow the example of Zacchaeus who gave half his possessions to the poor and repaid anyone he defrauded four times over.

According to Luke, Jesus calls his disciples first to undertake a visible socio-political, economic restructuring of relations among themselves. As this begins to take place, the Christian community will be able to function in the larger society as an agent of social change. While they are engaged in the task of creatively transforming the world, Christians must follow the example of Jesus and reject the use of violence. The way of Jesus is the way of love and forgiveness, not the way of violence.

9

The Importance of
Luke-Acts for Us Today

Christians realize that Luke-Acts is not primarily a work of
ancient history or literature, although Luke is often referred to
as an ancient historiographer and his two-volume work is
literary in nature. Luke is a Christian theologian who has
taken the stories about Jesus and the early church that he
found in his tradition and presented them in such a way as to
make them relevant for his audience. The Christian of today
and Luke's original reader, in the last quarter of the first
century, have at least two things in common. Both live in
between the first and second coming of Christ. And both want
an answer to the question, "What does Christian discipleship
entail?"

In order to understand Christian discipleship in Luke-Acts
one must recognize that Luke presents the reign of God as
both present and future. Luke agrees with Mark that the
Kingdom of God has come in the person of Jesus (cf. Mk.
1:15). Jesus instructs the Seventy to announce that "the Kingdom of God has come near" (Lk. 10:9,11). And later, when the
Pharisees ask when the Kingdom of God will come, Jesus
replies, "The Kingdom of God is among you" (17:21). The
miracles of Jesus also demonstrate that the Kingdom has
arrived. Jesus answers the Pharisees' contention that he
exorcises by the power of Beelzebul by saying, "But if it is by
the finger of God that I cast out demons, then the Kingdom of
God has come upon you" (11:20).

The future dimension of the Kingdom of God is suggested when Jesus teaches his disciples to pray for the coming of the Kingdom (Lk. 11:2), when the two men inform Jesus' disciples that "this Jesus, who was taken up from you into heaven, will come in the same way as you saw him go into heaven" (Acts 1:11; cf. Lk. 21:27,36), and when Luke speaks of Jesus as the Messiah still to come (Acts 3:19-21; cf. 17:31):

> 3[19]"Repent, therefore, and turn again, that your sins may be blotted out, that times of refreshing may come from the presence of the Lord, [20]and that he may send the Christ appointed for you, Jesus, [21]whom heaven must receive until the time for establishing all that God spoke by the mouth of his holy prophets from of old."

Because the Kingdom is now present, it is possible for individuals, through the grace of God, to participate in his reign. The one who is transformed by the redemptive, healing presence of God can allow God to continue to work through him/her to redeem and heal others. What this means is that the salvation of God is available now, not only at some far distant time; the reign of God can and should become manifest in the Christian community. But because the Kingdom is not here in its eschatological fullness, individuals can still sin. It remains possible for the Christian to act against this fundamental choice for God. Conversion, therefore, is not a once-for-all total change. It is a process that has to be worked out within the Christian community as both the church and the disciple journey toward God.

As important as membership in the visible community of disciples is for one who is called to acknowledge the Lordship of Jesus, it does not by itself guarantee salvation. What is necessary for salvation is membership in the Kingdom of God which: (1) exists within the Christian community but is not identical with it and (2) should be made visible in the lives of the disciples.

For those who are called to Christian discipleship, submitting to God's will means participating in the new type of human community made possible by the arrival of the Kingdom of God. But the church itself is still on the journey.

Because it is possible for those called to acknowledge the Lordship of Jesus to sin, both the church and the disciple stand in constant need of renewal and reform. In spite of its failings, however, the community gathered in Jesus' name remains the primary location where the grace of God manifests itself as love and reconciliation. Luke's presentation of Jesus and the early church must guide us as we seek to answer the question, "What does Christian discipleship entail?" This does not mean that we should uncritically apply to our own situation the answers Luke presents to his original readers. After all, Luke himself uses both the journey theme and the growth and development model to present the story of Jesus and the church. While there must be continuity between what Luke and the twentieth century reader see as the important components of Christian discipleship, there is also the possibility of development. The people of God, as individuals and as the church, continue to grow and develop as they journey with Jesus.

Individuals, from the time of the early church until today, receive the call of Jesus through his earthly representatives, Christian disciples. While one's initial attraction to Christianity may result from hearing the words of and about Jesus and his powerful deeds, in many cases it is the words and deeds of the Christian disciple that first attract the future convert. This suggests that we not take a narrow view of our missionary responsibility as Christians. Luke tells us that Jesus sent out as missionaries the Twelve and the Seventy. This implies that the universal church has an obligation to send out missionaries. In Acts one learns that the church at Antioch sponsored its own missionaries. This suggests that the local church, each parish or diocese, has an obligation to commission missionaries. Can we also conclude that every individual disciple is also called upon to engage in missionary activity?

Prior to the Second Vatican Council the role and importance of the ordained was exaggerated at the expense of the missionary responsibility of the entire community. Luke tells us that the one who prays will receive the gift of the Holy Spirit. And it is this same Holy Spirit that guided Jesus during his earthly ministry and the early church in its missionary efforts. It seems reasonable to suggest that, since all Christians are urged to pray for the gift of the Holy Spirit, the Holy Spirit motivates each Christian to engage in missionary activity. It is possible to conclude, therefore, that the disciple who follows Jesus' example of loving and compassionate service is taking part in the missionary enterprise; and that the words of Jesus, "The one who hears you hears me" (Lk. 10:16), apply to those who follow the example set by Jesus in their oral interchange with others. Our conclusion, therefore, is that the universal church, each local church, and each individual Christian has a missionary responsibility. One benefit of this broader understanding of mission is that it does not stress preaching and the celebration of the sacraments at the expense of the church's social and political responsibilities. The missionary obligation can be fulfilled in foreign lands or in one's local community, by publically preaching the good news of God's salvation or by following the example of Jesus and leading a life of humble service.

Because the church itself is in the process of becoming, growing and developing as it journeys toward God, it too should be seen as mission territory. Judas, Ananias, and Sapphira, are powerful reminders that reception of the Eucharist and membership in the church do not guarantee salvation. Because it is possible for the baptized Christian to sin, the words of Jesus, the good news of God's salvation, must continue to be heard.

Of course, the one who is attracted to the behavior of the Christian disciple has just begun the journey. This person must be introduced to the words and deeds of Jesus himself. Just as in Luke's day, the one who listens to the words of and about Jesus, God's agent of salvation, should be led to repentance, faith, and baptism. Because the will of God is present in the words and deeds of Jesus, they remain important for the disciple long after this initial pre-baptismal encounter; the words and deeds of Jesus are not meant only for the missionary enterprise.

Today one hears the words of and about Jesus proclaimed in Christian worship services. Many Christians also encounter the words and deeds of Jesus as they engage in private or group Bible-reading and reflection. The importance Luke places on hearing and seeing Jesus suggests that these practices should be encouraged. The example of Jesus who guides his disciples to a correct understanding of the Hebrew Scriptures, is followed by Philip when he helps the Ethiopian comprehend the text from Isaiah. One way in which this important aspect of listening to the words of Jesus (i.e., understanding them) is accomplished today is through the homily or sermon. An analogy is often drawn between the modern homilist and the apostles. The disciple of today listens to the teaching of the homilist just as the early Christian in the Jerusalem church listened to the teaching of the apostles (Acts 2:42; cf. 4:33).

It would be a mistake, however, to see the sermon as the only setting in which the words and deeds of Jesus and the early church are to be explained. According to Luke, insight and enlightenment are provided in different settings by a variety of individuals. Jesus becomes present as the two disciples relate their experience of the risen Lord to the eleven and those who were with them (Lk. 24:36). Philip provides help to the Ethiopian on the way from Jerusalem to Gaza (Acts 8:26ff.); Paul preaches to the Jews at Rome (Acts 28:23); and Priscilla and Aquila teach Apollos after his speech in the synagogue at Ephesus (Acts 18:26).

While God does speak to the individual through the words of Scripture, Luke-Acts suggests that a trustworthy guide is needed to insure the correct understanding of the text. Jesus himself provides the interpretation in the Gospel; Christian missionaries fulfill this role in Acts. The Second Vatican Council suggests that, in its widest sense, the teaching authority belongs to the whole church as the People of God. It is possible, therefore, that any member of the church could provide the necessary insight and enlightenment. There is no indication in Luke's two-volume work that the teaching authority resides exclusively with celibate males. After all, among the teachers in Luke-Acts are a married couple (Acts 18:26) and a man with four daughters (21:8-9). In Luke-Acts, however, these teachers are usually portrayed as men and women who are recognized as leaders by the Christian community.

The possibility that children were baptized members of the Christian community draws attention to the growth and development theme and reinforces the importance of conducting a mission to the baptized. Faith is not something that is possessed once and for all; it must be constantly renewed. The disciple's personal relationship with the risen Lord must continually grow, or it weakens and perhaps dies. Whether or not one begins the journey with Jesus as a child, the individual who wishes to travel along the way of the Lord must listen to his words. Hearing is not enough, of course, since many who hear do not become disciples. One must not only hear the word, but also hold it fast in an honest and good heart and bring forth fruit with patience (Lk. 8:15). This is not something that happens only once; it happens throughout an entire lifetime. In order to progress in the life of faith, the disciple must listen to and obey the word of the Lord as a child, an adolescent, and an adult.

People of every age need to hear the good news of God's salvation. They must hear the message of the forgiveness of sins and the restoration to wholeness or completeness. They must understand that it is now possible to be reconciled with and to establish a correct relationship with both God and our neighbor. Those who understand and accept God's saving action in Jesus Christ cannot continue behaving in the same sinful way. Jesus announces that he has come to call "sinners to repentance" (Lk. 5:32). Would-be followers of Jesus, therefore, must cease to do evil and strive to conduct their lives according to the will of God.

In Luke-Acts, those who wish to do the will of God must place themselves at the service of others. This service ethic includes adopting a lifestyle which, in many respects, is radically opposed to the standards of the world. The greatest disciple is not the one with the most economic or political power, authority, and prestige, but rather: (1) the one who is the best servant, (2) the one who is not selfish, but uses wealth and possessions for the benefit of those in need, and (3) the one who suffers injustice rather than inflicting it on others.

Christian discipleship, therefore, is eminently practical. The follower of Jesus does not adopt the hopeless and irresponsible position that the future is shaped by the power of God alone. The Christian is aware that we human beings have the capacity to shape our own physical and social environment. Because we are co-creators with God (cf. Gen. 1:28), we have the power to transform nature or to be the despoilers of nature; we can value human beings for themselves, realizing that human dignity comes from God (cf. Gen. 1:27) or we can be exploitive, viewing human beings merely as a labor force. Christians must realize that the obligation to "love our neighbor" requires a social commitment to the common good. We have the fundamental obligation to work for an end to hunger, injustice, exploitation and the denial of life. The only place where human dignity can be realized and protected is in community. This is why Christians must insure that all people have an opportunity to participate in the economic and political life of society. Luke understands that human dignity comes from God, not from nationality, race, sex, economic status or human accomplishment. Membership in the community that confesses Jesus as Lord and Savior is open to all, regardless of race, gender, or economic status. In a society dominated by wealthy and powerful men, a society that views the marginalized as relatively unimportant, Jesus demonstrates a preferential option for the poor, the powerless, and women as he preaches the good news of salvation to all. This must remind us today that racism, sexism, and ageism have no place within the Christian community.

Within the various Christian communities which appear in Luke-Acts there is a hierarchy of roles, titles, and authority. There is little evidence, however, that any role or function, except membership in the Twelve, was limited by racial, economic, or gender factors. As the early church begins and continues its journey, new roles and functions emerge. Luke presents the reader with a church that is in the process of growing and developing as it is guided through history by the Holy Spirit in accordance with the plan of God. Luke takes for granted that a hierarchy exists within the Christian community. However, he does not appear to be interested in presenting the reader with an ideal structural model. What Luke is concerned with is the appropriate behavior of those in authority, whether they be bishops, elders, prophets, teachers, or apostles. This leads him to point out quite clearly that church leaders must pattern their behavior after Jesus, who gave himself as servant, and must conduct themselves humbly as servants of all (Lk. 22:25-27).

The Christian community grows and develops as it journeys

toward God. If we accept this Lukan insight then we will not seek to cling almost desperately to the past. Christians must show a sensitivity about both the validity and the limitations of the past as well as an openness to the present and the future. The church of the first century grew and developed into the church of the second century which, in turn, grew and developed into the church of the third century, etc. If we understand that the Holy Spirit is guiding the church on its journey, then we will be open to the possibility of change. Some past decisions will be viewed as normative, yet under the continued guidance of the Holy Spirit others will be seen as inappropriate or incomplete understandings of the will of God for the present. This raises the possibility of new church structures, new models of leadership in the church, the ordination of women, accepting the insights of liberation theology, etc. The Holy Spirit, given to those who pray, will lead the Christian disciple and the Christian community to understand the will of God for the present.

The one who accepts the call to become a disciple of Jesus is baptized into the community that confesses him as Lord and Savior. This community recognizes the dignity of women and the importance of marriage. While Luke does not have the final word on marriage and divorce in the New Testament, he does present Jesus as speaking out against divorce and remarriage. At the very least, this rules out for Christians any cavalier attitude toward divorce and demands that marriage be taken quite seriously. Luke also presents a generally positive picture of the family. Jesus welcomes children and teaches his audience that the Kingdom of God belongs to children and to adults who are like them.

The Christian community, young and old, rich and poor, Jew and Gentile, frequently breaks bread together. Luke-Acts highlights the importance and centrality of the Eucharistic celebration. Instituted by Jesus himself at the Last Supper, this meal symbolizing peace, trust, and community is joyfully celebrated by Jesus' disciples in response to his command, "Do this in remembrance of me" (Lk. 22:19). After the ascension, the community is united through the Lord's Supper to the risen one who is present in the Eucharist. While the community is hierarchial and logic suggests that someone presided at the Eucharistic celebrations, there is no clear indication in Luke-Acts who presided at these ritual meals. Who should preside at the communal Eucharistic celebration today? What is unclear in Luke-Acts becomes clear as the church grows and develops. According to the Didache, a late first-century manual on Christian morals and practice, prophets were permitted to celebrate the Eucharist. Eventually, however, only bishops and presbyters had the right to preside at the Eucharistic celebration. Does this mean that today only a bishop or "priest," someone who has been publically ordained by a bishop, can preside at the communal Eucharistic celebration? Since historical and sociological factors played a role in the emergence of a more regular clergy, perhaps the Holy Spirit is leading us to respond in a new way to our own situation in life. As the church continues its journey with Jesus perhaps it will be led by the Holy Spirit to recognize a different set of candidates (i.e., women, those who are married) as appropriate presiders at the Eucharist. The Holy Spirit might also lead us to recognize as acceptable a different method for choosing those who would preside at the Eucharistic celebration. Perhaps those men and women who emerge as leaders of the Christian base communities in the so-called Third World should be seen as logical candidates to preside at the communal Eucharistic celebration.

Mention of the communal Eucharist causes one to think of the various parts of that celebration (e.g., prayer, listening to the words of Jesus, etc.). One must remember, however, that in order to inherit eternal life you must "love the Lord your God with all your heart, and with all your soul, and with all your strength, and with all your mind; and your neighbor as yourself" (Lk. 10:25-28). In our world there are those who latch on to the first commandment, forgetting the second, and those who do just the opposite. The ideal, according to Jesus, is to live the two commandments.

The command to love one's neighbor must be put into practice. One way in which this happens is when the Christian addresses economic injustice, both inside and outside the Christian community. The poor and the oppressed must be set at liberty. The willingness of Jesus and his disciples to help those in need set them at odds with the values of the pagan world in which they lived. If one has material possessions, one must freely give to those who are in need. This can take many different forms, e.g., communal living in common, like the Jerusalem church, or private possessions and almsgiving. The point is that for the Christian, sharing material goods must replace possessing them as a value. Regardless of the model adopted, one must remember that in Luke's eyes how one handles possessions is an indication, a symbol, of one's interior disposition, whether one is responding positively or negatively to the word of God.

While the wealthy have a right to use their possessions for the necessities of life, that which is superfluous belongs to the poor. The story of the rich man and Lazarus (Lk. 16:19-31) teaches us that the rich are in possession of the goods of the poor even if they have aquired them honestly or inherited them legally. If they are to be saved, the wealthy must follow the example of Zacchaeus who gave half his possessions to the poor and repaid anyone he defrauded four times over. The stories in Acts lead unmistakably to the conclusion that Christians are not called to contribute to the poor merely what they do not need, but rather truly to share their goods.

Luke-Acts actually leads the modern Christian to a radical conclusion when it comes to possessions and economic justice. Luke's growth and development model and his teaching about the continued guidance of the Holy Spirit require that the Christian pay close attention to modern, as well as ancient, insights into God's will. One modern insight is that the poor and oppressed suffer because of human-made, and therefore changeable, structures. It is widely recognized today that there is a need to change social and economic structures in order to achieve justice. Feeding the hungry and clothing the naked can be achieved in the long run only by way of profound economic transformations. In addition to feeding the hungry, the Christian must question the reason for hunger. The disciple of Jesus must become an active agent of social change. Luke-Acts challenges us to reassess our lifestyle and to take the steps necessary to restructure our lives and our society in accordance with the will of God.

As we modern Christians examine our discipleship in light of Luke-Acts, a personal response is required to Jesus' question, "Who do you say that I am?" (Lk. 9:20). Luke presents Jesus as the Messiah/Christ promised in the Hebrew Scriptures. But he reinterprets this title, presenting Jesus as the suffering Messiah, not a political king and military leader who would drive out the Romans. Luke's presentation of Jesus as the suffering Messiah, suffering Son of Man, and Suffering Servant, suggests that hardship is not alien to Christian discipleship. The one who wishes to travel with Jesus on the journey to God must realize that the road is often difficult and demanding. The suffering Messiah, not the royal military leader, is the model Luke presents for his Christian readers to follow.

In his use of the Servant theme, however, Luke does not dwell exclusively on suffering. While Luke admits that suffering and death might be the lot of the faithful disciple, he is much more interested in presenting the disciple as one who serves. In Luke-Acts Jesus is seen as the Servant who lives a life of service and teaches his disciples to do the same (e.g., Lk. 22:24-30). The Christian must follow the example of Jesus, the one who serves. With mercy and compassion the disciple must take care of the weaker members of society. This includes providing food for widows (cf. Acts 6:1-6), ministering to the poor who are hungry and covered with sores (cf. Lk. 16:19-31), and providing medical care for those in need, even if they are outside one's religious community (cf. 10:25-37).

Only a correct understanding of Jesus leads to the adequate practice of Christian discipleship. The parallels between Jesus and his disciples in Luke-Acts point unmistakably to the fact that Luke sees Jesus as a model for his followers. And the example he gives them is one of service. Doing the will of God means loving God and loving our neighbor. The Christian who prays and celebrates the Eucharist in community must also act with mercy and compassion toward those in need.

The requirement to be active in the social and political sphere on behalf of the marginalized is difficult for some to accept and put into practice. But it has always been that way. "If they do not hear Moses and the prophets, neither will they be convinced if some one should rise from the dead" (Lk. 16:31). Throughout the Hebrew Scriptures the messengers of God repeatedly urged the Israelites to care for the widow, the orphan, and the stranger in their midst. In the New Testament, Jesus shows by word and deed that one's goal must be justice for the poor, the maimed, the lame, and the blind. If we believe that Jesus of Nazareth is the risen Lord, why do we refuse to obey him and follow his example?

Luke's presentation of Jesus as the Suffering Servant who "had done no violence" (Isa. 53:9) raises the same question. Why do some refuse to follow the example of Jesus of Nazareth, whom they proclaim as risen Lord and Savior? The presence of the Kingdom of God requires Christians, with the help of God's grace, to conform their lives to the will of God. Jesus commands his followers "take up your cross daily" (Lk. 9:23) and teaches them not to impose their will on others by force (22:25-30). Christians should use whatever power they have for the benefit of the marginalized. The followers of Jesus should prefer to suffer injustice themselves rather than impose their rights on others through the use of violence. By both word and deed Jesus taught his disciples the meaning of Christian discipleship. Near the end of his earthly life, Jesus summarized this teaching when he told his disciples, "I am among you as one who serves."

Bibliography

Achtemeier, P. J., "The Lukan Perspective on the Miracles of Jesus: A Preliminary Sketch." In *Perspectives on Luke-Acts*, ed. C. H. Talbert. Danville: ABPR, 1978.

Baab, O. J., "Woman." *IDB* 4:864-67.

Bamberger, B. J., "Tax Collector." *IDB* 4:522.

Barrett, C. K., *Luke the Historian in Recent Study*. London: Epworth, 1961.

Bearsley, P. J., "Mary the Perfect Disciple: A Paradigm for Mariology." *TS* 41 (1980) 461-504.

Beasley-Murray, G. R., *Baptism in the New Testament*. Grand Rapids: Eerdmans, 1962.

Behm, J., "μετανοέω and μετάνοια." *TDNT* 4:975-1006.

Bernadicou, P. J., "Christian Community According to Luke." *Worship* 44 (1970) 205-219.

_____, "The Spirituality of Luke's Travel Narrative." *RevRel* 36 (1977) 455-466.

Best, E., *Following Jesus: Discipleship in the Gospel of Mark*. JSNTS. Sheffield: JSOT, 1981.

Bovon, F., *Luc le theologian: vingt-cinq ans de recherches (1950-1975)*. Neuchatel: Delachaux & Niestle, 1978.

Brandon, S. G. F., *Jesus and the Zealots*. New York: Charles Scribner's Sons, 1967.

Brown, R. E., *The Birth of the Messiah*. Garden City: Doubleday, 1977.

_____, *The Gospel According To John I-XII* AB 29. Garden City: Doubleday, 1966.

————, *The Gospel According To John XIII-XXI* AB 29A. Garden City: Doubleday, 1970.

————, et al. *Mary in the New Testament.* NY: Paulist, 1978.

————, "The Meaning of Modern New Testament Studies for an Ecumenical Understanding of Mary." In *Biblical Reflections on Crises Facing the Church.* NY: Paulist, 1975.

————, et al. *Peter in the New Testament.* New York: Paulist and Minneapolis: Augsburg, 1973.

————, *Priest and Bishop: Biblical Reflections.* New York: Paulist, 1970.

————, "Roles of Women in the Fourth Gospel." *TS* 36 (1975) 688-699.

Brown, S., *Apostasy and Perseverance in the Theology of Luke.* AnBib 36. Rome: Pontifical Biblical Institute, 1969.

Bultmann, R., "πιστεύω." *TDNT* 6:197-228.

Cadbury, H. J., "The Greek and Jewish Traditions of Writing History." In *The Beginnings of Christianity. Part I. The Acts of the Apostles,* 5 vols., ed. F. J. Foakes-Jackson and K. Lake. London: Macmillan, 1920-1935.

————, *The Making of Luke-Acts.* New York: Macmillan, 1927.

————, "The Speeches in Acts," In *The Beginnings of Christianity. Part I. The Acts of the Apostles,* 5 vols., ed. F. J. Foakes-Jackson and K. Lake. London: Macmillan, 1920-1935.

Caird, G. B., *Saint Luke.* Baltimore: Penguin, 1963.

Cassidy, R. J., *Jesus, Politics, and Society: A Study of Luke's Gospel.* Maryknoll: Orbis, 1978.

————, and Scharper, P. J., *Political Issues in Luke-Acts.* Maryknoll: Orbis, 1983.

Conzelmann, H., "The Address of Paul on the Areopagus." In *Studies in Luke-Acts*, ed. L. E. Keck and J. L. Martyn. Nashville: Abingdon, 1966.

_____, *The Theology of St. Luke*. Trans. G. Buswell. New York: Harper & Row, 1961.

Creed, J. M., *The Gospel According to St. Luke*. London: MacMillan, 1957.

Cullmann, O., *Baptism in the New Testament*. London: SCM, 1964.

_____, *The Christology of the New Testament*. Trans. S. C. Guthrie and C. A. M. Hall. Philadelphia: Westminster, 1959.

Danker, F. W., *Jesus and the New Age according to St. Luke*. St. Louis: Clayton, 1972.

_____, *Luke*. Proclamation Commentaries. Philadelphia: Fortress, 1976.

Degenhardt, H.-J. *Lukas-Evangelist der Armen: Besitz und Besitzverzicht in den lukanischen Schriften*. Stuttgart: Katholisches Bibelwerk, 1965.

Dibelius, M., *Studies in the Acts of the Apostles*, ed. H. Greeven. New York: Scribner's, 1956.

Dillon, R. J., *From Eye-Witnesses to Ministers of the Word*. AnBib 82. Rome: Biblical Institute, 1978.

Dodd, C. H., *The Apostolic Preaching and Its Developments*. London: Hodder and Stoughton, 1936.

Dupont, J., "Repentir et conversion d'apres les Actes des Apôtres." *ScEccl* 12 (1960) 137-173.

_____, *The Salvation of the Gentiles*. Trans. J. Keating. New York: Paulist, 1979.

_____, *The Sources of the Acts*. New York: Herder & Herder, 1964.

Durken, D., ed. *Sin, Salvation, and the Spirit*. Collegeville: Liturgical, 1979.

Edwards, G. R., *Jesus and the Politics of Violence.* New York: Harper, 1972.

Ellis, E. E., *The Gospel of Luke.* Camden: Nelson, 1966.

Farmer, W. R., *The Synoptic Problem.* Philadelphia: Fortress, 1982.

Filson, F. V., "The Journey Motif in Luke-Acts." In *Apostolic History and the Gospel,* ed. W. W. Gasque and R. P. Martin. Grand Rapids: Eerdmans, 1970.

Fitzmyer, J. A., *The Gospel According To Luke I-IX.* AB 28. Garden City: Doubleday, 1981.

_____, *The Gospel According To Luke X-XXIV.* AB 28A. Garden City: Doubleday, 1985.

Flanagan, N., "The What and How of Salvation in Luke-Acts." In *Sin, Salvation, and the Spirit,* ed. D. Durken. Collegeville: Liturgical, 1979.

Flender, H., *St. Luke: Theologian of Redemptive History.* Philadelphia: Fortress, 1967.

Foerster, W., "εἰρήνη." *TDNT* 2:400-420.

Ford, J. M., *My Enemy is My Guest: Jesus and Violence in Luke.* Maryknoll: Orbis, 1984.

_____, "Zealotism and the Lukan Infancy Narratives." *NovT* 18 (1976) 280-292.

Franklin, E., *Christ the Lord: A Study in the Purpose and Theology of Luke-Acts.* Philadelphia: Westminster, 1975.

Fuller, R. H., "Luke and the Theologia Crucis." In *Sin, Salvation, and the Spirit,* ed. D. Durken. Collegeville: Liturgical, 1979.

_____, *The Foundations of New Testament Christology.* New York: Scribner's, 1965.

_____, and Perkins, P. *Who Is This Christ?* Philadelphia: Fortress, 1983.

George, A., "Israel." In *Etudes sur l'oeuvre de Luc.* Paris:

Gabalda, 1978. Published originally as "Israel dans l'oeuvre de Luc." *RB* 75 (1968) 481-525.

_____, "Le sens de la mort de Jesus." In *Etudes sur l'oeuvre de Luc.* Paris: Gabalda, 1978. Published originally as "Le sens de la mort de Jesus pour Luc." *RB* 80 (1973) 186-217.

Giles, K. N., "The Church in the Gospel of Luke." *SJT* 34 (1981) 121-146.

Gill, D., "Observations on the Lukan Travel Narrative and Some Related Passages." *HTR* 63 (1970) 199-221.

Glockner, R., *Die Verkundigung des Heils beim Evangelisten Lukas.* Mainz: Matthias-Grunewald, 1976.

Goulder, M. D., *Type and History in Acts.* London: SPCK, 1964.

Grässer, E., "Die Parusieerwartung in der Apostelgeschichte." In *Les Actes des Apotres: traditions, redaction, theologie,* ed. J. Kremer. Gembloux: Duculot, 1979.

Grundmann, W., "σύν—μετά with the Genitive." *TDNT* 7:766-797.

_____, *Das Evangelium nach Lukas.* THKNT, 3. Berlin: Evangelische Verlaganstalt, 1963.

_____, "Fragen der Komposition des lukanischen 'Reiseberichte'." *ZNW* 50 (1959) 252-271.

Haenchen, E., *The Acts of the Apostles: A Commentary.* Philadelphia: Westminster, 1971.

Hardon, J. A., "The Miracle Narratives in the Acts of the Apostles." *CBQ* 16 (1954) 303-318.

Hezel, F. X., "Conversion and Repentance in Lucan Theology." *TBT* 37 (1968) 2596-2602.

Hinnebusch, P., *Jesus, The New Elijah.* Ann Arbor: Servant, 1978.

Hubbard, B. J., "Commissioning Stories in Luke-Acts: A Study of Their Antecedents, Form and Content." *Semeia* 8 (1977) 103-126.

————, "The Role of Commissioning Accounts in Acts." In *Perspectives on Luke-Acts*, ed. C. H. Talbert. Danville: ABPR, 1978.

Jeremias, J., *The Eucharistic Words of Jesus*. Philadelphia: Fortress, 1977.

————, *Infant Baptism in the First Four Centuries*. Trans. D. Cairns. Philadelphia: Westminster and London: SCM, 1960.

Jervell, J., "The Divided People of God." In *Luke and the People of God*. Minneapolis: Augsburg, 1972.

Johnson, L. T., *The Literary Function of Possessions in Luke-Acts*. SBLDS 39. Missoula: Scholars, 1977.

Jones, D. L., "The Title 'Servant' in Luke-Acts." In *Luke-Acts: New Perspectives from the Society of Biblical Literature Seminar*, ed. C. H. Talbert. New York: Crossroad, 1984.

Kariamadam, P., "Discipleship in the Lucan Journey Narrative." *Jeevadhara* 10 (1980) 111-130.

Karris, R. J., *Invitation to Acts*. Garden City: Doubleday, 1978.

————, *Invitation To Luke*. Garden City: Doubleday, 1977.

Käsemann, E., "Ministry and Community of the New Testament." In *Essays on New Testament Themes*. London: SCM, 1964.

Keck, L. E. and Martyn, J. L., eds. *Studies in Luke-Acts*. Nashville: Abingdon, 1966.

Kilmartin, E. J., *The Eucharist in the Primitive Church*. Englewood Cliffs: Prentice-Hall, 1965.

Kingsbury, J. D., *Jesus Christ in Matthew, Mark, and Luke*. Philadelphia: Fortress, 1981.

Kodell, J., "Luke's Theology of the Death of Jesus." In *Sin, Salvation, and the Spirit*, ed. D. Durken. Collegeville: Liturgical, 1979.

_____, "'The Word of God grew': The Ecclesial Tendency of Λόγος in Acts 1,7; 12,24; 19,20." *Biblica* 55 (1974) 505-519.

Kraybill, D. B. and Sweetland, D. M., "Possessions in Luke-Acts: A Sociological Perspective. *PRS* 10 (1983) 215-239.

Kümmel, W. G., *Introduction to the New Testament.* Nashville: Abingdon, 1975.

Kurz, W., *Following Jesus: A Disciple's Guide to Luke and Acts.* Ann Arbor: Servant, 1984.

_____, "Luke-Acts and Historiography in the Greek Bible." In *SBL Seminar Papers.* Chico: Scholars, 1980.

_____, "Luke 3:23-38 and Greco-Roman and Biblical Genealogies." In *Luke-Acts: New Perspectives from the Society of Biblical Literature Seminar*, ed. C. H. Talbert. New York: Crossroad, 1984.

Lampe, G. W. H., "The Holy Spirit in the Writings of St. Luke." In *Studies in the Gospels*, ed. D. E. Nineham. Oxford: Blackwell, 1957.

LaVerdiere, E. A. and Thompson, W. G., "New Testament Communities in Transition: A Study of Matthew and Luke." *TS* 37 (1976) 567-597.

Lohfink, G., *The Conversion of St. Paul: Narrative and History in Acts.* Trans. and ed. B. J. Malina. Chicago: Franciscan Herald, 1976.

_____, *Die Sammlung Israels: Untersuchung zur lukanischen Ekklesiologie.* Munich: Kosel, 1975.

_____, *Jesus and Community: The Social Dimension of Christian Faith*, trans. J. P. Galvin. Philadelphia: Fortress and New York: Paulist, 1982.

Lohse, E., "Lukas als Theologe der Heilgeschichte." *EvT* 14 (1954) 256-275.

_____, "Missionarisches Handeln Jesu nach dem Evangelium das Lukas." *TZ* 10 (1954) 1-13.

Manson, T. W., *The Servant-Messiah: A Study of the Public Ministry of Jesus.* New York: Cambridge, 1953.

Marshall, I. H., *The Acts of the Apostles: An Introduction and Commentary.* TynNTC. Leicester: Inter-Varsity and Grand Rapids: Eerdmans, 1980.

_____, *The Gospel of Luke: A Commentary on the Greek Text.* Grand Rapids: Eerdmans, 1978.

_____, *Luke: Historian and Theologian.* Exeter: Paternoster, 1970.

Matera, F. J., "The Death of Jesus According to Luke: A Question of Sources." *CBQ* 47 (1985) 469-485.

Mattill, A. J., Jr., "The Jesus-Paul Parallels and the Purpose of Luke-Acts: H. H. Evans Reconsidered." *NovT* 17 (1975) 15-46.

Metzger, B. M., "Seventy or Seventy-Two Disciples." *NTS* 5 (1958-1959) 299-306.

_____, *A Textual Commentary on the Greek New Testament.* New York: UBS, 1971.

Michiels, R., "La conception lucanienne de la conversion." *ETL* 41 (1965) 42-78.

Miyoshi, M., *Der Anfang des Reiseberichts, Lk 9:51-10:24: Eine redaktionsgeschichtliche Untersuchung.* AnBib 60. Rome: Pontifical Biblical Institute, 1974.

Mullins, T. Y., "New Testament Commission Forms, Especially in Luke-Acts." *JBL* 95 (1976) 603-614.

Munck, J., *The Acts of the Apostles.* AB 31. Garden City: Doubleday, 1967.

Navone, J., *Themes of St. Luke.* Rome: Gregorian, 1970.

Neyrey, J., *The Passion According to Luke: A Redaction Study of Luke's Soteriology.* New York: Paulist, 1985.

O'Brien, P. T., "Prayer in Luke-Acts." *TB* 24 (1973) 111-127.

O'Toole, R. F., "Christian Baptism in Luke." *RevRel* 39 (1980) 855-866.

————, *The Christological Climax of Paul's Defense.* AnB 78. Rome: Biblical Institute, 1978.

————, "Christ's Resurrection in Acts 13:13-52." *Biblica* 60 (1979) 361-372.

————, "Luke's Notion of 'Be Imitators of Me As I Am of Christ' in Acts 25-26." *BTB* 7 (1978) 155-161.

————, "Parallels between Jesus and His Disciples in Luke-Acts: A Further Study." *BZ* 27 (1983) 195-212.

————, *The Unity of Luke's Theology: An Analysis of Luke-Acts.* Wilmington: Michael Glazier, 1984.

Ott, W., *Gebet und Heil: Die Bedeutung der Gebetsparänese in der lukanische Theologie.* Munchen: Kosel Verlan, 1965.

Perrin, N., *Rediscovering the Teaching of Jesus.* New York: Harper and Row, 1967.

Pilgrim, W. E., *Good News to the Poor: Wealth and Poverty in Luke-Acts.* Minneapolis: Augsburg, 1981.

Plevnik, J., "'The Eleven and Those with Them' According to Luke." *CBQ* 40 (1978) 205-211.

Plümacher, E., "Wirklichkeitserfahrung und Geschichtsschreibung bei Lukas." *ZNW* 68 (1977) 2-22.

Plummer, A., *A Critical and Exegetical Commentary on the Gospel According To S. Luke.* ICC. Edinburgh: T. & T. Clark, 1922.

Quesnell, Q., "The Women at Luke's Supper." In *Political Issues in Luke-Acts*, ed. R. J. Cassidy and P. J. Scharper. Maryknoll: Orbis, 1983.

Rahner, K., "Theos in the New Testament." In *Theological Investigations.* NY: Seabury, 1974.

Rengstorf, K. H., "μαθητής." *TDNT* 4:457-459.

Reumann, J., *Jesus in the Church's Gospels.* Philadelphia: Fortress, 1968.

Rhoads, D. M., *Israel in Revolution 6-74 C. E.* Philadelphia: Fortress, 1976.

Richard, E., *Acts 6:1-8:4: The Author's Method of Composition.* Missoula: Scholars, 1978.

————, "The Creative Use of Amos by the Author of Acts." *NovT* 24 (1982) 37-53.

————, "The Divine Purpose: The Jews and the Gentile Mission." In *Luke-Acts: New Perspectives from the Society of Biblical Literature Seminar,* ed. C. H. Talbert. New York: Crossroad, 1984.

Richardson, A., *An Introduction to the Theology of the New Testament.* London: SCM, 1958.

Robbins, V. K., "By Land and by Sea: The We-Passages and Ancient Sea Voyages." In *Perspectives in Luke-Acts,* ed. C. H. Talbert. Danville: ABPR, 1978.

Robinson, W. C., Jr., "On Preaching the Word of God (Luke 8:14-21)." In *Studies in Luke-Acts,* ed. L. E. Keck and J. L. Martyn. Nashville: Abingdon, 1966.

————, "The Theological Context for Interpreting Luke's Travel Narrative (9:51ff.)." *JBL* 79 (1960) 20-31.

————, *The Way of the Lord.* Basel: Dissertation, 1962.

Ross, J. F., "Meals." *IDB* 3:315-318.

Schmid, J., *Das Evangelium nach Lukas.* RNT 3. Regensburg: Pustet, 1960.

Schnackenburg, R., "Lukas als Zeuge verschiedener Ger-meindestrukturen." *Bibel und Leden* 12 (1972) 232-47.

Schubert, P., "The Final Cycle of Speeches in the Book of Acts." *JBL* 87 (1968) 1-16.

Schürmann, H., *Jesu Abschiedsrede.* Münster: Aschendorff, 1957.

Schweizer, E., "Concerning the Speeches in Acts." In *Studies in Luke-Acts,* ed. L. E. Keck and J. L. Martyn. Nashville: Abingdon, 1966.

Sheridan, M. "Disciples and Discipleship in Matthew and Luke." *BTB* 3 (1973) 235-255.

Smith, C. W. F., "Prayer." *IDB* 3:857-867.

Streeter, B. H. *The Four Gospels: A Study of Origins.* Rev. ed., London: Macmillan, 1930.

Swartley, W. M., "Politics or Peace (Eirēnē) in Luke's Gospel," in *Political Issues in Luke-Acts,* ed. R. J. Cassidy and P. J. Scharper. Maryknoll: Orbis, 1983.

Sweetland, D. M., "Discipleship and Persecution: A Study of Luke 12:1-12." *Biblica* 65 (1984) 61-79.

_____, "The Good Samaritan and Martha and Mary." *TBT* 21 (1983) 325-330.

_____, "The Lord's Supper and the Lukan Community." *BTB* 13 (1983) 23-27.

_____, *Our Journey With Jesus: Discipleship according to Mark.* Wilmington: Michael Glazier, 1987.

Talbert, C. H., *Acts.* Atlanta: John Knox, 1984.

_____, "Discipleship in Luke-Acts." In *Discipleship in the New Testament,* ed. F. F. Segovia. Philadelphia: Fortress, 1985.

_____, *Literary Patterns, Theological Themes and the Genre of Luke-Acts.* SBLMS 20. Missoula: Scholars, 1974.

_____, *Luke and the Gnostics.* Nashville: Abingdon, 1966.

_____, "Martyrdom in Luke-Acts and the Lukan Social Ethic." In *Political Issues in Luke-Acts,* ed. R. J. Cassidy and P. J. Scharper. Maryknoll: Orbis, 1983.

_____, ed. *Perspectives on Luke-Acts.* Danville: ABPR, 1978.

_____, *Reading Luke.* New York: Crossroad, 1984.

_____, "The Way of the Lukan Jesus: Dimensions of Lukan Spirituality," *PRS* 9 (1982) 237-249.

Taylor, V., *The Passion Narrative of St. Luke: A Critical and Historical Investigation*. SNTSMS 19. Cambridge: University Press, 1972.

Tiede, D. L., *Prophecy and History in Luke-Acts*. Philadelphia: Fortress, 1980.

Toombs, L. E., "Clean and Unclean." *IDB* 1:641-48.

Trites, A., "The Prayer Motif in Luke-Acts." In *Perspectives on Luke-Acts*, ed. C. H. Talbert. Danville: ABPR, 1978.

Udick, W. S., "Metanoia as Found in the Acts of the Apostles." *TBT* 28 (1967) 1943-1946.

van Unnik, W. C., "The 'Book of Acts' the Confirmation of the Gospel." *NovT* 4 (1960) 26-59.

von Soden, H., *Geschichte der christlichen Kirche. 1: Die Entstehung der christlichen Kirche*. Leipzig: Teubner, 1919.

Wanke, J., *Beobachtungen zum Eucharistieverstandnis des Lukas auf Grund der lukanischen Mahlberichte*. Leipzig: St. Benno, 1973.

Weinert, F. D., "The Meaning of the Temple in Luke-Acts." *BTB* 11 (1981) 85-89.

Wilson, S. G., *The Gentiles and the Gentile Mission in Luke-Acts*. SNTSMS 23. Cambridge: Cambridge University, 1973.

_____, "Law and Judaism in Acts." In *SBL Seminar Papers*. Chico: Scholars, 1980.

Yoder, J. H., *The Politics of Jesus*. Grand Rapids: Eerdmans, 1972.

Zehnle, R. F., *Peter's Pentecost Discourse: Tradition and Lukan Reinterpretation in Peter's Speeches of Acts 2 and 3*. SBLMS 15. Nashville: Abingdon, 1971.

Endnotes

Notes, Introduction

[1]For a detailed history of the problem, see W. G. Kümmel, *Introduction to the New Testament* (Nashville: Abingdon, 1975) 38-80.

[2]However, some continue to defend the priority of Matthew. See, e.g., W. R. Farmer, *The Synoptic Problem* (Philadelphia: Fortress, 1982).

[3]See B. H. Streeter, *The Four Gospels: A Study of Origins*, rev. ed. (London: Macmillan, 1930).

[4]See J. Dupont, *The Sources of the Acts* (New York: Herder & Herder, 1964).

[5]So, e.g., C. K. Barrett, *Luke the Historian in Recent Study* (London: Epworth, 1961) 22.

[6]V. K. Robbins, "By Land and by Sea: The We-Passages and Ancient Sea Voyages," in *Perspectives on Luke-Acts*, ed. C. H. Talbert (Danville: ABPR, 1978) 215-242. Cf. E. Plümacher, "Wirklichkeitserfahrung und Geschichtsschreibung bei Lukas," *ZNW* 68 (1977) 2-22, and H.J. Cadbury, *The Making of Luke-Acts* (New York: Macmillan, 1927) 230.

[7] See, e.g., J. A. Fitzmyer, *The Gospel According To Luke* (Garden City: Doubleday, 1981 & 1985) 1:35-53 and E. E. Ellis, *The Gospel of Luke* (Camden: Nelson, 1966) 40-55; .

[8] See Dupont, *Sources*, 166

[9]See Cadbury, *Making 8-9,* and W.C. van Unnik, *"The 'Book of Acts' the Confirmation of the Gospel,"* NovT 4 (1960) 26-59. Cf. I. H. Marshall, *The Acts of the Apostles: An Introduction and Commentary* (Leicester: Inter-Varsity and Grand Rapids: Eerdmans, 1980) 55.

Notes Chapter 2

[1]See D. M. Sweetland, *Our Journey with Jesus: Discipleship according to Mark* (Wilmington: Michael Glazier, 1987) 16-23.

[2]

Mark		Luke
		Infancy Narrative (1-2)
(1:1-8)	John the Baptist	(3:1-20)
(1:9-11)	Baptism of Jesus	(3:21-22)
		Genealogy of Jesus (3:23-28)
(1:12-13)	The Temptation	(4:1-13)
(1:14-15)	Jesus Preaches in Galilee	(4:14-15)
		Rejection at Nazareth (4:16-30)
Call of the First Disciples (1:16-20)		
(1:21-28)	Synagogue at Capernaum	(4:31-37)
(1:29-31)	Simon's Mother-In-Law	(4:38-39)
(1:32-34)	Sick Healed at Evening	(4:40-41)

(1:35-38)	Departure from Capernaum	(4:42-43)
(1:39)	Preaching Journey of Jesus	(4:44)
		Call of First Disciples (5:1-11)

[3]The same body of water is being referred to in both Gospels. That this is both a call and a commissioning story is shown by B. J. Hubbard, "Commissioning Stories in Luke-Acts: A Study of Their Antecedents, Form and Content," *Semeia* 8 (1977) 103-126, and "The Role of Commissioning Accounts in Acts," in *Perspectives on Luke-Acts*, ed. C. H. Talbert (Danville: ABPR, 1978) 187-198. Cf. T. Y. Mullins, "New Testament Commission Forms, Especially in Luke-Acts," *JBL* 95 (1976) 603-614.

[4]It is widely recognized that Luke has composed this story on the basis of Mark 1:16-20 and other traditional material (cf. Jn. 21:1-14). See e.g. R. E. Brown, *The Gospel According To John* (Garden City: Doubleday, 1966 & 1970) 2:1090. For a discussion of the seven well-known Lukan transpositions of Markan material see J. A. Fitzmyer, *The Gospel According To Luke* (Garden City: Doubleday, 1981 & 1985) 1:71-72.

[5]P. J. Achtemeier, "The Lukan Perspective on the Miracles of Jesus: A Preliminary Sketch," in *Perspectives*, 156-157.

[6]C. H. Talbert, *Reading Luke* (New York: Crossroad, 1984) 58-59.

[7]Luke 5:17-26; 7:18-23; 8:2; 19:37-38.

[8]Acts 9:35,42; 13:12; 16:25-34; 19:17.

[9]S. Brown, *Apostasy and Perseverance in the Theology of Luke*, AnBib 36 (Rome: Pontifical Biblical Institute, 1969) 58 n.213, argues that Luke leads his readers to this conclusion when he uses "after this" *(μετὰ ταῦτα)* in 5:27 to connect the call of Levi (5:27-32) with the miraculous cure of the paralytic (5:17-26). Achtemeier, "Miracles," 161, agrees and suggests that Luke's use of "strange things" *(παράδοξος)* in 5:26 supports this understanding of miracle. Cf. Talbert, *Reading*, 59.

[10]See I. H. Marshall, *The Gospel of Luke: A Commentary on the Greek Text* (Grand Rapids: Eerdmans, 1978) 205.

[11]On the understanding of ἔσῃ ζωγρῶν (you shall be taking them alive) suggested here see Fitzmyer, *Luke*, 1:563, and Marshall, *Commentary*, 205-206.

[12]R. E. Brown, *Peter in the New Testament* (New York: Paulist and Minneapolis: Augsburg, 1973) 119, and Fitzmyer, *Luke*, 1:563-564.

[13]See e.g. Brown, *Peter*, 119; Marshall, *Commentary*, 206; and A. Plummer, *A Critical and Exegetical Commentary on the Gospel According To S. Luke*, ICC (Edinburgh: T. & T. Clark, 1922) 147.

[14]W. C. Robinson, Jr., is usually credited with drawing attention to this in his doctoral dissertation, *The Way of the Lord* (Basel: Dissertation, 1962).

[15]While it is generally agreed that this section begins at 9:51, several different termination points have been suggested (18:30; 19:10; 19:27 [28]; and 19:44 [48]). The goal of the journey, Jerusalem, is reached only in the last suggested ending as the group is still "drawing near the city" (ἤγγιζόν τὴν πόλιν) in 19:29,37,41.

[16]See E. E. Ellis, *The Gospel of Luke* (Camden: Nelson, 1966) 125, and P. J. Bernadicou, "The Spirituality of Luke's Travel Narrative," *RevRel* 36 (1977) 456. It is widely recognized that in Acts Luke presents Paul as a missionary with a specific itinerary and purpose.

[17]It is widely recognized that the substantive ἀνάλημψις (a taking up, assumption) in Luke 9:51 refers to the passion, death, resurrection, and ascension of Jesus. The

movement of Jesus toward the ultimate goal of the ascension, therefore, should be
seen as providing the overall framework for Luke 9:51–Acts 1:11.

[18]See e.g. Marshall, *Commentary*, 205.

[19]See Sweetland, *Mark*, 51-69.

[20]In many instances Mark clearly uses ἀκολουθεῖν to indicate entry into special
communion with Jesus (Mk. 2:14,15; 8:34; 9:38; 10:21,28; cf. 10:32,52 and 15:41).
Luke often emphasizes this aspect of discipleship by his use of the preposition σύν
(with) (8:1,38; 9:32; 22:14,56; 24:44; Acts 4:13). In Luke 23:49, for example, the
evangelist has changed Mark's comment that the women who witnessed the crucifixion
had "followed" (ἀκολουθεῖν) Jesus "when he was in Galilee" (Mk.
15:41) to say that the women had "accompanied" (συνακολουθεῖν) Jesus "from Galilee." See W. Grundmann,
"σύν-μετά with the Genitive," *TDNT* 7:766ff.; K. N. Giles, "The Church in the Gospel
of Luke," *SJT* 34 (1981) 140-141; and Brown, *Apostasy*, 56,82f., who states that there
can be "no doubt that in συνελθόντων (who have accompanied) in Acts 1:21 the
exterior association with Jesus expresses the interior commitment of discipleship"
(56).

[21]See Sweetland, *Mark*, 23-25.

[22]Marshall, *Commentary*, 217; cf. R. J. Karris, *Invitation To Luke* (Garden City:
Doubleday, 1977) 80.

[23]See e.g., Ellis, *Luke,* 106-107, and Fitzmyer, *Luke,* 1:590.

[24]Marshall, *Commentary*, 219.

[25]Ibid., 217.

[26]Talbert, *Reading*, 63, and W. Kurz, *Following Jesus: A Disciple's Guide to Luke
and Acts* (Ann Arbor: Servant, 1984) 25. Cf. E. Best, *Following Jesus: Discipleship in
the Gospel of Mark*, JSNTS 4 (Sheffield: JSOT, 1981) 178, who suggests that the call of
Levi in Mark be understood in this way.

[27]Talbert, *Reading*, 63.

[28]J. Behm, "μετανοέω and μετάνοια," *TDNT* 4:1002.

[29]See J. Kodell, "'The Word of God Grew': The Ecclesial Tendency of *logos* in Acts
1,7; 12,24; 19,20," *Biblica* 55 (1974), 514, who follows R. Michiels, "La conception
lucanienne de la conversion," *ETL* 41 (1965) 42-78.

[30]Luke frequently presents Jesus in banquet or dinner scenes (Lk. 7:36-50; 9:10-17;
10:38-42; 11:37-54; 14:1-24; 19:1-10; 22:4-38; 24:29-32, 41-43). See Marshall, *Commentary*, 221, and Talbert, *Reading*, 64-65. Cf. J. Neyrey, *The Passion According to
Luke: A Redaction Study of Luke's Soteriology* (New York: Paulist, 1985) 9.

[31]B. J. Bamberger, "Tax Collector," *IDB* 4:522.

[32]On the function of this pericope in Mark's Gospel see Sweetland, *Mark*, 25-28.

[33]See A. Trites, "The Prayer Motif in Luke-Acts," in *Perspectives*, 168-186.

[34]H. J. Cadbury, *The Making of Luke-Acts* (London: S.P.C.K., 1968) 269; Fitzmyer,
Luke, 1:244-247; Talbert, *Reading*, 102-104,132; and R. F. O'Toole, *The Unity of
Luke's Theology: An Analysis of Luke-Acts* (Wilmington: Michael Glazier, 1984) 72.

[35]In the parallel text, Mark does not refer to the Twelve as "apostles" (cf. Mk. 6:30).
Although there is some disagreement over the identity of "the disciples" and "the
Twelve" in Mark, most commentators believe that Mark, like Luke, pictures Jesus
choosing twelve from a larger group of disciples (cf. Mk. 3:13-19). See Sweetland,
Mark, 36-50.

[36]See G. Lohfink, *Jesus and Community: The Social Dimension of Christian Faith,*

trans. J. P. Galvin (Philadelphia: Fortress and New York: Paulist, 1982) 10, 89ff.

[37]Brown, *Apostasy*, 56.

[38]Ibid., 88.

[39]Cf. Sweetland, *Mark*, 28-29.

[40]Talbert, *Reading*, 96-97, and Marshall, *Commentary*, 350. For a different view see E. Franklin, *Christ the Lord: A Study in the Purpose and Theology of Luke-Acts* (Philadelphia: Westminster, 1975) 167, who states that the journey of the Twelve "does not prefigure either their activity after Pentecost or the life of the Church as a whole.... They are therefore not portrayed as examples to later missionaries."

[41]There is an obvious connection between much of what is promised prophesied in the Gospel and what occurs in Acts. For example, Luke tells his readers that the early Christian missionaries Paul and Barnabas followed Jesus' charge (Lk. 9:5) and "shook off the dust from their feet" (Acts 13:51) after they were persecuted in Pisidian Antioch.

[42]The manuscript evidence is evenly divided between "seventy" and "seventy-two." Most scholars point to the fact that the number of those sent corresponds to the number of Gentile nations in Genesis 10 (70 in the Massoretic Text and 72 in the LXX). Whether seventy or seventy-two, therefore, these missionaries symbolize all the nations of the world and foreshadow the universal mission. For a discussion see B. M. Metzger, "Seventy or Seventy-Two Disciples," *NTS* 5 (1958-1959) 299-306, which is summarized in *A Textual Commentary on the Greek New Testament* (New York: UBS, 1971) 150-151.

[43]See e.g. M. Miyoshi, *Der Anfang des Reiseberichts, Lk 9:51-10:24: Eine redaktionsgeschichtliche Untersuchung*, AnBib 60 (Rome: Pontifical Biblical Institute, 1974) 74-75; Ellis, *Luke*, 154-155; and Fitzmyer, *Luke*, 2:842f.

[44]See e.g. W. Grundmann, "Fragen der Komposition des lukanischen 'Reiseberichte'," *ZNW* 50 (1959) 260, and *Das Evangelium nach Lukas*, HTKNT, 3 (Berlin: Evangelische Verlaganstalt, 1963) 208; E. Lohse, "Lukas als Theologe der Heilgeschichte," *EvT* 14 (1954) 272, and "Missionarisches Handeln Jesu nach dem Evangelium das Lukas," *TZ* 10 (1954) 12; R. F. Zehnle, *Peter's Pentecost Discourse: Tradition and Lukan Reinterpretation in Peter's Speeches of Acts 2 and 3*, SBLMS 15 (Nashville: Abingdon, 1971) 107,130; and Talbert, *Reading*, 114-115. Even S. G. Wilson, *The Gentiles and the Gentile Mission in Luke-Acts*, SNTSMS 23 (Cambridge: Cambridge University, 1973) 45-47, who insists that "in the immediate context the mission of the Seventy is clearly to Israel," grudgingly admits that "Luke may well have had one eye on the later mission of the Church."

[45]H.-J. Degenhardt, *Lukas-Evangelist der Armen: Besitz und Besitzverzicht in den lukanischen Schriften* (Stuttgart: Katholisches Bibelwerk, 1965) 60-66, argues that it is Luke's intent in this pericope to portray, for the benefit of the missionaries of his own day, what he believes to be the ideal attitude toward possessions. Before one can agree with this conclusion both Luke 22:35 and Luke's picture of the missionaries' use of possessions in Acts must be examined.

[46]See Brown, *Apostasy*, 119-120; P. J. Bearsley, "Mary the Perfect Disciple: A Paradigm for Mariology," *TS* 41 (1980) 477-478; and D. M. Sweetland, "The Good Samaritan and Martha and Mary," *TBT* 21 (1983) 325-330.

[47]See Metzger, *Textual Commentary*, 186-187 on the inclusion of καὶ λέγει αὐτοῖς· εἰρήνη ὑμῖν (and he said to them, "Peace to you!").

[48]W. Foerster, "εἰρήνη," *TDNT* 2:413.

[49]Fitzmyer, *Luke*, 1:225 and 2:847; cf. Brown, *John*, 2:1021.

[50]e.g. Lk. 5:25-26; 6:20-23; 15:4-32; 19:37-44; 24:50-53.

[51]e.g. Acts 2:26-27,42-47; 13:48,52; 15:3,31.

[52]Cadbury, *Making*, 267-268; J. Navone, *Themes of St. Luke* (Rome: Gregorian, 1970) 71-87; P. J. Bernadicou, "Christian Community According to Luke," *Worship* 44 (1970) 213ff., and "Spirituality," 460-463; and O'Toole, *Unity*, 225-260.

[53]For an explanation of how this pericope functions in Mark's Gospel see Sweetland, *Mark*, 29-34.

[54]Luke has already told the reader about the disciples who left everything to follow Jesus (Lk. 5:11,28). Here he changes Mark's "sell what you have" (*implying* the need to leave everything behind) and has Jesus state *explicitly* that one must sell "all" (πάντα).

[55]Most commentators conclude that the invitation of Jesus was refused. See e.g. G. B. Caird, *Saint Luke* (Baltimore: Penguin, 1963) 205; Marshall, *Commentary*, 683; Karris, *Invitation to Luke*, 207; and Talbert, *Reading*, 172. Fitzmyer, *Luke*, 2:1200, however, after drawing the reader's attention (*pace* Caird and Marshall) to the fact that Luke does not tell his audience that the ruler "went away," admits that Luke "implies" that this individual "could not bring himself to follow Jesus in the specific way that was proposed to him."

[56]A conclusion is also missing in the story of the Prodigal Son (Lk. 15:11-32). This leads each reader to identify with the elder son and his dilemma. Should the father's invitation to rejoice with him and the rest of the community over the return of the prodigal be accepted? Is the reader/elder brother able to respond joyfully over a sinner's repentance? If not, why not?

[57]In Mark (Mk. 10:28; cf. Mt. 19:27) Peter says to Jesus, "we have left everything (πάντα)." Luke replaces "everything" (πάντα) with τὰ ἴδια (literally "[our] own things"). Luke's use of τὰ ἴδια here is best seen as a stylistic variation for πάντα and should be translated as "property" or "possessions" and not "home." See BAGD, 370. This use of τὰ ἴδια also anticipates the language about possessions in Acts 4:32ff.

[58]So Talbert, *Reading*, 173, and Fitzmyer, *Luke*, 2:1205-1206.

[59]Although no crowd is mentioned, Luke seems to assume that the disciples (Lk. 18:15), Peter (18:28), the Twelve (18:31), Pharisees (17:20), the ruler (18:18), and others (18:1,9,15) are present with Jesus during this period. See e.g. Fitzmyer, *Luke*, 2:1197. On the literary unity of Luke 17:11-18:30 see Talbert, *Reading*, 164ff.

[60]Plummer, *Luke*, 421. Cf. Fitzmyer, *Luke*, 2:1196.

[61]Talbert, *Reading*, 171-172.

[62]Caird, *Saint Luke*, 205.

[63]Marshall, *Commentary*, 683.

[64]L. T. Johnson, *The Literary Function of Possessions in Luke-Acts*, SBLDS 39 (Missoula: Scholars, 1977) 155, n.1.

[65]While our interest lies primarily in the words of Jesus here, it should be noted that verses 44-49 are actually part of a larger literary unit (24:36-53) that recounts this appearance of the risen Lord.

[66]There is also a close connection between the resurrection appearance stories and the missionary commissioning in Matthew and John. In Matthew 28:16-20, the risen Lord appears to his disciples and commands them to go and "make disciples of all nations." In John 20:21, the resurrected Jesus says to his disciples, "As the Father has sent me, even so I send you."

[67]Cf. J. Plevnik, "'The Eleven and Those with Them' According to Luke," CBQ 40 (1978) 205-211.

[68]While the "we" in 18:28 is unspecified, one can argue that it refers at least to Peter, James and John (cf. Lk. 5:11), probably to Levi (cf. 5:28), and possibly to the last group mentioned, i.e. "the disciples" (cf. 18:15).

[69]Talbert, *Reading*, 176f., states that the Zacchaeus story is a "paradigm of what conversion entails," while Marshall, *Commentary*, 694, notes that in this pericope "the meaning of discipleship, especially in regard to wealth, is clearly expressed." For a different interpretation see Fitzmyer, *Luke*, 2:1218ff.

[70]Discipleship might be suggested in Acts 13:43, but not in 12:8,9 or 21:36.

[71]Acts 1:8,22; 2:32; 3:15; 5:32; 10:39,41; 13:31; 22:15,20; 26:16.

Notes Chapter 3

[1]We will examine Peter's five missionary sermons (Acts 2, 3, 4, 5, and 10) and Paul's missionary speeches to the Jews (13) and Gentiles (17). Paul's farewell address to the Ephesian elders at Miletus (20) will also be discussed in this chapter. The four well-known apologetic speeches of Paul in Acts 21-28 (22:1-21; 23:1ff.; 24:10-21; 26:1-23) differ in form and content from the missionary speeches and will not be examined in detail in this chapter.

[2]See "Paul on the Areopagus," and "The Speeches in Acts and Ancient Historiography," in *Studies in the Acts of the Apostles*, ed. H. Greeven (New York: Charles Scribner's Sons,1956) 26-77 and 138-185. At about the same time H. J. Cadbury arrived at similar conclusions. See "The Greek and Jewish Traditions of Writing History," in *The Beginnings of Christianity. Part I. The Acts of the Apostles*, 5 vols., ed. F. J. Foakes Jackson and K. Lake (London: Macmillan, 1920-1935) 2, 7-29, "The Speeches in Acts," *Beginnings*, 5, 402-427, and *The Making of Luke-Acts*. The important contribution to this discussion made by C. H. Dodd, *The Apostolic Preaching and Its Developments* (London: Hodder and Stoughton, 1936) must not be ignored.

[3]See Talbert *Acts* (Atlanta: John Knox, 1984) 6; cf. Marshall, *Acts*, 55.

[4]G. W. H. Lampe, "The Holy Spirit in the Writings of St. Luke," in *Studies in the Gospels*, ed. D. E. Nineham (Oxford: Blackwell, 1957) 159-200.

[5]Ellis, *Luke*, 109.

[6]Zehnle, *Peter's Pentecost Discourse*, 17.

[7]In "Parallels between Jesus and His Disciples in Luke-Acts: A Further Study," *BZ* 27 (1983) 195-212, R. F. O'Toole argues that Luke uses the same words to describe the preaching and message of both Jesus and his followers.

[8]Luke frequently draws attention to the fact that individuals and groups heard the word that was preached to them (Acts 2:37; 4:4; 8:6; 10:33; 13:44,48; 17:32; 18:8; 19:5,10; cf. 13:12; 16:14; 17:4,11).

[9]E. Haenchen, *The Acts of the Apostles: A Commentary* (Philadelphia: Westminster, 1971) 98, cf. 49. See also P. Schubert, "The Final Cycle of Speeches in the Book of Acts," *JBL* 87 (1968) 4, n.7, and R. J. Dillon, *From Eye-Witnesses to Ministers of the Word*, AnBib 82 (Rome: Biblical Institute, 1978) 155, who states that it is Jesus' voice that continues to be heard in the ministry of the early church, "for it is only *in personal encounter with him*, and from that perspective, that the whole mystery of God's plan of salvation is opened to the eye of faith."

[10]It is possible to be familiar with Scripture and yet misunderstand the Christ-event. See Sweetland, "Good Samaritan," 329.

[11]In Luke's second volume the miracles of Jesus are referred to twice (Acts 2:22 and 10:38) and there are numerous references to "signs and wonders" performed by the disciples (e.g. 2:43; 4:30; 5:12; 6:8; 8:13; 14:3; 15:12). Cf. Achtemeier, "Miracles," 165, n.22. Johnson *Literary Function*, 60-78, argues that Moses is the model for Luke's portrayal of Jesus and the apostles, because all are filled with the Spirit, speak God's word, perform signs and wonders, and stimulate a response of acceptance/rejection.

[12]J. A. Hardon, "The Miracle Narratives in the Acts of the Apostles," *CBQ* 16 (1954) 311.

[13]See I. H. Marshall, *Luke: Historian and Theologian* (Exeter: Paternoster, 1970) 87 n.2.

[14]J. Dupont, "Conversion in the Acts of the Apostles," in *The Salvation of the Gentiles*, trans. J. Keating (New York: Paulist, 1979) 61-62.

[15]N. Flanagan, "The What and How of Salvation in Luke-Acts," in *Sin, Salvation, and the Spirit*, ed. D. Durken (Collegeville: Liturgical, 1979) 212. Cf. I. H. Marshall, *The Acts of the Apostles: An Introduction and Commentary*, TynNTC (Leicester: Inter-Varsity and Grand Rapids: Eerdmans, 1980) 81,194, and Zehnle, *Peter's Pentecost Discourse*, 63-66.

[16]Wilson, *Gentiles*, 95, states that "On Luke's definition, a Church with no missionary activity is not a true Church."

[17]See C. H. Talbert, *Luke and the Gnostics* (Nashville: Abingdon, 1966) 17-32, who claims, "It is no overstatement to say that Acts is dominated by the theme of 'witness'" (17) and "Above all, the witness guarantee is intended to cover the resurrection of our Lord" (29). Cf. R. F. O'Toole, *The Christological Climax of Paul's Defense*, AnBib 78 (Rome: Biblical Institute, 1978) 102-104.

[18]One must remember, as Dillon states in *Eye-Witnesses*, 215-217, 281, witnessing is not just a vouching for the tradition about Jesus, but involves the total reenactment of Jesus' "journey" (cf. Acts 10:39), including his passion and death.

[19]Cadbury, "The Speeches in Acts," 402.

[20]Cf. W. C. Robinson, Jr., "The Theological Context for Interpreting Luke's Travel Narrative (9:51ff.)," *JBL* 79 (1960) 20-31; Talbert, *Gnostics*, 17-32; J. Navone, *Themes of St. Luke* (Rome: Gregorian, 1970) 199-210; and Fitzmyer, *Luke*, 1:243.

[21]Navone, *Themes*, 206.

[22]Johnson, *Literary Function*, 183, is referring to Acts 2:41-47. See also Marshall, *Acts*, 83.

[23]Discipleship might be suggested in Acts 13:43, but not in 12:8,9 or 21:36.

[24]BAGD, 31.

[25]See Lampe, "Holy Spirit," 197.

[26]Fitzmyer, *Luke*, 1:241.

[27]C. H. Talbert, "The Way of the Lukan Jesus: Dimensions of Lukan Spirituality," *PRS* 9 (1982) 237-249.

[28]J. Kodell, "'The Word of God grew'."

[29]See Fitzmyer, *Luke*, 1:235.

[30]Degenhardt, *Evangelist der Armen*, 167. Cf. Brown, *Apostasy*, 98ff.; Marshall, *Acts*, 84; D. B. Kraybill and D. M. Sweetland, "Possessions in Luke-Acts: A Socio-

logical Perspective, *PRS* 10 (1983) 215-239; and W. E. Pilgrim, *Good News to the Poor: Wealth and Poverty in Luke-Acts* (Minneapolis: Augsburg, 1981) 148ff.

[31]Johnson, *Literary Function,* 158-161, 183-190, 210f., 221-222.

[32]Trites, "Prayer-Motif," 181.

[33]See Cadbury, *Making,* 267-268; Navone, *Themes,* 71-87; P. J. Bernadicou, "Christian Community According to Luke," *Worship* 44 (1970) 213ff., and "Spirituality," 460-463; and O'Toole, *Unity,* 225-260.

[34]See O'Toole, *Unity,* 86-94.

[35]Johnson, *Literary Function,* 66, and Marshall, *Acts,* 89. See also Talbert, *Acts,* 21, who argues that witness to Jesus must include both word and deed.

[36]Lk. 2:13-14, 20; 2:28; 4:15; 5:26; 7:16; 13:13; 17:15, 18; 18:43; 19:37-38; 23:47; 24:52-53.

[37]F. J. Matera, "The Death of Jesus According to Luke: A Question of Sources," *CBQ* 47 (1985) 480.

[38]Numerous passages in the Gospels suggest that Jesus is the fulfillment of the prophecies about the suffering Servant of Yahweh. In Acts (3:13, 26; 4:27, 30) this identification is made explicitly. The various titles applied to Jesus in this speech (e.g. Servant, Prophet like Moses, etc.) will be examined below when we discuss the Christology of Luke-Acts.

[39]Cf. Dupont, "Conversion," 80, who believes this word play is intentional.

[40]BAGD, 301. See Dupont, "Conversion," 79.

[41]The Sanhedrin (Acts 4:7) ask by what "power" (δύναμις) this miracle was done, so the immediate reference to the Spirit in verse 8 suggests not only that the Spirit is responsible for the speech Peter is about to give but for the healing as well (cf. Spirit and δύναμις in 1:8).

[42]R. H. Fuller, "Luke and the Theologia Crucis," in *Sin, Salvation, and the Spirit,* 218.

[43]It is widely accepted that Luke understands the silence of the council in Acts 4:14, "they had nothing to say in opposition (ἀντειπεῖν)," as the fulfillment of Jesus' promise in Luke 21:15, "I will give you a mouth and wisdom, which none of your adversaries will be able to withstand or contradict (ἀντειπεῖν)." This verb, ἀντειπεῖν (to say against or contradict), occurs only at these two places in the New Testament (Lk. 21:15; Acts 4:14).

[44]F.W. Danker, *Luke,* Proclamation Commentaries (Philadelphia: Fortress, 1976) 58.

[45]Marshall, *Acts,* 104, cf. 104-107.

[46]See C. H. Talbert, *Literary Patterns, Theological Themes and the Genre of Luke-Acts,* SBLMS 20 (Missoula: Scholars, 1974) 35-39, for a discussion of parallels, both in content and in sequence, between Acts 1:2-4:23 and 4:24-5:42.

[47]See Acts 13:26 where Paul states that "to us has been sent the message of this salvation."

[48]See E. Schweizer, "Concerning the Speeches in Acts," in *Studies in Luke-Acts,* ed. L. E. Keck and J. L. Martyn (Nashville: Abingdon, 1966) 208-216.

[49]In its original location, Joel 2:28-32 (LXX 3:1-5), "Lord" undoubtedly referred to God the Father. There can be no doubt, however, that Luke understands "Lord" to refer to the risen Christ who Christians call upon at baptism (cf. Acts 2:38-41).

[50]The Greek word for witness, μάρτυρες, is the source for our English word "martyr."

[51]In his second volume, Luke mentions both the miraculous deeds of Jesus (Acts 2:22; 10:38) and the numerous miracles performed by his disciples. Cf. Achtemeier, "Miracles," 165, n.22.

[52]See Trites, "Prayer-Motif," 179ff.

[53]See Hubbard, "Commissioning Accounts," 193.

[54]Our point here is that Luke has Paul describe this activity, which he presents in a positive light, as almsgiving. From Paul's own account of his activities (1 Cor. 16:1-4; 2 Cor. 8-9; Rom. 15:25-33), we know that he brought to Jerusalem a substantial amount of money which he had collected from the Gentile Christian churches as a gift "for the poor among the saints at Jerusalem" (Rom. 15:26).

[55]For a discussion of the similarities and differences in these three accounts see G. Lohfink, *The Conversion of St. Paul: Narrative and History in Acts*, trans. and ed. B. J. Malina (Chicago: Franciscan Herald, 1976).

[56]Cf. Brown, *Apostasy*, 135-145.

[57]See R. Bultmann, "πιστεύω" *TDNT* 6, 211f.

[58]The parallels between Jesus and Paul in Luke-Acts are widely acknowledged. See e.g. Cadbury, *Making*, 231-232; M. D. Goulder, *Type and History in Acts* (London: SPCK, 1964) 46-53, 61-62, 98-110; A. J. Mattill, Jr., "The Jesus-Paul Parallels and the Purpose of Luke-Acts: H. H. Evans Reconsidered," *NovT* 17 (1975) 15-46; R.F. O'Toole, "Luke's Notion of 'Be Imitators of Me As I Am of Christ' in Acts 25-26," *BTB* 7 (1978) 155-161, *Christological Climax, passim*, and *Unity*, 67-72; and Neyrey, *Passion*, 43, 98, 104-105.

[59]This emphasis on bearing witness has been found throughout Acts.

[60]O'Toole, *Christological Climax*, 68-69, and "Parallels," 207-209. Cf. P. Kariamadam, "Discipleship in the Lucan Journey Narrative," *Jeevadhara* 10 (1980) 118.

[61]J. Dupont, "The Salvation of the Gentiles and the Theological Significance of Acts," in *Salvation*, 28-29.

[62]The term "work" (ἔργον) is used in Acts 14:26 and 15:38 to indicate missionary activity.

[63]R. F. O'Toole, "Christ's Resurrection in Acts 13:13-52," *Biblica* 60 (1979) 362-364.

[64]Luke only uses σωτήρ (Savior) four times in his two volumes. In the Gospel it refers both to God (Lk. 1:47) and to Jesus (2:11). When Peter and Paul use σωτήρ in their speeches, the term refers to Jesus (Acts 5:31; 13:24).

[65]Some see this speech as a climatic point in the book, see e.g. Dibelius, "Paul on the Areopagus," in *Studies*, 26-77, and H. Conzelmann, "The Address of Paul on the Areopagus," in *Studies in Luke-Acts*, 217-230. For a different view, see Marshall, *Acts*, 281.

[66]Thus Luke portrays a unity of faith from Jesus to the apostles to Paul to the Ephesian elders.

[67]Talbert, *Literary Patterns*, 96-99.

[68]When Paul refers to the conclusion of his ministry as completing his "course" (δρόμος; Acts 20:24; cf. 13:25), the reader is once again reminded of the way (ὁδός) motif.

[69]See Dillon, *Eye-Witnesses*, 190, n.100, and Brown, *Apostasy*, 128. Cf. Marshall, *Luke*, 210f.

[70]Following H. von Soden, *Geschichte der christlichen Kirche. 1: Die Entstehung der christlichen Kirche* (Leipzig: Teubner, 1919) 73, C.H. Talbert, "Discipleship in Luke-Acts," in *Discipleship in the New Testament*, ed., F.F. Segovia (Philadelphia: Fortress, 1985) 62-75," states that "Luke-Acts is similar to the biographies of certain founders of philosophical schools, that contained within themselves not only the life of the founder but also a list or brief narrative of his successors and selected other disciples" (63). In writings such as these, especially when a narrative is given, the emphasis is frequently on the successor(s) emulating the founder (64). See also Talbert, "Martyrdom in Luke-Acts and the Lukan Social Ethic," in *Political Issues in Luke-Acts*, eds. R. J. Cassidy and P. J. Scharper (Maryknoll: Orbis, 1983) 99-110, and "The Way of the Lukan Jesus: Dimensions of Lukan Spirituality," *PRS* 9 (1982) 237-249; and Neyrey, *Passion*, 161.

[71]Acts 2:14-36; 4:2; 8:4-8, 12, 35; 10:34-43; 13:12, 46; 16:14, 31-34; 17:2-4, 11, 22-31; 18:5; 19:4, 8-10.

Notes, Chapter 4

[1]R. H. Fuller and P. Perkins, *Who Is This Christ?* (Philadelphia: Fortress, 1983) 77.

[2]See Fitzmyer, *Luke*, 1:196-197, who concludes that there are four phases of Christ's existence, from conception to parousia, in Lukan Christology.

[3]O'Toole, *Christological Climax*, 14. Cf. Fitzmyer, *Luke*, 1:197.

[4]Other less frequently used titles will not be examined at length: King, Son of David, Leader, Holy One, Righteous One, Judge, Teacher.

[5]See Sweetland, *Mark*, 146-151.

[6]In addition to the two verses cited, Luke has no parallel to the possible inclusion of "Son of God" in Mark 1:1. Because this is a questionable reading and may be a scribal expansion the lack of a Lukan parallel will not be treated here as significant. See B. M. Metzger, *A Textual Commentary on the Greek New Testament* (New York: UBS, 1971) 73.

[7]While Jesus is identified as the Son of God in Acts 8:37 it is unlikely that this variant reading was part of the original text. See Metzger, *Textual Commentary*, 359-360.

[8]Sweetland, *Mark*, 146-151.

[9]J. Reumann, *Jesus in the Church's Gospels* (Philadelphia: Fortress, 1968) 290. Cf. O. Cullmann, *The Christology of the New Testament*, trans. S. C. Guthrie and C. A. M. Hall (Philadelphia: Westminster, 1959) 270, and Fitzmyer, *Luke*, 1:208, who states that this emphasis on obedience is seen especially in Luke's Gospel.

[10]See Fitzmyer, *Luke*, 1:207-208.

[11]Lk. 2:11,26; 3:15; 4:41; 9:20; 20:41; 22:67; 23:2,35,39; 24:26,46; Acts 2:31,36; 3:18; 4:26; 5:42; 8:5; 9:22; 17:3; 18:5,28; 26:23.

[12]E.g. Acts 2:38; 3:6; 4:10,33; 8:12; 9:34; 10:36,48; 11:17; 15:26; 16:18; 20:21; 24:24; 28:31.

[13]See Sweetland, *Mark*, 140-141.

[14]Fitzmyer, *Luke*, 1:200.

[15]See O'Toole, *Christological Climax*, 23, 111f.

[16]In the Old Testament this title was also applied to the judges (Jdg. 3:9,15) as

people raised up by God for the deliverance of his people. In the Greek Bible the title is applied thirty-five times to God and only five times to human beings.

[17]In the Gospel Luke uses the title "Lord" fourteen times for Jesus. Matthew and Mark each use this title only once for Jesus.

[18]R. E. Brown, *The Birth of the Messiah* (Gardan City: Doubleday, 1977) 390.

[19]This theme is further highlighted when Luke places the journey to Bethlehem immediately after this passage which mentions the "way of peace."

[20]Zacchaeus identifies Jesus as the "Lord" and Jesus responds that "the Son of Man came to seek and to save the lost" (19:10).

[21]See, e.g., A. Richardson, *An Introduction to the Theology of the New Testament* (London: SCM, 1958) 145-146.

[22]See, e.g., T. W. Manson, *The Servant-Messiah: A Study of the Public Ministry of Jesus* (New York: Cambridge, 1953) 72-73; R. H. Fuller, *The Foundations of New Testament Christology* (New York: Scribner's, 1965) 34-43; and N. Perrin, *Rediscovering the Teaching of Jesus* (New York: Harper and Row, 1967) 164-99.

[23]For two different views on Luke's use of this title for Jesus, see Fitzmyer, *Luke*, 1:208-211, and J. D. Kingsbury, *Jesus Christ in Matthew, Mark, and Luke* (Philadelphia: Fortress, 1981) 106-110.

[24]For an examination of how Mark uses this title for Jesus, see Sweetland, *Mark*, 151-154.

[25]For the extensive parallels between Jesus and Stephen see O'Toole, *Unity*, 63-67. For a thorough analysis of the Stephen story see E. Richard, *Acts 6:1-8:4: The Author's Method of Composition* (Missoula: Scholars, 1978).

[26]So Fitzmyer, *Luke*, i:211-212. Cf. Kingsbury, *Jesus Christ*, 105-106. For a different interpretation see D. L. Jones, "The Title 'Servant' in Luke-Acts," in *Luke-Acts: New Perspectives from the Society of Biblical Literature Seminar*, ed. C. H. Talbert (New York: Crossroad, 1984) 148-165.

[27]Marshall, *Commentary*, 183. See also, Ellis, *Luke*, 98 and J. Schmid, *Das Evangelium nach Lukas*, RNT 3 (Regensburg: Pustet, 1960) 112. For a different opinion, see Fitzmyer, *Luke*, 1:529.

[28]On Acts 26:23 see O'Toole, *Christological Climax*, 109-110.

[29]See, e.g., P. Hinnebusch, *Jesus, The New Elijah* (Ann Arbor: Servant, 1978).

[30]See Fitzmyer, *Luke*, 1:207-208.

Notes, Chapter 5

[1]See Brown, *Apostasy*, 119-20, and P. J. Bearsley, "Mary the Perfect Disciple: Paradigm for Mariology," *TS* 41 (1980) 477-78.

[2]For an explanation of how Luke has radically changed the meaning of his source (Mk. 3:31-35) in this pericope, see Fitzmyer, *Luke*, 1:722-25.

[3]See Sweetland, "The Good Samaritan."

[4]See, e.g., R. E. Brown, "The Meaning of Modern New Testament Studies for an Ecumenical Understanding of Mary," in *Biblical Reflections on Crises Facing the Church* (NY: Paulist, 1975) 93-95, and *The Birth of the Messiah* (NY: Doubleday, 1977) 318, 343; R. E. Brown et al., *Mary in the New Testament* (NY: Paulist, 1978)

137, 168, 174-75, 287; O'Toole, *Unity*, 125-26; Talbert, *Reading*, 22-24; Bernadicou, "Spirituality," 465; and Bearsley, "Mary," 472-78.

[5]Sweetland, *Mark*, 89-91.

[6]Fitzmyer, *Luke*, 1:725. See also Brown, *Mary*, 167-170.

[7]The "all" of Acts 2:1 is understood by most to refer to the group of 120 mentioned in 1:14 and not merely to Matthias and the Eleven (1:26). See, e.g., Marshall, *Acts*, 68; Karris, *Invitation to Acts* (Garden City: Doubleday, 1978) 32; Munck, *The Acts of the Apostles*, AB 31 (Garden City: Doubleday, 1967) 14-15.

[8]These speeches include the five missionary sermons of Peter (Acts 2, 3, 4, 5, and 10), the missionary speeches of Paul to the Jews (13) and the Gentiles (17), Paul's four apologetic speeches (21-28), and Paul's farewell address to the Ephesian elders (20).

[9]E.g., Acts 4:20; 5:20f., 32; 7:2; 9:4; 11:7; 19:4, 10; 22:7, 14ff.; 24:24; 26:14.

[10]E.g., Acts 4:4; 10:33, 44; 14:9; 15:7; 16:14; 19:5; 21:19ff.; 26:29; 28:28.

[11]See Sweetland, *Mark*, 51ff.

[12]Most scholars conclude that this is a vague messianic reference, although it has also been suggested that "the one who is to come" should be understood as the eschatological prophet or the messenger of Yahweh. See Fitzmyer, *Luke*, 1:666 and Marshall, *Commentary*, 289-290.

[13]It is likely that Luke has included these verses from Isaiah because of the universalism theme. Thus, as far as Luke is concerned, "all flesh" is probably more important here than "shall see."

[14]The resurrection appearances also function as commissioning events in Matthew 28:19f. ("Go therefore and make disciples of all nations") and in John 20:21 ("As the Father has sent me, even so I send you").

[15]Talbert, *Reading*, 55.

[16]Cf. Fitzmyer, *Luke*, 1:223-4, and O'Toole, *Unity*, 51.

[17]It was mentioned earlier that while μετάνοια, in a general sense, involves a radical conversion from all that is evil and a total commitment to God, Luke understands this not as a once-for-all total change, but as a process to be worked out within the Christian community.

[18]Luke uses the noun "repentance" (μετάνοια) both in the Gospel (Lk. 3:3, 8; 5:32; 15:7; 24:47) and in Acts (5:31; 11:18; 13:24; 19:4; 20:21; 26:20). The verb "to repent" (μετανοεῖν) also appears in the Gospel (Lk. 10:13; 11:32; 13:3, 5; 15:7, 10; 16:30; 17:3, 4) and in Acts (2:38; 3:19; 8:22; 17:30; 26:20).

[19]R. Bultmann, "πιστεύω," *TDNT* 6:208.

[20]See Sweetland, *Mark*, 51-69, 138-161.

[21]Relying primarily on Mark, Luke identifies Jesus as the Son of Man who will be delivered into the hands of "men" and Gentiles (Lk. 9:44; 18:32; 22:22; 24:7), be killed, and be raised (9:22; 18:33; 24:7).

[22]Luke's obvious dependence on the Isaian servant songs (cf. Lk. 2:32; 22:32; Acts 8:32ff.) suggests that he identifies Jesus as the "Servant" of God in Acts 3:13, 26; 4:27, 30. Especially important here is Jesus' explicit quotation of Isaiah 53:12 in Luke 22:37.

[23]See O'Toole, "Parallels," 195-212, and *Unity*, 63-67, 82-86. Cf. D. M. Sweetland, "Discipleship and Persecution: A Study of Luke 12:1-12," *Biblica* 65 (1984) 76ff., and R. F. O'Toole, "Luke's Notion of 'Be Imitators of Me as I Am of Christ' in Acts 25-26," *BTB* 8 (1978) 155-61.

²⁴It is unclear whether Luke understands these people, who are obviously disciples of John, to be Christians. It is at least possible that Luke has this in mind given his use of the term "believe" (19:2) and his habit of referring to Christian believers as "disciples" elsewhere in Acts.

²⁵In spite of this fact, however, R. F. O'Toole, "Christian Baptism in Luke," *RevRel* 39 (1980) 858, believes that "Luke clearly views Pentecost as a baptism" (cf. Acts 1:5).

²⁶Fitzmyer, *Luke*, 1:240-41.

²⁷There has been considerable debate about the Samaritan episode. See F. Bovon, *Luc le theologian: vingt-cinq ans de recherches (1950-1975)* (Neuchatel: Delachaux & Niestle, 1978) 244-52, 397-99. Only in Acts 8 does one meet individuals who believe and are baptized, but do not receive the Holy Spirit as a result.

²⁸Acts 2:41-47; 8:12, 13, 37; 10:43; 11:17; 16:31, 34; 18:8; 19:2, 4.

²⁹Acts 2:38; 11:18.

³⁰Acts 1:14; 2:1-4; 9:11; 10:2, 4, 9, 30, 31; 11:15; 16:13, 16, 25 (cf. Luke 3:21).

³¹Acts 2:38; 10:43; 22:16.

³²Acts 8:39; 16:34.

Notes, Chapter 6

¹See I. H. Marshall, *Luke: Historian and Theologian* (Exeter: Paternoster, 1970) 103-15.

²Ultimately, Luke's conception of God differs from both the Jewish and Greek conceptions. See, e.g., Marshall, Ibid., and K. Rahner, "Theos in the New Testament," in *Theological Investigations* (NY: Seabury, 1974) 1:79-148.

³See Richard, *Acts 6:1-8:4*.

⁴While prophecies found in Isaiah play an extremely important role in Luke-Acts (e.g., Lk. 4:16-21; cf. 7:22f. and 9:35), it should be noted that as part of his "proof from prophecy" theme Luke also cites both the prophets as a whole (e.g., Lk. 18:31; Acts 3:18; 13:27) and specific prophecies found in Malachi (Mal. 3:1; 4:5-6; cf. Lk. 1:13-17), Micah (Mic. 5:2; cf. Lk. 2:4), Joel (Joel 2:28-32; cf. Acts 2:16-21), Amos (Acts 15:15f.), 2 Samuel (2 Sam. 7:9-14; cf. Lk. 1:30-33), the Psalms (Psalm 2; cf. Acts 4:25 and Psalm 118; cf. Lk. 20:17f.), and Deuteronomy (Deut. 18:15f.; cf. Acts 3:22f.).

⁵Few scholars would defend this position today. One who would, however, is E. Grässer, "Die Parusieerwartung in der Apostelgeschichte," in *Les Actes des Apotres: traditions, redaction, theologie*, ed. J. Kremer (Gembloux: Duculot, 1979) 99-127.

⁶*The Theology of St. Luke*, trans. G. Buswell (New York: Harper & Row, 1961) 230.

⁷Ibid., 201; cf. 197, n.3. See also E. Käsemann, "Ministry and Community of the New Testament," in *Essays on New Testament Themes* (London: SCM, 1964) 91-94, who argues that Luke has replaced a theology of the cross with a theology of glory.

⁸See, e.g., A. George, "Le sens de la mort de Jesus," in *Etudes sur l'oeuvre de Luc* (Paris: Gabalda, 1978) 201-11 (published originally as "Le sens de la mort de Jesus pour Luc," *RB* 80 [1973] 186-217); R. Glockner, *Die Verkundigung des Heils beim Evangelisten Lukas* (Mainz: Matthias-Grunewald, 1976) 155-95; and Neyrey, *The Passion*, 129-92.

⁹See J. Kodell, "Luke's Theology of the Death of Jesus," in *Sin, Salvation, and the Spirit*, 221-30.

[10]See, e.g., Neyrey, *The Passion According to Luke* 137-38; N. Flanagan, "The What and How of Salvation in Luke-Acts," *Sin, Salvation, and the Spirit*, 212-13; and O'Toole, *Unity*, 23-32.

[11]See George, "Israel," in *Etudes*, 87-125 (originally published as "Israel dans l'oeuvre de Luc," *RB* 75 [1968] 481-525).

[12]See S. G. Wilson, "Law and Judaism in Acts," in *SBL Seminar Papers* (Chico: Scholars, 1980) 251-65, and F. D. Weinert, "The Meaning of the Temple in Luke-Acts," *BTB* 11 (1981) 85-89.

[13]See, e.g., Johnson, *Literary Function;* Richard, *Acts 6:1-8:4* and "The Creative Use of Amos by the Author of Acts," *NovT* 24 (1982) 37-53; and W. S. Kurz, "Luke-Acts and Historiography in the Greek Bible," in *SBL Seminar Papers* (Chico: Scholars, 1980) 283-300 and "Luke 3:23-38 and Greco-Roman and Biblical Genealogies," in Talbert, *Luke-Acts*, 169-87.

[14]O'Toole, *Unity*, 21; cf. 17, 22, 160-61; see also *Acts 26: The Christological Climax of Paul's Defense (Acts 22:1-26:32)* (Rome: Pontifical Biblical Institute, 1978) 94, 98.

[15]Fitzmyer, *Luke*, 1:188.

[16]See E. Haenchen, *The Acts of the Apostles* (Philadelphia: Westminster, 1971) 102; cf. G. Lohfink, *Die Sammlung Israels: Untersuchung zur lukanischen Ekklesiologie* (Munich: Kosel, 1975).

[17]S. G. Wilson, *The Gentiles and the Gentile Mission in Luke-Acts* (NY: Cambridge, 1973) 227.

[18]"The Divided People of God," in *Luke and the People of God* (Minneapolis: Augsburg, 1972) 41-74.

[19]Ibid., 43.

[20]See Lohfink, *Jesus and Community*, 22, 25, 90-91, who argues that Jesus' death on behalf of Israel is an alternative to rejection and judgement.

[21]See Richard, "The Divine Purpose: The Jews and the Gentile Mission," in *Luke-Acts*, 197-99, and D. L. Tiede, *Prophecy and History in Luke-Acts* (Philadelphia: Fortress, 1980) 121ff.

[22]Richard, "Divine Purpose," 199.

[23]Franklin, *Christ the Lord*, 119-42, and Jervell, "The Divided People of God," 56.

[24]See Richard, "Amos," 51-52, and "Divine Purpose," 200-201.

[25]B. J. Bamberger, "Tax Collector," *IDB* 4:522.

[26]L. E. Toombs, "Clean and Unclean," *IDB* 1:641-48.

[27]See Kraybill and Sweetland, "Possessions," 231-233.

[28]See O. J. Baab, "Woman," *IDB* 4:864-67.

[29]See, e.g., Cadbury, *Making*, 234, 263-265; H. Flender, *St. Luke: Theologian of Redemptive History* (Philadelphia: Fortress, 1967) 9ff.; and O'Toole, *Unity*, 118ff.

[30]This must be understood in light of our comments on discipleship and possessions in chapter 8.

[31]Cf. Acts 2:17-21 where Peter interprets the Pentecost event as the fulfillment of Joel 3:1-5. Luke sees the present time, therefore, as a time when God will pour out his Spirit upon "all flesh" and "whoever" calls on the name of the Lord shall be saved.

Notes, Chapter 7

1See Sweetland, *Mark*, 85-105.

2See W. C. Robinson, Jr., "On Preaching the Word of God (Luke 8:14-21)," in *Studies in Luke-Acts*, 133; and R. E. Brown, "Roles of Women in the Fourth Gospel," *TS* 36 (1975) 697, and *Mary*, 167-170.

3For a detailed explanation of how this passage functions in Mark's Gospel see Sweetland, *Mark*, 92-95.

4Talbert, *Reading*, 173, and Fitzmyer, *Luke*, 2:1205-1206.

5This could be either a Lukan creation or a pre-Lukan name for the community. Cf. Fitzmyer, *Luke*, 1:242-243.

6Cf. Robinson, "On Preaching," 131-132.

7See Sweetland, *Mark*, 23, 44-45.

8Haenchen, *Acts*, 160, n.2.

9This term, which occurs 9 times in Luke-Acts, appears only three times in Matthew (19:21; 24:47; 25:14) and not at all in Mark.

10See D. B. Kraybill and D. M. Sweetland, "Possessions in Luke-Acts: A Sociological Perspective," *PRS* 10 (1983) 224-27.

11D. M. Sweetland, "The Lord's Supper and the Lukan Community," *BTB* 13 (1983) 25.

12Cf. K. H. Rengstorf, "μαθητής," *TDNT* 4:457-459, and Q. Quesnell, "The Women at Luke's Supper," in *Political Issues*, 67-69.

13Lk. 8:1; 9:1, 12; 18:31; 22:3, 47. (Mt. 10:5; 26:14, 20, 47; Mk. 3:16; 4:10; 6:7; 9:35; 10:32; 11:11; 14:10, 17, 20, 43.)

14Lk. 24:9, 33. (Matthew 28:16 refers to "the eleven disciples.")

15Lk. 6:13; 9:10; 11:49; 17:5; 22:14; 24:10. (Mt. 10:2; Mk. 3:14; 6:30.)

16Scholars are divided over whether or not this reference to "the Twelve" was originally part of Mark's Gospel. See Metzger, *Textual Commentary*, 80-81.

17Ellis, *Luke* 109, and Lohfink, *Jesus and Community*.

18See Quesnell, "Women," 64-65, who interprets the lack of a specific number in Luke's account to mean that there was a larger group than Jesus and the Twelve who participated in the Last Supper.

19See e.g., Plummer, *St. Luke*, 551; and Fitzmyer, *Luke*, 2:1561, who concludes that while Cleopas is not an apostle, "one cannot exclude the possibility that the unnamed disciple is one of the Eleven."

20See Ellis, *Luke*, 132, who states that this is "almost certainly" the case.

21Lk. 9:54; 10:23; 11:1; 12:1, 22; 16:1; 17:1, 22; 18:15; 19:29, 37, 39; cf. 14:26, 27, 33.

22See H. Schürmann, *Jesu Abschiedsrede* (Münster: Aschendorff, 1957) 63-99; V. Taylor, *The Passion Narrative of St. Luke: A Critical and Historical Investigation*, SNTSMS 19 (Cambridge: University Press, 1972) 61-64; and D. M. Sweetland, "The Lord's Supper and the Lukan Community," *BTB* 13 (1983) 23-27.

23See Quesnell, "Women," 59-79, who argues "(1) that Luke thought a larger group than just the Twelve were at the Supper with Jesus; and (2) that within that larger group Luke included the women" (59).

24See R. E. Brown, *Priest and Bishop: Biblical Reflections* (New York: Paulist, 1970) 48-59.

[25]Cf. Wilson, *Gentiles*, 117, who suggests that "the title 'Apostle' as such was not important to Luke."

[26]O'Toole, "Parallels," 210.

[27]Ibid., 211.

[28]See, e.g., R. Schnackenburg, "Lukas als Zeuge verschiedener Germeindestrukturen," *Bibel und Leden* 12 (1972) 232-47.

[29]Elsewhere in Acts they are mentioned only in the Pentecost account (2:14) and in the story about the selection of the seven table servers (6:2ff.).

[30]Although these seven individuals are appointed specifically to "serve" tables so that the Twelve might devote themselves "to prayer and to the ministry of the word" (Acts 6:4), two of their number, Stephen (6:8-7:53) and Philip (8:4-13) are pictured later as preaching and disputing with the Jews.

Notes, Chapter 8

[1]E.g., Plummer, *St. Luke*, 469; Fitzmyer, *Luke*, 2:1305; and Marshall, *Commentary*, 741.

[2]While children, and especially infants, are never mentioned in these texts it is very likely that these households did include small children. See G. R. Beasley-Murray, *Baptism in the New Testament* (Grand Rapids: Eerdmans, 1962) 312-320, and J. Jeremias, *Infant Baptism in the First Four Centuries* (Philadelphia: Westminster and London: SCM,1960) 19-24.

[3]Ibid., 312-314.

[4]For a different view see, O. Cullmann, *Baptism in the New Testament* (London: SCM, 1964) 25f., 71-80; Jeremias, *Infant Baptism*, 49ff.; and W. Grundmann, *Evangelium nach Lukas*, 353.

[5]Plummer, *Luke*, 42. Cf. Fitzmyer, *Luke*, 2:1196.

[6]Fitzmyer, *Luke*, 2:1185

[7]Caird, *Saint Luke*, 205.

[8]On the originality of Luke 22:19b-20 see Sweetland, "Lord's Supper," 24.

[9]J. F. Ross, "Meals," *IDB* 3:315-318.

[10]See E. J. Kilmartin, *The Eucharist in the Primitive Church* (Englewood Cliffs: Prentice-Hall, 1965).

[11]See J. Jeremias, *The Eucharistic Words of Jesus* (Philadelphia: Fortress, 1977) 224.

[12]This reference to the "new covenant" occurs in the Lukan and Pauline accounts. Mark and Matthew have "the blood of the covenant."

[13]See Sweetland, "Lord's Supper," 27. Cf. also J. Wanke, *Beobachtungen zum Eucharistieverstandnis des Lukas auf Grund der lukanischen Mahlberichte* (Leipzig: St. Benno, 1973).

[14]Fitzmyer, *Luke*, 2:1559.

[15]See Marshall, *Acts*, 83.

[16]Cf. Haenchen, *Acts*, 584, who agrees that this passage refers to the celebration of the Lord's Supper.

[17]Bernadicou, "Community," 205-19; E. A. LaVerdiere and W. G Thompson, "New

Testament Communities in Transition: A Study of Matthew and Luke," *TS* 37 (1976) 591f.; and O'Toole, *Unity*, 255.

[18]The issue is more complex if Quesnell, "Women," is correct in concluding that Luke thought a larger group than just the Twelve were at the Supper and that within that larger group Luke included the women.

[19]Brown, *Priest and Bishop*, 41. This conclusion does not contradict the fact that Luke shows a continuous line running from God, through Jesus Christ, through the church in Jerusalem, to Paul and the churches he founded outside Palestine.

[20]See C. W. F. Smith, "Prayer," *IDB* 3:857-867.

[21]See Sweetland, *Mark*, 133-136.

[22]See Trites, "The Prayer Motif."

[23]Cadbury, *Making*, 269; Fitzmyer, *Luke*, 1:244-47; Talbert, *Reading*, 102-104, 132; and O'Toole, *Unity*, 72.

[24]P. T. O'Brien, "Prayer in Luke-Acts," *TB* 24 (1973) 120-121, 126-127.

[25]See W. Ott, *Gebet und Heil: Die Bedeutung der Gebetsparänese in der lukanische Theologie* (Munchen: Kosel Verlan, 1965).

[26]See Lampe, "Holy Spirit," 159.

[27]See Navone, *Themes*, 71-87.

[28]Cf. the parallel verse in Matthew where God gives "good things" to those who ask (Mt. 7:11).

[29]See Fitzmyer, *Luke*, 2:900, 904-906. Cf. Marshall, *Commentary*, 458-460, and Talbert, *Reading*, 129.

[30]For Luke, "temptation" is not restricted to an eschatological trial. See Fitzmyer, *Luke*, 2:907, Talbert, *Reading*, 130.

[31]Fitzmyer, *Luke*, 2:899.

[32]See Marshall, *Commentary*, 457-458, and Talbert, *Reading*, 130-131.

[33]For what follows see Kraybill and Sweetland, "Possessions," 228-35.

[34]See Sweetland, *Mark*, 29-34, 130-133.

[35]See Pilgrim, *Good News*, 129-34, who regards the Zacchaeus story "as the most important Lukan text on the subject of the right use of possessions."

[36]Jesus speaks favorably of almsgiving in the Zacchaeus story and in Luke 11:41; 12:33; 16:9; and 18:22.

[37]Johnson, *Literary Function*, 127-71.

[38]See R. J. Cassidy, *Jesus, Politics and Society: A Study of Luke's Gospel* (Maryknoll: Orbis, 1978) 40-41.

[39]The term "zealot" was traditionally used in Old Testament times and in the intertestamental period to describe those who were zealous for God's law. "Zealot" is currently used to designate the more radical and warlike Jewish rebels against foreign, especially Roman, rule after the uprising of Judas in 6-7 A. D. See S. G. F. Brandon, *Jesus and the Zealots* (New York: Charles Scribner's Sons, 1967) 26ff.; J. M. Ford, *My Enemy is My Guest: Jesus and Violence in Luke* (Maryknoll: Orbis, 1984) 1-12; and Cassidy, *Jesus, Politics, and Society*, 123-125.

[40]See Ford, *Guest*, vii-x, and J. H. Yoder, *The Politics of Jesus* (Grand Rapids: Eerdmans, 1972) 90-93.

[41]Cassidy, *Jesus, Politics, and Society*, 122-123. Cf. D. M. Rhoads, *Israel in Revolution 6-74 C. E.* (Philadelphia: Fortress, 1976) 154-156.

[42]It is not certain that Luke understands Simon to be a member of the Zealot party. See Fitzmyer, *Luke*, 1:619, and Marshall, *Commentary*,240.

[43]Brandon, *Zealots*, 316. For an argument against Brandon's claim that the historical Jesus was a violent revolutionary, see G. R. Edwards, *Jesus and the Politics of Violence* (New York: Harper, 1972).

[44]See Ford, *Guest*, 98-101.

[45]Cassidy, *Jesus, Politics, and Society*, 43.

[46]Ibid., 45. Cf. Fitzmyer, *Luke*, 2:1434; Marshall, *Commentary*, 827; and Ford, *Guest*, 113-116.

[47]See Fitzmyer, *Luke*, 2:1261; Marshall, *Commentary*, 719; Ford, *Guest*, 111-112; and Talbert, "Martyrdom," 108.

[48]"Martyrdom," 107-108.

[49]*St. Luke*, 140.

[50]Ibid., 138.

[51]*Jesus, Politics, and Society*, 129.

[52]Ibid., 41.

[53]Ibid., 78-79.

[54]Ibid., 79.

[55]*The Politics of Jesus*.

[56]Ibid., 39.

[57]Ibid., 157.

[58]Ibid., 46.

[59]W. M. Swartley, "Politics or Peace (Eirēnē) in Luke's Gospel, in *Political Issues in Luke-Acts*, 18-37.

[60]"Martyrdom," 108.

Index of Scripture References

OLD TESTAMENT

NEW TESTAMENT

Index of Authors

GOOD NEWS STUDIES

Consulting Editor: Robert J. Karris, O.F.M.

Volume 30